GENTLECARE

Changing the Experience of
Alzheimer's Disease
in a Positive Way

GENTLECARE™

*Changing the Experience of
Alzheimer's Disease
in a Positive Way*

MOYRA JONES

SECOND EDITION, REVISED

MOYRA JONES
RESOURCES LTD.

CATALOGING IN PUBLICATION DATA:
A catalog for this publication is available from the National Library of Canada

Published by
MOYRA JONES RESOURCES LTD
Suite 605 – 121 10th Street
New Westminster, B.C. V3M 3X7

Second Edition, Revised
ISBN 978-0-9680584-1-1

GENTLECARE is the registered trademark of
Moyra Jones Resources Ltd.

Set in SCALA and SCALA SANS by The Typeworks
Cover design by Diane McIntosh
Printed in the U.S.A.

NOTICE TO THE READER

This book is sold with the understanding that neither the author nor the publisher is engaged in tendering legal, accounting, medical, or other professional advice. If such advice or other assistance is required, the personal services of a competent professional should be sought.

This one is for Rob,
who is always there
when it matters

GENTLECARE™

In geology, a discontinuity is a break in the ordered layering of the earth's strata, often caused by the tectonic forces which bend the strata until it breaks. We know these breaks as earthquakes.

Alzheimer's disease is not unlike the tectonic forces which cause earthquakes. Alzheimer's disease strips away the humanity of those afflicted by the disease, layer by layer. It exhorts from family caregivers a level of involvement beyond their ability to provide, and it causes major and minor seismic events within health care systems which are poorly prepared to manage the crisis.

The Gentlecare Life Care Prosthetic System (Gentlecare™) offers support in living to the individual suffering from the disease, and knowledge, skills, and support for family and professional care providers.

There is an old Chinese saying:

> *A butterfly flaps its wings*
> *Once and the air all over*
> *The earth is changed forever*

Gentlecare has adopted the butterfly as its logo in an effort to depict the gentle and complex approach advocated in the care of people with dementing illnesses.

Each one of us, in whatever our role, who helps recall a memory, restores dignity, or rights a wrong for any of these vulnerable people, changes the world forever in ways we may never know.

I appreciate your company on this journey of exploration, challenge, and success. I can be contacted at:

Moyra Jones Resources Ltd.
~~Suite 605 – 121 10th Street~~
New Westminster, British Columbia V3M 3X7
Canada

Phone: 604-421-1680
Fax: 604-421-1753
E-mail: moyrajonesresourcesltd@shaw.ca
Website: www.Gentlecare.com

...dream, believe, experience

Contents

Acknowledgments

No book is the result of the author's efforts alone. So my grateful acknowledgment is offered to many people who have given of their time, energy, expertise, experiences, and suggestions.

I want to thank:

The families and victims of Alzheimer's disease who welcomed me into their lives and courageously shared their stories. They are true heroes.

My two men: Robert, who never faltered in his belief that this book was possible; and Marc, my son and soul mate, who spent more hours at the computer, and made more cups of tea, than I care to remember.

Joyce Wright, whose love and support gives new meaning to the word friendship.

Lorna Seaman, for her generous contributions to my understanding of nutrition, and the joy she brought to our creative endeavors.

My former colleague Alix McGinity, for her support and editorial comments on the subject of assessment.

Sandy Telford, an outstanding Gentlecare practitioner, who bravely tested my ideas and generously shared her experiences.

John Piacitelli, a unique and precious advocate for elderly people, who believed in Gentlecare, and urged me to write about it.

Olga Greenwell, who encourages me through good times and bad, and always comes up with the right word.

The professional care providers who work each and every day "in the trenches" and who understand the challenges of providing Alzheimer's care.

My dear friends Michael J. and Hardtimes Morgan who unfailingly kept me company through every hour of writing.

I shall always be grateful to Douglas Gray, who with great generosity of spirit went out of his way to provide me with wise counsel.

Every author should be lucky in their choice of publishing house. I am very grateful to the people at Hartley & Marks for their caring, persistence, and spirit; to my publisher Vic Marks who believed in this book; to Susan Berlin, my lion-hearted editor who helped move my ideas to a different level; to managing editor Susan Juby, for awesome support in the final stages; indeed all the fine people who contributed to bringing this book into being.

The hundreds and hundreds of people who have taken the time to write to me with ideas, anecdotes, stories, butterflies, and good wishes.

This book would not have been possible without everyone's love.

—Moyra
Ajijic, Mexico
February 1999

Foreword

The biggest disease today is not leprosy or tuberculosis,
but rather the feeling of being unwanted.
—Mother Teresa, *Observer,* 3 October 1971

The prevalence of Alzheimer's disease in the older population is a tragedy unmatched in any other age group. This tragedy is compounded by the type of care they frequently receive when placed in long-term care facilities.

Moyra Jones was faced with this situation when her father and other family members fell victim to the disease. Based on this personal experience and her own professional expertise, she dedicated herself to developing a system of care that expresses her conviction that dementia does not rob an individual of his or her individuality. In Moyra's Gentlecare system for dementia care, the caregiver is required to treat the person with dementia as a unique human being with the same need for respect, recognition, and self-worth as a person without dementia.

Her philosophical approach emphasizes the need for everyone involved in the care of the impaired person, regardless of function or job description, to accept and value the dignity and worth of the impaired person. Caregivers are further expected to contribute to the creation of a prosthetic environment free of physical restraint that provides the person with dementia the support needed to make up for the progressive loss of functions resulting from the illness.

The benefits of the Gentlecare system have been felt not only by people with Alzheimer's disease, but by fellow residents, family members, and staff as well.

In this book, Moyra shares her philosophy on which her care system is based, and provides much-needed practical guidelines for families and other caregivers to use in their care of people with dementia, and in their relationships with one another. Whether you are a caregiver or not, this book will challenge you to examine your beliefs and feelings about being old, and about having dementia or some other mental illness. You will be asked to look at your attitudes, your expectations, and the behaviors you encourage and reinforce in the older people you serve.

By so doing, you will gain the satisfaction of knowing that you have encouraged in them the discovery of new meaning and purpose in their lives, without a feeling of being unwanted, regardless of their age or mental status.

—John D. Piacitelli, MSW, MPH
Mental Health Program Administrator
Elderly Services, Washington State
Mental Health Division
Tacoma, WA, USA

Alzheimer's disease is a progressive disease that we cannot really change, nor can we avoid its ultimate outcome. The disease is frightening for professionals and relatives because we cannot stop its destructive effects.

Among both professional and lay caregivers, some think that Alzheimer's disease is incurable, that the afflicted person cannot be helped, and that custodial care is the only kind of care possible. Others believe that people with Alzheimer's can be rehabilitated if they are involved in intensive activities to improve their mental and physical capacities. In reality, however, inappropriate activities compromise afflicted people and often trigger aggressive reactions.

I had difficulties caring for people with Alzheimer's disease, and doubts about the possibility of improving the level of care in my facility.

Then I was introduced to Moyra and Gentlecare. I experienced a paradigm shift, and am now an enthusiastic supporter of the need for special care for dementia victims based on the Gentlecare prosthetic model.

My thinking changed because of the evidence put before me. Alzheimer's disease is incurable—but the Alzheimer patient is not untreatable! Gentlecare provides an alternative to patient neglect or the traditional, and unreachable, rehabilitation goal of functional improvement. Gentlecare is based on a prosthetic model aimed at maximizing the well-being of Alzheimer patients by using a three-pronged program: adapted environments, personal contact, and supportive activities. We, doctors and families, could not accept the unhappy conclusion that there was nothing we could do. For us, Gentlecare is a new and powerful alternative. In her book, Moyra explains how these three elements elevate the quality of care for Alzheimer patients.

The main surprise for the reader will be the book's rich and detailed review of the everyday life of people with Alzheimer's, their families, and caregivers. *Gentlecare* offers many useful suggestions on every aspect of daily routine, from nutrition to sleep patterns. But for me, the best part is the new mind-set and the new approach to people with Alzheimer's that one gets from reading Moyra's book: build new supportive environments, find new solutions for behavioral problems, imagine new ways of improving well-being, and you will succeed in taking care of them. Every person is an individual, and caring for people is not simply a matter of applying a formula, but rather of recognizing each individual's uniqueness. That, I think, is the main lesson to be learned from this book, from Gentlecare, from Moyra Jones.

—Antonio Guaita, MD
Medical Director
Instituto Geriatrico,
Camillo Golgi,
Abbiategrasso (Milano), Italy

Prologue

This book began a long time ago. My family and I became caught up in caring for my father in the 1960s, long before Alzheimer's disease became a household word. No one in our circle of acquaintances had ever heard of Alzheimer's. There were no books, no journals, no articles, and no health services available to help us sort through the complex problems that confronted us. I was told the disease was rare, non-hereditary, that it affected only memory. I was told, in fact, that it did not exist!

My mother was encouraged to stay at home in the small village where she and my father had always lived and to call the church if she needed help with my father. We soon learned that no one wanted to be involved in my father's health problems. The physicians encouraged rest and a change of pace, and finally, massive doses of anti-psychotic medication, which left my father rigid and as brain-dead as a zombie. There was "no room at the inn" in any health care facility. Even years later I can vividly remember every detail of our journeys through the corridors of emergency services, acute medical/surgical wards, and palliative care units. There were brief sojourns in the empty rooms of pediatric departments, and finally four years of moves to and fro within extended care units.

My father and me.

I remember going to visit my father in hospital one day in the beginning, when he still knew where he was and what was happening to him. He was stretched flat on his back with a double layer of sheeting wrapped around him from his chin to his toes, pinning him to the bed. His face was blue. He was making pitiful choking sounds like a small trapped animal. I remember my frantic search for scissors, and the paralyzing anxiety that hampered me as I cut the sheets that bound him. I can still feel his breath on my face when he finally responded to my resuscitation efforts. And I will never forget his eyes looking at me and asking, "Why?"

What had happened to the health care system that I had worked in since I was 13 years old? How could the organizations I had later studied and worked within be failing my father when he needed them most? Why were some people receiving superb health care and treatment at the same time that my father was being treated like a leper by the very same system?

Why? Why? Why? These same questions are still being asked by families today.

Later on, when my father's Alzheimer's disease had progressed, I learned that the problems we had encountered in the beginning were just the tip of the iceberg. Things got worse, much worse. Sometimes in my ignorance and despair I thought I had done my father a disservice by rescuing him from asphyxiation.

My mother and father enjoyed a unique relationship.

And today, in hindsight and the light of knowledge cast by our growing understanding of Alzheimer's, I think, "If only I had known then what I know now!"

My father was a gentle, caring man who adored his wife, his daughter, and his dogs. He had a fine sense of community, believing that each of us had a bounden duty to extend our own good fortune to those less fortunate in our community. I have lovely images of him at dusk in our backyard, leaning on the pump as he talked to a farmer about money to buy some needed equipment, or counseled some young couple on ways to manage the purchase of a home.

He was a naturalist who practiced conservation long before it became the popular thing to do. He adored roaming outdoors on foot or by canoe. His love of space, freedom, and movement became his deadly enemies later in his dance with dementia. He loved people, animals, plants, jobs, projects, emergencies, challenges, music, fun, teasing, travel, his church, his home, his garden, and especially butter tarts!

My dad was a fine problem solver. He would consider a problem for days, trying various strategies or approaches until he found a solution that was just right. As a little girl I remember watching in fascination as he built stone walls. He selected each stone with great care, seeing colors and images in the stone that my untrained eye could not see. Sometimes he would abruptly turn the stone completely upside down and find the perfect fit. Then he would grin at me, drawing me into a lovely feeling of satisfaction.

As Alzheimer's disease invaded his mind, my father followed these same lifelong patterns—touching, moving, fitting, taking apart, stacking, tearing, turning things upside down, until he had the whole house in one awful mess. For the most part my mother and I followed him, trying to restore order and get him to sit down and be quiet!

My dad was a wonderful gardener, so I was aghast the day he began to dig holes in his beautiful lawn. At first I tried to entice him into the house, the car, anywhere, just so long as I could keep him from ruining the lawn. Then suddenly I realized what was happening: he was working! This man was engaged in a job, and not about to be distracted from it by my protestations. Where once he had created wonderful flower beds, now he dug holes. It was hard for me to regard the destructive act of digging holes in the same way I viewed gardening, but given the nature of the disease consuming his mind, this activity was the best version of his former skills that he could manage: digging holes equaled gardening.

This insight was infinitely liberating for me. It allowed me to understand his concentration and persistence. It helped me to see life through his eyes. It took me behind the disease, and gave me back my father.

And so I encouraged him to dig holes—and I filled them in. We spent endless joyful hours at this activity. Once I was able to look beyond the specific activity, I was able to appreciate and even enjoy this limited, distorted version of his former skills.

I was able to laugh with him and celebrate our shared accomplishments. We could stop for a tea break, clean up together, and go into the house with that tired glow that only gardening can give.

Years later, as my father sat restrained in a chair, my heart broke as I sensed his frustration and despair. Where could I find the words to explain to hospital staff that he wanted to dig holes, to have a job, to be free, to feel again a sense of accomplishment and self-worth? Within the hospital setting there was no possibility of an old man digging holes. When he tried, he was given medication and restrained in a wheelchair.

And so we lost him—not so much to the disease, but rather to the system. He was in the wrong place, with the wrong disease, at the wrong time.

I remember going to visit him each evening after work, untying his restraint, helping him find his balance, and then trying to keep up with him as he raced down the corridors and out into the fresh air. My father was an outdoors man: strong, active, utterly tireless. It must have been sheer hell for him to sit confined for days on end, not permitted to stand or move about. I can remember a staff member saying to me as we passed by, "Is that Len? I didn't know he could walk!" But how could she? She had only seen him in a wheelchair. She was a part of the system that fed, changed, and tidied patients, gave them their medications, and focused on urgent matters. She was one of an insufficient number of people doing endless tasks in a limited amount of time. How could she be expected to know my father? And how could I, knowing her work routine, say to her: "Please, he needs to be digging holes"?

So what was this physically strong man, with no need of medical treatment, doing in the middle of a facility designed to treat and manage physical illness? Talk about square pegs in round holes! No wonder he couldn't fit in. No wonder everyone was at their wits' end in trying to "cope" with him.

Most staff I talked to didn't really understand my father's illness. When I explained some of his behaviors in terms of his disease process, they would say, "Oh, that makes sense! That's why he does so-and-so!" And I would think how hard it must be to care for people in

If you don't know the kind of person I am, and I don't know the kind of person you are, a pattern that others made may prevail in the world, and following the wrong god home, we may miss our star.

—WILLIAM STAFFORD

such an intimate way without knowing who they were or why they acted the way they did.

It took my father a long time to die. Some days I could not find him in the fog of drugs and dementia. And some days he was with me in an eerie fashion that made me think, "Oh my God! He's still here. He still feels. He knows." One night, in preparing him for sleep, I adjusted the restraint jacket that held him flat on his back on the bed. And he looked straight at me and said, "Why are you doing this to me?"

Why, indeed? I had no answer for him then.

Somewhere in the system of which he was a part, it had been decided that this physically well man would now be tied to a bed on his back for hours and hours during the night. Sometimes he would lie in his own waste, sometimes he would shout and swear. Always he would tear at the restraint, pleading for release or crying, "Why are you doing this to me?" Those words, and his image, burn in my brain even to this day.

I believe there is a better way.

Throughout my father's illness, significant people emerged for him. His grandson Marc who visited and chatted a blue streak with him, a homemaker who had a knack for making him laugh, a nurse from Hong Kong who forged an unlikely and lasting bond with him. And I, as his only daughter, connected with him in ways that changed both our lives. But it was my mother who mattered most. She was his touchstone, his security. She tried to be with him all the time because when she was, he was content. When he was upset, it was she who could calm him. He would do anything she asked. Even when he could no longer utter her name, he would smile, or whistle, or on some occasions touch her hand.

At the time, none of us really appreciated the drain of my father's illness on my mother. Fixated as we were on the horror of my father's unfolding disease, we neglected to notice her physical and emotional exhaustion. We failed to identify her overwhelming grief at the loss of her life partner. Because he was alive, we never addressed the losses we were all feeling until it was much too late, and my mother, too, was tragically ill. Today, medical journals abound with articles on caregiver burnout. But careful study is required before we truly understand the complexity of the caregiving relationship throughout the continuum of the disease.

Though surrounded by me and wonderfully caring staff, my father waited until my mother was at his side before he died. How could this be when the disease destroys all cognition? I don't know—I only know it happened. In those few moments I learned how powerful and enduring the familial relationship really is, and what a potent, irreplaceable therapeutic force it can be.

A few years ago, I was privileged to help one of my mother's old friends at the time of her death. She laughed and said, "Oh honey! I can hardly wait to see your mother and father tonight. [They had both predeceased her.] I'm going to tell them what you are doing and all the progress that's been made with your dad's disease." I remember marveling at a faith so strong and comforting.

Two friends to the very end.

Sometimes in the quiet, I imagine these three old friends observing all the positive efforts being made to change the way we care for people experiencing dementing illness and their family members. I imagine my father's delight when he sees old men in Gentlecare units moving furniture, piling wood, even digging holes! And it surely would please my mother to see caregivers taking care of themselves, gaining the knowledge and skills they need to do the job of caregiving, and also attending to their grieving, and to a life after dementia.

A lot has changed in 30 years—but much remains the same. This book is about Gentlecare: a system designed to make changes.

PART ONE

UNDERSTANDING ALZHEIMER'S DISEASE

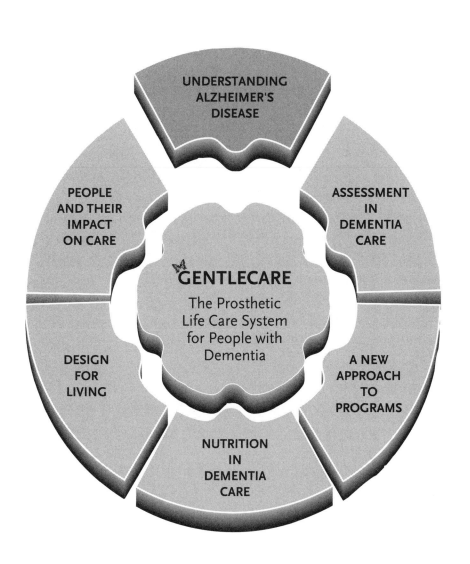

1

Old Problems, New Issues

If only, when one heard
That Old Age was coming,
One could bolt the door,
Answer "not at home!"
And refuse to meet him!
        —Old Chinese drinking song

It has been said that societies are judged by the way they treat their very old and their very young. Old age is a fact of life. All of us have fathers, mothers, husbands, wives, lovers, and friends who have lived beyond mid-life. In 2002, 7 percent of the world's population was aged 65 or over. This percentage is expected to grow to 9 percent by 2020 and to almost 17 percent by 2050, according to the U.S. Census Bureau. Most of those people—70 percent of them—will be active, wise, strong, and dynamic, living independently in their communities, and enjoying life fully. However, increasing numbers of elderly people are not aging in accordance with conventional expectations.

Older people are becoming the principal client group for all health care services, acute and chronic care alike. And 10 to 12 percent of those elders 65 years and older requiring any kind of health care services will do so because of a dementing illness. As the average age of the population rises, the number of people so afflicted will increase dramatically, until nearly half of all people over 85 will suffer from some form of progressive dementia—most often Alzheimer's disease. For every one of these unfortunate people, at least one family member and often more will be involved in providing care.

People with dementia deeply disturb our ideas about old age and how it should unfold. The eccentricities of the cognitively alert can be looked upon as charming quirks. Those same behaviors in dementia sufferers are judged as further evidence of their incompetence. Cognitively impaired elders—perhaps our parents—defy our expectations. For many grown children, the notion of a parent being less than "parent-like" is unthinkable. People with dementia don't fit the mold of "normal aging." More importantly, they don't fit into our existing health care system. For people with dementing illness, there is no refuge—not in their own homes, their communities, or within our social service and health care systems. Consequently, they are overwhelmed by fear and anxiety; they are deprived of normal roles and relationships, surrounded by a conspiracy of silence, and unable to affect the outcome of events in their own lives.

Many theories of disease assign to the luckless ill the ultimate responsibility both for falling ill and for getting well.

—SUSAN SONTAG,
*ILLNESS AS A
METAPHOR*

DEMENTIA

Dementia refers to over 70 diseases that cause a grouping of symptoms which results in progressive deterioration of brain cells, particularly those responsible for memory and thought. The cause is often unknown, and therefore a cure is currently unavailable. Dementing illness results in dysfunction in all aspects of daily living and interpersonal relationships. This category of diseases often was referred to as senility.

People with dementia are oppressed by the recognition that they are a problem to their families and to others—a situation they are helpless to alter. At the most vulnerable time in their lives they are often abandoned by the very systems they have counted on and contributed to all their lives: their families, their churches, and their health care systems.

An estimated 70 percent of all care given to persons with dementia is provided by elderly women, who are often ill themselves and certainly exhausted. Their ability to advocate on behalf of impaired family members is questionable. Trained in the importance of maintaining dignity and surviving through resignation and fortitude, older women often don't make waves. Because current health care practices fail to meet the needs of people with dementia, 80 percent of caretakers choose instead simply to care for their family members at home, often at a tragic cost to their own health.

As dementing illnesses like Alzheimer's disease spread more widely, the advocacy torch is being passed to a younger, more vocal group of caregivers: daughters and daughters-in-law who make up the fastest-growing group of new caregivers. Younger family members trying to come to grips with the problem of dementia are less willing to settle for inadequate health care for their family members. The challenge for those of us on the front line is to focus our anger and find a better—a different—way to meet the needs of people with dementia and their families.

Alzheimer's disease exists in two forms: *early onset disease,* which normally shows its first signs between the ages of 45 and 60; and *late onset disease,* which can become evident at any time after the age of 60. Both types of the disease are on the increase.

As yet, the cause of the increase in early onset Alzheimer's (or presenile dementia of the Alzheimer's type) is unknown. The increase in the late onset form of the disease (*senile dementia*) is probably explained in part by the fact that people are simply living longer. As well, it is known that about 10 to 15 percent of people with Alzheimer's come from families in which significant numbers of people have had the disease; this is known as Familial Alzheimer's disease.

In his Global Deterioration Scale, Dr. Barry Reisberg suggests that Alzheimer's disease parallels *in reverse* the developmental stages of childhood. As a child gains developmental mastery over his life, so a person experiencing dementia declines through the same stages, losing control over the various aspects of life. As people live through the process of Alzheimer's disease, it is possible to correlate their functional levels with those of children at similar stages. For example, by the time a person with Alzheimer's requires 24-hour supervision, he or she is probably operating at the *developmental* level of a child of 7 or 8 while being 73 years old chronologically. Such a person is not a child, but rather childlike in terms of the ability to manage life tasks and need for appropriate supports.

CHAPTER
ONE

*Nothing she did or said
was quite what she meant
but still her life could be
called a monument
shaped in a slant of
available light and set
to the movement of
possible music.*

—JUDITH DOWNING,
"THE GRAND-
MOTHER CYCLE"
CONVERSE QUARTERLY

It's worth noting that, as a rule, when children become ill our health care system goes to exquisite lengths to prepare them for hospitalization, to allay their fears, to develop an environment that helps them get well and does not frighten them, and to ensure that a family support system is in place. But when an elderly man with dementia becomes so dysfunctional that he requires round-the-clock supervision, his admission to hospital is often very different. Not infrequently, he is transported to hospital in an emergency vehicle or a stranger's car. He is placed in a communal living situation, surrounded by large numbers of people he doesn't know. Often it is suggested that his spouse or other family member leave, "until he settles in," which in some cases can be for a period of several weeks. He is shown to a bedroom, directed to a dining room, and then expected to manage in a strange and complex environment that may resound with telephones, intercoms, emergency buzzers, and alarm systems. There is not a familiar face in sight.

The person has no idea what is happening to his family, his pets, his house, or any of the responsibilities he may feel he has. Even if he is reassured on these matters, the disease causes him to forget the information as soon as he hears it. Fear and anxiety are the natural result, and often medication is administered to calm or quiet him. Medication creates even more confusion and disorientation, and so the fear and anxiety escalate.

It is curious that the health care system responds so very differently to people from two generations with very similar needs. On the one hand, the child is cherished and supported; on the other hand, the older person is treated with insensitivity and disregarded.

Although it is often painful, even unacceptable, for us to regard our elders with dementia as childlike, awareness of Alzheimer's reverse development process helps us to understand their vulnerability and need for special support. Furthermore, since we have gone through exactly the same stages of development that people with dementia traverse in reverse, we can recall how it feels to be helpless, afraid, to have one's opinions discounted, and be unable to make decisions independently. Those of us who have supported children through their developmental stages have already had the experience of how to give just the right amount of help, and how to withdraw support as they develop confidence and skills. This experience is invaluable in caring for people with dementia—if only caregivers learn to use it in reverse.

With such awareness, we can see how unreasonable we have been in our expectations of these frightened, vulnerable old people. We begin to see that they really require life care—not medical care—as their disease inevitably progresses. We begin to understand the pain and dilemma of family caregivers, and their power to help family members.

Evil thrives on apathy and cannot exist without it.

—HANNAH ARENDT

All we have learned about special, age-appropriate environments can help us design comfortable and comforting accommodation for older people with dementing illnesses. By using existing resources from families, communities, and the health care system, we can devise care strategies and support systems that truly and humanely meet the needs of these people.

It is no longer appropriate to regard elderly people as a homogeneous group who require the same type of environment, the same health care strategies, and the same solutions for dealing with their life problems. Whether they are "young-old" or "old-old," "young-old" with physical problems or "old-old" with cognitive problems, "over-all old" or simply aging "problem-old," our elders deserve appropriate responses and care from individuals, social structures, institutions, and communities.

The provision of appropriate services to the elderly requires a new commitment on the part of society at all levels. It is not so much a question of right or wrong, but rather a determination to do things differently.

Changes in the Older Population

Aging is everyone's tomorrow. It may be that one of us is beginning to experience the challenge of changes in health, status, or role that accompany older age. Or perhaps in mid-life we find ourselves caught up in the lives of our parents or grandparents. For many of us who work in

TYPICAL BREAKDOWN
OF ELDERS IN
HEALTH CARE FACILITIES

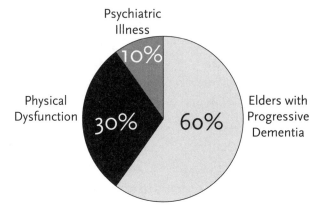

Psychiatric
Illness

10%

Physical
Dysfunction

30%   60%

Elders with
Progressive
Dementia

FIGURE 1-1

health care services, older people are becoming our principal client group, whether we provide acute or chronic care.

In the past, the health care problems of older people were generally seen as complex physical illnesses associated with aging. Today older people with physical illnesses are living longer, responding to ever-expanding medical and technological strategies, and asking to live in their own homes or in alternative arrangements within their communities. Older people with exclusively physical illnesses now form a minority group in chronic care, total care, or palliative care institutions. Elders who suffer from psychiatric disorders other than dementia now also form a minority in the health care system, as large psychiatric institutions downsize and send mentally ill people back to their local communities. These people are referred to as "psychogeriatrics," a pejorative term applied only to older people who experience psychiatric illness. (Children are never referred to as "psychopaediatrics!")

A disturbing proportion of older people in our communities, however, are elders experiencing some type of dementia or cognitive impairment. They are ultimately referred to our health systems for care. Older people with dementias may comprise up to 60 to 70 percent of all elders who use health care services.

For example, two out of three older people who use emergency services may have a dementing illness in addition to other health problems. Acute care medical facilities care for significant numbers of older people with dementia who require medical or surgical services, or who are awaiting placement in long-term care facilities. And three-quarters of the people who live in intermediate long-term care facilities have a dementing illness alone or in combination with other illnesses.

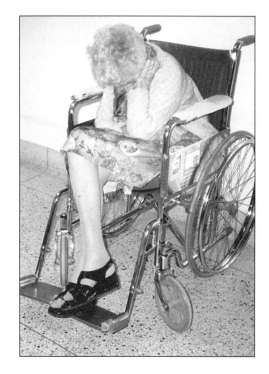

Chronic care, extended care, or total care facilities provide services for those who are greatly at risk of developing, or who already have, primary dementias. The challenge of providing appropriate care for these people is compounded by the fact that any of these conditions may exist together with other illnesses. For instance, it is not uncommon to find someone with Alzheimer's disease who is profoundly depressed, or someone with Parkinson's disease who also has cardiac dysfunction.

Furthermore, each of these people has at least one caregiver, often elderly as well, who is very likely to be exhausted and ill. The provision of gerontological care for the elderly has become as challenging and complex as delivery of acute medical care.

Forces That Shape the Care We Give

As people live longer, more of them develop some of the diseases of aging. Since the causes of many of these diseases remain obscure, effective treatment is elusive, and in some cases impossible. The traditional ways of caring for elderly people are proving inadequate and even inappropriate for the "new" types of illness and dysfunction we are encountering.

Suddenly, health services that were designed for other purposes are faced with providing residential and personal care to growing numbers of cognitively impaired mid-life and elderly persons—as well as providing advice and support to their family caregivers. The focus is shifting from health care to life care.

The challenge of the next decade is to evolve a new way of thinking about health and disease. The dehumanization of health care becomes especially critical when we consider services for older people. We need to re-conceptualize the way we think of illness. We can no longer think of it as just a physical condition that can be cured, or at least managed. If illness includes limited cognitive abilities, as it more frequently does among older people, we need to consider how to best preserve the whole person, and support a lifestyle that is meaningful and whole-some.

Is it reasonable to believe that structures and systems designed to ameliorate physical illness will work effectively for persons who are cognitively impaired, but relatively fit physically?

Troubling questions follow from this, and raise deep clinical and ethical problems—problems that quick-fix approaches won't solve. To achieve the necessary changes within health care systems requires that we change our perceptions regarding old age, and most especially, our view of progressive dementing illness and mental illness in the elderly. The services and practices we offer people with cognitive impairment and their families must be based on new and current knowledge, combined with effective management practices. Having recognized that most of the old paradigms, structures, and beliefs about caring for people with dementias were based on an incomplete understanding of their real needs, we must learn to approach problems differently. If people with dementia don't respond to the type of care we offer, then we have to change the type of care we give.

Is it reasonable, for example, to expect an elderly person experiencing dysfunction due to brain cell death to be able to live comfortably within existing health care facilities? Is it even possible?

I MET AN ELDERLY MAN AT HIS HOME, *and we walked in his garden. He pointed with delight to various trees that were his favorites. His family was seeking assistance in choosing a facility because his wife was ill and could no longer manage his care on her own.*

Three months later, I visited him in an institution, where he sat in a geriatric chair (a chair with a lock-down tray used for restraint purposes). When he saw me he began to cry, and said, "I am imprisoned in this machine. Please, please set me free!" When we did release him from the restraint, it was evident that he could no longer walk. His legs and ankles were swollen and his knees and hips had lost their range of movement. He had been changed into a "total care" patient by the system—not by the disease.

The North American approach to care of the elderly employs a *biomedical model* of care—a perspective that focuses on pathology and interventions that relieve symptoms or cure disease. This emphasis defines and shapes the systems we create, and the attitudes and behaviors we experience within the system.

In this model, people become "patients" and "patients" become their disease—"the gallbladder in room 203." The spectacular success of new technology and medical practices has overshadowed the harm that such highly technological and disease-specific systems can cause.

The reliance on the biomedical model to explain the experience of dementing illness has resulted in the medicalization of dementia. We have attempted to control dementia with medication, which can actually exacerbate problems if improperly used.

Can professional and lay personnel, without appropriate education or understanding of clinical issues, be expected to meet the challenges of Alzheimer's care?

The biomedical approach overlooks the social construction of dementia, in terms of changes in a person's functional deterioration, and the subsequent dynamics of caregiving relationships and community roles. The model also fails to take into account the impact of treatment contexts and environmental pressures on both the person with dementia and caregivers.

A place to live one's life to the fullest.

Viewing dementia as a medical problem that must be "fixed" has led us to focus on managing the problem behaviors that result

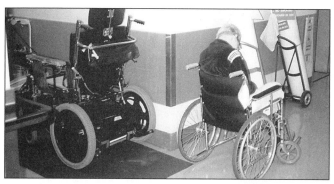

Not a place to wait for life's end.

CHAPTER
ONE

Is it reasonable to expect that elderly family caregivers—on their own—can meet the needs of persons devastated by dementia on a 24-hour basis for years and years?

from brain dysfunction. Consequently, problem behavior has come to be seen as an inevitable part of dementing illness, when in fact this need not be the case. For example, wandering, which has come to be seen as a pivotal aspect of Alzheimer's disease (Does he wander or not? Does he wander into someone else's room? Does he wander at night? Outdoors?), is not part of the clinical definition of Alzheimer's disease. Do we discuss causes? No. Instead, we are preoccupied with wandering! And wandering may be a function of being afraid, lonely, disoriented, anxious, or just going about one's business. Wandering may be simply explained as thirst, the need to find a bathroom, or boredom. Thus, behavior not considered abnormal if displayed by others is often judged harshly if exhibited by someone known to be cognitively impaired. Who among us has not wandered through a mall, or a mountain meadow, or the ancient part of a city?

The biomedical view of dementia is narrow, limited, and distorted in that it disregards the social forces that affect the progression of dementia. For example, we expect older people with dementia to live communally with other elders who may be cognitively alert, or who may suffer from psychiatric disorders. At this most vulnerable time of their lives, people with dementia are expected to adapt to and comply with living situations that people without dementia would find daunting. The psycho-social experience of dementing illness simply cannot fully be addressed within the confines of biomedical concepts.

For example, if a person with dementia exhibits problematic behavior, harmful to others or herself, she is eligible for admission to a Special Care Dementia Unit (SCDU). Once admitted, if the stress-free environment together with support offered by knowledgeable staff results in the person no longer displaying "violent" or problematic behavior, then she is no longer eligible to remain in the specialized environment. She is regarded as being "cured" of difficult behavior, and no longer in need of dementia care. It is not unusual to see such people transferred back to exactly the same situation that first caused the problem. And it is very common to see this tragic cycle played out again and again during the course of the disease.

CHARACTERISTICS OF THE
ACUTE BIOMEDICAL CARE PARADIGM

- The biomedical model of treatment is preoccupied with the treatment of symptoms and signs of disease and cures.
- Primary interventions are invasive strategies such as medication and surgery.
- Staff are encouraged to be emotionally neutral.
- The body and mind are regarded as separate entities.
- Environments are institutional in nature and technologically intensive.
- Patient dependency and compliance with medical treatment is encouraged.
- The health care professional is the authority and custodian of pertinent information and solutions.
- Labor is divided along professional or territorial lines.
- The emphasis is on efficiency.

*Aging is not a disease—
it's a lifelong process
that's very individual.*

—MARY FEDNIK

FIGURE 1-2

Attitudes and Malignant Myths that Shape the Way We React

Ageism

Ageism is discrimination on the basis of age. Older persons are often rendered invisible in life, in literature, and in films, or stereotyped as decrepit, lonely, or mean-spirited members of society who have little or nothing to contribute. Older persons are denied their individuality or often allowed only a very narrow spectrum of activities or acceptable behaviors.

Ageism can also be the social construction of aging. Rather than viewing aging as a normal process, we see it in terms of disease and dysfunction. This shapes the way we think and talk about old age, and the way we design health care systems. Biases are often so ingrained that we fail to recognize or identify our prejudices.

A YOUNG DOCTOR *who supervised an emergency department in a large hospital told me he felt older persons with dementia "use up far too much of our available health care resources. Do you really expect me to treat an old man with dementia rather than a child, or before I attend to a younger person? Honestly, Moyra, I don't know why you bother!"*

Commonly, older persons really get no health care treatment at all. What they get is more like health care "management." In many countries, there are health care workers called "case managers" who are responsible for developing health care plans for elders assigned to them—whether they agree to be "managed" or not. Nowhere is the management of elders more obvious than in the way we deal with older people with cognitive impairment. When we apply attitudes, language, and actions informed by ageism to management of the elderly, we produce dysfunction and loss of quality of life at an alarming rate.

Therapeutic Nihilism

The treatment of disease in older people, particularly the treatment of dementing illness, is plagued by *therapeutic nihilism*: the belief that nothing can be done to arrest the inevitable decline of intellectual and self-care abilities. It is true that no medical protocol currently exists to treat or cure progressive dementing illness. This does not mean, however, that nothing can be done to help people live through the process of dementia, or to help their families provide effective support. Therapeutic personal care, if appropriately applied, can dissipate problem behavior and assist the person with dementia to enjoy a relatively decent quality of life.

Infantilization

Let's get the potty line over with.

—ONE CARE AIDE TO ANOTHER

Being old in some cultures still carries with it the notion of respect. However, in our North American culture, status-giving roles and functions for the elderly are being destroyed, without satisfactory replacements. Tragically, many elderly people have accepted the negative social attitude about aging. One such attitude, *infantilization* of the elderly, is systemic in our health care programs. It can be defined as providing care activities for an elderly person beyond what is required by the person's needs or capacities. Infantilization results in learned helplessness. A vicious cycle is established whereby patronizing the elderly reduces their self-esteem, causing them to want to do less for themselves, which in turn makes them more helpless and childlike, and more in need of help.

Health care personnel, especially, are in a strategic position to affect the self-image of the institutionalized elderly. The negative attitudes and expectations of staff are frequently conveyed to elderly people, resulting in institutionally induced dependency. Troubling examples include the increasing numbers of elderly persons who are fed by staff or pushed about in wheelchairs, even though they are able to feed or walk by themselves. A classic example of infantilization is the children's high chair, modified for use by adults—the geriatric chair with the lockdown tabletop. It is a common restraint measure.

Losing people before they die is one of the most stressful aspects of dementia.

—NANCY MACE, THE 36-HOUR DAY

Much more obvious and poignant examples are to be found in the experience of older persons with dementing illnesses. As they grow progressively more dependent, and their capacity for adaptation diminishes, they are regarded as persons who have lost their "adultness." As they begin to act like children in their helplessness, power is transferred to health care personnel. With a dismaying disregard for the remaining potential of afflicted people, elders are:

- excluded from decision-making about their care;
- patronized;
- fed, dressed, bathed, and put to bed, although capable of performing many of these functions independently; and
- reprimanded and subjected to other forms of punishment when behavior deviates from the norms of the institution.

I REMEMBER VIVIDLY *a conversation with an old gentleman who was participating in a summer respite vacation for Alzheimer caregivers and their afflicted family members. I had been advised by the man's professional caregiver that he always went to bed directly after supper. When I offered to show him to his room, he became very reluctant and upset, so I asked him what was bothering him. He said, "I am a person! I want to stay up with the other people. Why do I have to go to bed?" When I encouraged him, by all means, to join us in front of the fireplace, he reached in his pocket and produced a mouth organ, with which he entertained us for several hours.*

Along with many other social, cultural, and moral issues, the myths of ageism and the models of care we use create serious problems for older people when they seek help from the existing health care system. And the cultural framework of the health care system limits and distorts the work of health care providers, including medical personnel, architects, interior designers, and people using the system.

One must wait until the evening to see how splendid the day has been.

—SOPHOCLES

Let's remember that the longer we live, the more we know; and the more we know, the more beautiful we are. We can actively create a new context for the experience of aging by shifting the outlook towards older people in our society. We are a cold and uncaring culture in our treatment of [North] Americans. In China, elders are respected and revered, which is a large part of why the Chinese live so long as healthy and productive citizens. We have thought that youth is better, and "thinking makes it so." Not because it is an objective truth, but only because it is a thought we carry and manifest in our collective experience.

—MARIANNE WILLIAMSON,
RETURN TO LOVE

2

Models are Maps for Action

*A model or paradigm is the set of ideas
that serves as a blueprint
or pattern for action.*

Older adults clearly need health care provided in a different way. To design more appropriate services, health care providers must first ask, "Why do we do things the way we presently do them?" Unless we examine the ideas that govern our actions—past and present—we are doomed to live with systems in the future that serve neither older people who need care, nor their families, nor professional care providers. Health care providers will continue to waste their creative energy on crisis management, finding Band-Aid solutions and never addressing the real problems, never asking older people themselves how they would like help to make their lives more fulfilling.

To generate ideas and guide our thinking in finding solutions we need new models. A model is a device we can use to find our way in the practice of care. We need to dust off our maps! This chapter examines the various models health care providers presently use to deliver care to people with dementing illness. So often, health care providers are driven not by the needs of people but by a sense of urgency. We just want to do something to fix the situation. We want to get the work done. We need to meet a deadline. We feel pressure to comply with rules, standards, schedules. We busy ourselves with paperwork or non-productive tasks. As a result, we frequently find ourselves working without any model or map. Perhaps worse, we may find that we are all using different maps. The work we do becomes fragmented, contradictory, frustrating, and most of all, ineffective. But we get on with it, even though it may be unclear what philosophy or principle drives our activities. We fail to ask ourselves:

- Who are these people whom we move, feed, and medicate?
- Where are their families?
- What are we doing for them?
- Why am I so tired and frustrated?
- What is the plan?
- Is there a plan?

A great many competent people are employed in providing health care to elderly people. New and renovated institutions are developed every day. Policies and procedures, standards and regulations, and guidelines are being written by the ton. Health policies are being developed. Budgets are being formulated; committees, associations, societies, teams, and consultants are being formed, all of them constantly meeting and conferencing. In short, there is a fierce focus on dementing diseases and what we should do about them.

But the bottom line in all of this activity is very simple. It is not a policy bottom line, financial bottom line, industrial relations bottom line, or regulatory bottom line. The definitive bottom line is:

- How well are they doing—the elderly people entrusted to our care?
- What is the quality of their daily existence?
- How are their families managing?

These questions must echo in our institutions, our policies, and our minds as we go about our daily responsibilities, no matter what level of work we do with people who suffer from dementia. Furthermore, the question, "How do my personal actions affect the lives of the people whose care is entrusted to me?" needs to be asked by researchers, ministers of health, housekeepers who shine the floors in care facilities, board members of societies that support and educate families, visiting homemakers, members of curriculum committees at universities, family caregivers, congregations in churches, dieticians, neighbors, union shop stewards, directors of care, grandchildren, and health care staff of institutions.

Until a medical cure for progressive dementing illnesses like Alzheimer's disease is found, the most effective way to help people who suffer the effects of such illnesses is to develop appropriate care systems. If the way we care for people with dementia is not a way that we ourselves could tolerate—if they are not comfortable; if they are anxious, confused, frightened, frustrated, or restrained; if they are abused, crushed, or empty—then we must change the way we are doing things, for the sake of afflicted people, for their families, for care providers, for our communities. To do this we need a map or model.

Developing a Health Care Paradigm

A model for the practice of health care develops from several elements:
- a *philosophy* based on the values and beliefs we hold sacred, personally, professionally, and as members of society; and
- a *body of knowledge,* compounded of data, observations, and analysis.

Our philosophy and knowledge base enable us to develop:
- a *frame of reference,* which is the assumptions and concepts that shape the way we work; and
- a *conceptual model* that helps us understand why we carry out a given type of practice.

On the basis of our conceptual model, we propose:
- our *model of practice* or how we do what we do, such as the strategies and activities that translate our conceptual model into reality; and
- the *expected results* or objectives of our model of practice. Outcomes are promises about what our model of practice will accomplish.

A model or paradigm of care, therefore, is the map we use to help us design and deliver a certain kind of health care. Many different models

In life each man paints his own portrait. And there is nothing but the portrait. It is not what you would have done, could have done, or should have done. . . . [It is] just what you did.

—JEAN PAUL SARTRE

of care have been used or proposed. Several are currently in use, each based on a different set of principles or theories about care and treatment:

- The *custodial care model* focuses on maintaining the physical condition of a person in care for as long as possible.
- The *biomedical acute care* model centers on the treatment and elimination of symptoms which are signs of pathology. The emphasis is on efficiency and speedy resolution of the problem. Staff is trained to be emotionally neutral and objective. The primary interventions are invasive strategies, drugs, and surgery. Body and mind are regarded as separate entities, although this view is beginning to change. The acute care environment is institutional and technologically intensive. The sick person is regarded as a "patient" who is dependent upon professional staff for information and problem resolution. In acute care situations, the labor force is divided along professional or territorial lines, which is very costly. This model of care has been very successful in the treatment of physical illness. The biomedical model is very costly.
- The *functional independence* model is concerned with a person's ability to function socially and psychologically with physical well-being.
- The *therapeutic model*'s goal is a person's successful integration of physical and social achievement.
- The *prosthetic model of care,* which I developed, is based on the premise that appropriate care can be given only when there has been an accurate assessment of the deficit a person is experiencing. Only then can the macro-environment (people, programs, and physical space) be organized into a *prosthesis of care* designed to compensate for the person's deficits, to support existing or residual function, and to maximize quality of life.

In this chapter we have been talking about various models of practice now in use, and the need to change them to respond to changing clinical issues and profiles. If we are to accomplish such change, we will have to ask ourselves:

GENTLECARE
PROSTHETIC MODEL OF CARE FOR DEMENTIA

Philosophy
- Elderly people have value.
- People with dementia suffer from a complex disease.
- Independence is better than dependence.
- Internal control is better than external control.
- Individuals have a right to a meaningful existence, whatever their level of development or health problem.
- People with dementia have diminished resources to control or direct their behavior.
- Care providers can change their behavior to be more effective.

Knowledge
- Precise diagnosis and identification of the dementing illness and its effects.
- Social history and context of people with dementia is known.

Gentlecare Frame of Reference
- Behavior can be affected by external stimulus.
- Behavior occurs within a context.

Conceptual Model
- Performance deficits can be compensated for by a prosthesis of support composed of people, programs, and physical space.

Model of Practice
- Know the person and the disease.
- Engage the family in therapeutic partnership.
- Educate the therapeutic agent(s).
- Identify and control external influences, and modify strategies.
- Modify the environment.
- Design meaningful opportunities for activity.
- Evaluate.

Outcomes
- Behavioral change can be achieved.
- Behavior can be shaped, changed, generalized, and/or extinguished.
- Functional levels can be altered to enhance independence.
- Personal resources can be preserved.
- Costs can be reduced.

FIGURE 2-1

- How does transformation from one paradigm to another happen?
- What can be usefully retained of the old models, and what must be created anew?

T.S. Kuhn, in his groundbreaking book, *The Structure of Scientific Revolutions* (University of Chicago Press, 1974), notes:

> Since new paradigms are born from old ones, they ordinarily incorporate much of the vocabulary and apparatus, both conceptual and manipulative, that the traditional paradigm had previously employed. But they seldom employ these borrowed elements in quite the traditional way. Within the new paradigm, old terms, concepts and experiments fall into what we must call, though the term is not quite right, a misunderstanding between the two competing schools.

The Gentlecare Prosthetic Life Care System is an example of a prosthetic model of care. It provides a new map that can lead us through the maze-like process of dementia care.

> *A human being is part of the whole, called by us the "Universe," a part limited in time and space. He experiences himself, his thoughts and feelings, as something separated from the rest—a kind of optical delusion of his consciousness. This delusion is a kind of prison for us, restricting us to our personal desires and to affection for a few persons nearest to us. Our task must be to free ourselves from this prison by widening our circles of compassion to embrace all living creatures and the whole of nature in its beauty.*
>
> —ALBERT EINSTEIN

CHARACTERISTICS OF THE PROSTHETIC HEALTH CARE PARADIGM

- The prosthetic model of care focuses on patterns of behavior and causes of problems.

- Human values, conversation, and connections are emphasized by staff whose method of caring is the major component of therapy.

- Noninvasive tools and techniques are used, with significant reliance on an appropriate person/environment fit; the focus is on the use of human interaction (music, massage, hugs, pets, walks, talks).

- Integration of body, mind, and spirit is critical to the care approach.

- Environments are simple, normalized, therapeutic, and prosthetic.

- Since many of the symptoms of dementing illness cannot be treated, the emphasis is on identifying and supporting remaining function.

- The objective of dementia care is to assist and support the client and his family.

- The social context is vital; professionals, families, and communities work in therapeutic partnership.

- All staff are the principal therapeutic agents; their way of caring is the major component of therapy.

- There is a mix of jobs by small groups.

FIGURE 2-2

3

An Overview of Gentlecare

My wish, indeed my continuing passion, would be not to point the
finger in judgment, but to part a curtain, that invisible shadow
that falls between people; the veil of indifference to each other's
presence, each other's wonder, each other's human plight.
—Eudora Welty,
American author

Gentlecare is a prosthetic system of dementia care designed to change the experience of a dementing illness such as Alzheimer's disease for those afflicted persons, their families, and professional caregivers. The system is based on my personal experience, as well as on the experience of hundreds of professional and family caregivers who, like me, are searching for more appropriate solutions to the devastating problems raised by dementia.

The challenge of providing appropriate services to older people with dementing illnesses preoccupies health care planners and practitioners alike. As knowledge of those illnesses grows, it is becoming clear that current health systems, policies, and models of care not only compromise quality of life for people with dementia; they are sources of *iatrogenic illness* as well. Iatrogenic illness is illness caused by the care, the environment, or factors other than the disease. It results in accelerated loss of function for people suffering from dementia, and therefore in excessive dependency on other people; ultimately such illness escalates the costs of care.

In addition, current health care practices distance family caregivers from their loved ones, causing untold anguish and frustration. Professional health care providers also report ever-increasing levels of personal stress, physical injury, and job dissatisfaction.

Gentlecare offers a positive approach not only to the relentless progress of dementing illness, but also to the unnecessary dysfunction and heartache of iatrogenic illness. The system is rooted in a recognition of the person with dementia as a unique and special human being with a rich history and a difficult future. This person is acknowledged to be experiencing devastating problems, and so deserves appropriate and compassionate assistance with the life challenges to come.

Unfortunately, there is a malignant myth in dementia care that family caregivers may take responsibility for people with dementia for the first few years of the illness, but then professional caregivers need to take over. On occasion, families have been encouraged to disappear from the caregiving scene, or to "have a rest." When this happens, family members sometimes feel impotent or unnecessary and may sever their relationship with the afflicted family member. This causes untold anguish and frustration.

In the Gentlecare system the person suffering from dementia is thought of as part of a family, and any intervention takes this into account. Gentlecare emphasizes that whole families, not just individuals, suffer from Alzheimer's disease. Effective dementia care must acknowledge the power of family by supporting and assisting family members, and involving them in the care process. If there is no existing family, it is sometimes necessary to create an artificial or surrogate family.

The Concept of a Prosthesis of Care: People, Programs, and Physical Space

Gentlecare is a comprehensive program designed to prepare professional staff and family caregivers to care for persons with primary progressive dementias. The system is applicable in acute care institutions, long-term care facilities, and day care programs; and it changes the way family caregivers see their role in a demented person's own home.

Gentlecare advocates a major shift in focus away from a concentra-

One of the most preva-
lent medical problems
of our times is iatrogenic
illness. It results from
surgical complications,
wrong medication, side
effects of drugs or other
treatments, and the
debilitating effects
of hospitalization.

—THE AQUARIAN
CONSPIRACY

tion on the behaviors of the person with dementia, and toward an adjustment of the physical and social environment in which the person must operate. It involves a significant paradigm shift in the way we think and act in caring for people with dementia.

This process begins by ensuring that staff and family members clearly understand the clinical process and implications of progressive dementia. The emphasis is on an awareness of the afflicted person's relationships and life context, in which the person lives, rather than on crisis intervention. Family members and staff are helped to identify and remove stressors in the environment of the person with dementia. They are encouraged to develop effective strategies and programs that will help the individual live more comfortably within the environment.

Gentlecare assists staff and families to evaluate the functional strengths and deficits of the person, and provides them with assessment methods, criteria for admission to special care units, strategies for problem-solving and stress reduction, and tools to alleviate troubling behaviors.

Caregivers learn how to maximize the afflicted person's existing abilities by designing and developing exciting activities and helpful programs, and integrating supportive care patterns into daily life. Suggestions are made for communication techniques that family caregivers and professionals can use with people experiencing dementia.

The Gentlecare system advocates a therapeutic partnership among care facilities, families, and community volunteers. Suggestions are offered on how to involve families and community volunteers in assisting with dementia care, creating a modified community for the afflicted person within the health care system.

Gentlecare advocates adapted "work" therapy strategies to help improve the demented person's quality of life. Such strategies can provide

Touch is the most powerful positive intervention.

Delta Habilitation Centre, Delta, BC, Canada.
This building was designed specifically to provide dedicated indoor and outdoor living space for people with dementia. It is composed of four living spaces, each of which opens onto a therapeutic garden.

people with meaningful activity while showing respect for former lifestyles and roles. The Gentlecare system accommodates and supports existing levels of function and development, rather than requiring people with dementia to perform in ways that are no longer possible.

Although I have sickness in me, if the focus is on my wellness, allow it to overshadow my sickness.

—AUTHOR UNKNOWN

Gentlecare is a system that focuses on using the *macro-environment* to achieve effective dementia care. Methods are outlined for developing prosthetic physical environments—both indoors and outdoors—that support rather than challenge dysfunctional persons. Suggestions are made for modifying existing environments, as well as for designing and developing purpose-built facilities. Gentlecare designs a prosthesis of care or *enviro-match* between people with dementing illness and:
- the physical space in which they live;
- their daily activities; and
- the significant people with whom they interact.

People with dementia are not asked to perform activities in ways they no longer can. Contrast this with the usual care facility environment. Most care facilities provide communal living arrangements, set up within buildings that are institutional in design and frequently technologically focused. Inside those buildings, an unbelievable array of activities takes place—maintenance and housekeeping, education, life-saving health care, public functions—all happening alongside the daily activities of people dealing with dementia. It is hard for us to even imagine our own lives being played out in the midst of such a hive of bewildering activity.

> ### PROSTHESIS
> A device or artificial structure (either external or implanted) that substitutes for, or supplements, a missing or defective part.

In the Gentlecare system, the environment is regarded as more than just the physical space in which people live. The macro-environment of people with progressive dementing illness consists of people, programs, and physical space, working in a dynamic interaction. The macro-environment forms the total context in which the person with dementing illness must live and function throughout the course of the disease.

Gentlecare introduces the concept of the *prosthesis of care,* in which the three components—people, programs, and physical space—work in harmony to produce a support, or *prosthesis* for the person with dementia. Such a prosthesis compensates for the deficits created by a dementing illness.

The replacement of physical body parts by prosthetic devices is a well-accepted procedure in health care. If someone sustains a spinal cord injury, for example, a wheelchair is prescribed to compensate for the resulting paralysis. With this prosthesis, the injured person can regain control over life; without the prosthesis, the person is dependent on others and quite helpless.

Dementia destroys people's ability to manage their needs and be in control in a way that closely parallels the effects of physical paralysis, since it, too, makes them dependent on others for daily care. Just as a wheelchair can recreate mobility for a spinal injury patient, an appropriate prosthesis can give a person with dementia an improved quality of life. Gentlecare manipulates those three vital components—people, programs, and physical space—in ways that assist and support people through the course of a dementing illness.

People: The First Element of the Prosthesis of Care

Of the three components of the person's macro-environment, by far the most critical is people. The person with dementia is surrounded by people, including the key family caregiver (usually a spouse or a mid-life daughter or son) and other significant family members. They form a vital support system that must be maintained throughout the disease process—regardless of where the person with dementia lives. Professional care providers form an artificial support system that needs to be specifically focused. And people with dementia are forced to live with large numbers of other ill people, which can make life very challenging. In addition to these key individuals, at any point in time the dysfunctional person's "home" may be invaded by any number of other people, such as volunteers, visitors, or administrative staff.

All these people can either be agents of help or forces of destruction in their impact on the health of a person with dementia. Their beliefs, attitudes, and language shape the life of the person with dementia; their level of education, skills, and judgment can make all the difference in the world. In Gentlecare, people are the essential therapeutic agents of dementia care.

Programs: The Second Element of the Prosthesis of Care

Programs include everything the person with dementia does or has done to him, in a 24-hour cycle. In place of the standard rigid activity schedule driven by artificial wake-up times, sleep times, and meal times, interspersed with sporadic social or recreational activities, Gentlecare uses *all* activity in the life of the person with dementia to enhance his experience and ensure he leads a meaningful life.

Programs designed for persons with dementia are most effective when they are an integral part of daily life, rather than "add-ons" or "take-outs," or activities parachuted into the daily routine. Programming that focuses on and supports self-care, communication, intimacy, relaxation, stress reduction, competency, and former life roles often has magical effects on persons with dementia. All program initiatives should be designed to support and celebrate the existing strengths of people in care.

Physical Space: The Third Element of the Prosthesis of Care

The physical environment of people with dementia needs to be simple, normalized, and therapeutic. It must be space designed to be lived in, and must resonate with familiar personal memorabilia.

Experience has shown that areas dedicated for the use of people with dementia most effectively support their needs. Many design features can help to enhance function and quality of life, such as secure perimeters; indoor and outdoor walking paths; appropriate wayfinding cues and signage; multiple small social and dining areas; avoidance of distracting patterns; reduction of glare, noise, and confusion; and family cluster living arrangements.

The Impact of the Prosthesis of Care

It has been said that the challenge for people with dementia is not in facing death—it is facing life.

The task of helping people with the formidable cognitive damage caused by dementing illness is daunting. Gentlecare takes on this task by first identifying the disease, and then assessing the specific deficits in function caused by the disease at a given moment in time. Then Gentlecare designs a personal prosthesis of care for each person with dementia, to help each of them manage daily life challenges. The components of the prosthesis of care—people, programs, and physical space—are not costly add-ons to existing programs; they are part of existing basic health care services. However, Gentlecare organizes those components differently, so that they support—rather than challenge—the person with cognitive impairment.

In Gentlecare, people, programs, and physical space are set up in creative, dynamic interaction. Gentlecare prostheses have as many variations as there are people needing help or people offering help. For example:

- In a Gentlecare unit, maintenance workers don't just walk into a room to fix a tap or hang a picture. As members of the Gentlecare team, they are aware of working in a person's "home." Therefore, they engage in conversation with the person with dementia, identify the project, ask for the host's opinion—in other words, attempt to involve the host, however marginally. Thanks is given for any contribution to the work, thereby enhancing self-esteem.

- In hospitals and health care facilities, public address systems are used to call people to telephones, make announcements, and alert people to emergencies. This practice is not viewed favorably in Gentlecare units, since sudden, loud voices issuing from the PA system are frightening, disorienting, intrusive, and confusing for people struggling with cognitive impairment. A Gentlecare environment eliminates this stress factor, and uses personal pagers or written messages instead of public address systems.

It works! It works!

—A CARE AIDE

- It is common practice in health care institutions for the night shift staff to get people up and dressed before the day shift staff arrives, in order to "get a head start on the day's work." This is one of the most unsettling of all institutional practices. Gentlecare units, in contrast, adapt the morning wake-up routine so that older, cognitively impaired people can wake up naturally. They are not rushed, they are helped to enjoy the beginning of their day, and they are appropriately oriented and prepared for the coming day's activities.

This is really common sense!

—A DIRECTOR OF NURSING CARE

These are but three examples of different ways to help. Gentlecare is a simple, common sense, affordable, "do-able" approach to care that can be practiced by family caregivers, professional caregivers, support staff, volunteers, friends, and neighbors alike.

The Gentlecare system enables people who are ill to lead tolerable, even comfortable, lives, avoiding confrontation and crises despite the devastation of their disease. It gives life back to family caregivers, and protects them against threats to their own health by helping them avoid crises.

Gentlecare empowers professional care providers, offering them new ways to address problems in their workplace. It reduces accidents and injuries, improves staff morale, and puts joy back into the workplace.

The Theater of Gentlecare

People often ask me how I think of solutions to the endless number of problems that arise in caring for people with dementia—how I visualize Gentlecare in action within a care facility. I often think of Gentlecare as a theatrical performance, one in which staff members, family caregivers, volunteers, and the people with dementia are engaged in the presentation of an ongoing play.

I see the people with dementia as the actors in the play. I see the unit manager, the care coordinator, or the supervisor as the director of the play—the person who pulls all the bits and pieces together to keep momentum. I see the people who work in activities and recreation, the custodial staff and volunteers, as the stage crew who prepare the stage and sets in which the play takes place.

The care aides and others who give direct care act as prompters. I imagine that each person with dementia has a prompter—a care aide, a family caregiver, a volunteer, or one of the support staff. The prompter is there to keep the actors (people with dementia) on track by giving cues, reminding them of lines, and giving them the information they need to carry out their daily "performance." The play takes place throughout all the working hours.

Everyone has to know the care plan, which is the manuscript for the play. The "director/unit manager" has the master copy of the script/ care plan, and everyone has the same script, and everyone follows it. The lines and the stage directions are all there.

If a change to the script is proposed by the director, one of the stage crew, or a prompter, or if a script change is made because of a change in the condition of the actor, it is the director's responsibility to ensure that the suggested change is suitable and effective. The director must also ensure that the whole crew knows what the change is, and that it is written into the script.

OUTCOMES OF GENTLECARE

Institutions and families using the Gentlecare Prosthetic Life Care System
report the following outcomes:

• improved levels of functioning in the person with dementia

• greater participation in self-care activities

• increased spontaneous socialization and communication

• reduced non-cognitive and assaultive behaviors

• less wandering

• fewer arguments and altercations

• fewer episodes of catastrophic behavior

• reduced incontinence

• improved family comfort and participation in care

• accelerated volunteer and community involvement

• trends indicating cost savings

FIGURE 3-1

At any given point in the day, one or more actors are on stage performing an activity. They could be having a bath, eating a meal, going to
an exercise program, or waking up and getting dressed for the day. The
people with dementia are helped to perform that activity.

When that scene is completed, they go off stage and rest, in the
same way that actors perform a scene and then exit and rest before they
come back on stage. The job of the director is to facilitate the whole theatrical event and to make sure that every person with dementia has a
prompter; that each actor has the necessary information and support to
perform appropriately; and that the whole environment supports the
role that each one plays.

Every single person on the unit—physician, board member, housekeeping staff, visitor, nurse, care aide, or rehabilitation staff member—
has to be aware of what play is being presented each day. They must
know the actors' abilities and their roles. They must know what kind of
props and sets are needed to perform properly. It's up to them to prepare all that—to support, encourage, and inspire people with dementia
to give the best performances of which they are capable.

*I feel as if a light bulb
had gone on in my
head. Now, when I
look at the person with
dementia through
different eyes, I know
how to help him.*

—A PHYSICIAN

4

Why Do They Do
What They Do?

I'm not stupid!
I have Alzheimer's disease!
　　　—a person with Alzheimer's

Fundamental to the design of the Gentlecare program or any dementia care program is an understanding of dementing disease. Dementia is the loss of intellectual functions—such as thinking, remembering, and reasoning—of sufficient severity to interfere with a person's daily functioning.

Dementia is not a disease in itself, but rather a group of symptoms that may accompany certain diseases or physical conditions. The degree of damage and rate of progression of dementias varies, depending on both the cause of the symptoms and the particular individual affected. Some of the more familiar diseases that produce dementia include Alzheimer's disease, multi-infarct dementia, Huntington's disease, and sometimes Parkinson's disease.

Dementia can present in either acute or chronic forms. Acute dementias (or acute deliriums) are metabolic or systemic in nature. They respond to treatment and the damage can often be reversed. Chronic dementias, on the other hand, for the most part cannot be treated successfully, since the damage that creates the dementia is structural and irreversible. There is permanent damage to brain tissue.

Alzheimer's disease (pronounced *Allts' hi-merz*) was first described by Dr. Alois Alzheimer in 1907. It is the most common of the dementing disorders, and is a progressive, degenerative disease that attacks brain cells and results in impaired memory, thinking, and behavior. The rate of progression, as with all dementias, varies from one person to another.

ALZHEIMER'S DISEASE

The time from diagnosis to death, on average, is eight years, but may range from five to twenty years.

Ten to fifteen percent of persons with Alzheimer's disease hallucinate or have delusions.

One in ten people with Alzheimer's disease has seizures.

—*US News and World Report,* August 1991

Not infrequently, when we first meet people with dementia, we know very little about the essential person behind the disease. It is not possible to treat such people appropriately until we know the answers to these basic questions:

- Who is this man or woman?
- What is important to him or her?
- Does he have different perceptions than I?
- How does she feel?

More often than not, professional caregivers know very little about the actual process of dementing disease, or how far the disease has progressed in an individual. Families rarely have the information they need to be able to react appropriately to their loved one's actions. Caregivers, both lay and professional, need to be aware that there is a direct correlation between the nature of disease the person is experiencing and the behavior they are exhibiting.

Behavior—especially problem behavior—does not occur at random or in isolation. Behavior follows a course that corresponds to the disease process. People suffering from a dementing disease behave the way they do because the disease has evolved to a particular stage. The symptoms and unusual behaviors that result from brain damage

DEMENTIA

Types

Acute/Delirium

- responds to treatment
- is metabolic/systemic
- damage may be reversed

Chronic

- cannot be reversed
- structural damage
- irreversible damage to
  the brain tissue

Causes

- drug toxicity
- alcoholism
- dehydration
- hypothyroidism
- vitamin B12 deficit
- depression
- sensory deficits
- infections
- congestive heart failure
- malnutrition
- stress
- compounded loss

- Alzheimer's disease
- multi-infarct/vascular
- Huntington's disease
- Pick's disease
- Parkinson's disease
- Korsakoff's syndrome
- AIDS-related dementia

(Diseases may occur in any combination.)

FIGURE 4-1

corresponds to the particular function of the damaged area of the brain. In fact, these effects are sometimes referred to as "physiological maps" of the brain, since they indicate what area of the brain has been affected.

The behavior of people with dementia is exacerbated by stressors such as terror, confusion, frustration, misconceptions, disorientation, and (justifiable) anger. Their actions are seldom premeditated, but are based on feelings rather than thought. *Their behavior is the best behavior they are capable of, given the circumstances they find themselves in.* Behavior is the window to a person's mind, and must be studied very carefully.

Most caregiver action or care plans developed for people with dementia are behavior driven: that is, a care strategy, intervention, or procedure is initiated in response to the fact that a person with dementia has behaved in a certain way—rather than as a response to the functional implications of the disease that caused the behavior.

For example, consider a person who is observed to be walking randomly. A typical behavior-driven strategy is to get the person to sit down and be quiet. But suppose the wandering person is trying to find a drink? As Alzheimer's disease progresses, the part of the brain that regulates body thirst is damaged, and people with Alzheimer's disease frequently experience terrible thirst. Suppose the person is trying to find a drink while disoriented and confused by a complex environment?

Behavior is the window to a person's mind. It allows us to understand why a person acts the way they do.

If our care strategy has been to ask the person to sit down or we have ensured compliance through the use of restraints, how effective have we been in meeting that person's actual needs? Thirst is a powerful need, and the person may be quite persistent in trying to quench it. How much will the control strategies need to be escalated to ensure that the person stays put? Will that require a verbal request, physical restraint, or control by drugs?

Alzheimer's disease progresses without visible "markers." We must therefore rely on the behaviors we can observe to give clues about a person's functional abilities. Only with that information can we build a plan of care that addresses the person's needs appropriately. If in devising a care plan strategy we fail to make the vital connection between the person, the disease he is experiencing, and the behaviors he is exhibiting as a result, then we will likely fall far short of giving appropriate care to that person. Making that connection changes the way we deliver dementia care.

Planning Care Using the Gentlecare Formula

The Gentlecare formula is a method of organizing thinking and action based on a comprehensive evaluation of the needs of a person with dementia—rather than on a reactive response to the person's behavior.

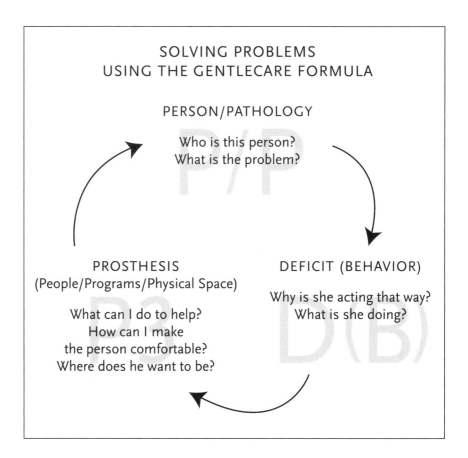

SOLVING PROBLEMS
USING THE GENTLECARE FORMULA

PERSON/PATHOLOGY

Who is this person?
What is the problem?

DEFICIT (BEHAVIOR)

Why is she acting that way?
What is she doing?

PROSTHESIS
(People/Programs/Physical Space)

What can I do to help?
How can I make
the person comfortable?
Where does he want to be?

FIGURE 4-2

The formula helps us to remember that all intervention should be designed for the individual, and based on the specific pathology the person is experiencing (person/pathology). Next, the deficit in functioning caused by the disease is reviewed; this is done by observing and monitoring the deficit the individual is experiencing as manifested or exhibited by his behavior (D(B)). Once the problem has been correctly identified, a prosthesis of care strategy can be developed (prosthesis). In Gentlecare this prosthesis consists of supportive people, meaningful strategies, and a residential environment that supports the person.

It should be noted that the Gentlecare formula works from any point in the triangle (see Figure 4-2). For example, we can observe a behavior and ask what deficit that represents before we plan strategies. It is not uncommon in health care facilities to observe elderly people engaging in unusual sexual behavior. When staff encounter such behavior, it is helpful if they are aware that such activity on the part of elderly people is usually due to damage to the part of the brain that provides emotional and sexual control, rather than being malevolent premeditated behavior. This information helps to devise an appropriate response rather than a judgmental or punitive one.

Alternatively, we can use the formula to examine the appropriateness of the prosthesis given the particular deficit of the individual in care. For example, if the strategy in a health care facility is to wake, groom, and dress individuals early in the morning, we might ask: Given an individual's personal preferences and habits, together with the damage caused by the disease, is this stressful care strategy contributing to this person's behavior? Could we devise a better strategy?

Understanding "Childlike" Behaviors

As discussed in Chapter 1, Dr. Barry Reisberg suggests that people suffering from a dementing disease experience loss of skills in a sequence not unlike that which a child follows in the development of skills, but in reverse order. As a result, although people with dementia are *not* children, they are childlike. We must respect them as elders at all times; however, if we want to help them appropriately, we need to understand that they are losing the abilities we normally assume older people have. Consequently, their behavior as adults may appear to be inappropriate or irresponsible.

> I REMEMBER AN *elderly lady saying to me, "Moyra, caring for my husband is like running around after an eight-year-old all day! I'm exhausted." And of course, given the stage of illness, his behavior did resemble that of an eight-year-old child.*

The following scale clearly outlines the performance deficits that a person with dementia will experience. It is very helpful as a guide to care planning.

Behind the idea
And the reality
Between the motion
And the Act
Falls the shadow

—T.S. ELIOT,
   THE HOLLOW MEN

REVERSE ORDER OF DEVELOPMENT SCALE

APPROX. AGE	ABILITIES	STAGE OF DISEASE
12 Yrs	Hold a job	Borderline
8–12 Yrs	Handle simple finances	Early (Stage 2)
5–7 Yrs	Select proper clothing	Moderate (Stage 3 & 4)
5 Yrs	Put on clothes Personal grooming	Severe (Stage 5)
4 Yrs	Go to toilet unaided	
3–4½ Yrs	Control urine	
3 Yrs	Control bowels	
15 Months	Speak 5–6 words	Late (Stage 6)
1 Yr	Speak 1 word	
1 Yr	Walk	
6–9 Months	Sit up	
2–3 Months	Smile	

ABILITIES INCREASE WITH AGE

ABILITIES DECREASE WITH DISEASE

FIGURE 4-3

Reference: Dr. Barry Reisberg

The information provided in the Global Deterioration Scale (pages 39 to 41) helps families and other care providers to understand the stages of Alzheimer's disease.

THE GLOBAL DETERIORATION SCALE FOR ASSESSMENT OF PRIMARY DEGENERATIVE DEMENTIA	
Level	Clinical Characteristics
I No cognitive decline	No subjective complaint of memory deficit. No memory deficit evident on clinical interview.
II Very mild cognitive decline (forgetfulness)	Subjective complaints of memory deficit, most frequently in the following areas: (a) forgetting where one has placed familiar objects; (b) forgetting names one formerly knew well. No objective evidence of memory deficit on clinical interview. No objective deficit in employment or social situations. Appropriate concern with respect to symptomatology.
III Mild cognitive decline (early confusional)	Early clear-cut deficits. Manifestations in more than one of the following areas: (a) patient may have gotten lost while traveling to an unfamiliar destination; (b) co-workers become aware of patient's relatively poor performance; (c) word- and name-finding deficit becomes evident to intimates; (d) patient may read a passage or book and retain little material; (e) patient may demonstrate decreased facility in remembering names upon introduction to new people; (f) patient may have lost or misplaced an object of value; (g) concentration deficit may be evident in clinical testing. Objective evidence of memory deficit obtained only with intensive interview. Decreased performance in demanding employment and social settings. Denial begins to become manifest in patient. Mild to moderate anxiety accompanies symptoms.

FIGURE 4-4

IV Moderate cognitive decline (late confusional)	Clear-cut deficits on careful clinical interview. Deficit manifest in the following areas: (a) decreased knowledge of current and recent events; (b) may exhibit some deficit in memory of personal history; (c) concentration deficit elicited on serial subtractions; (d) decreased ability to travel to familiar locations. Inability to perform complex tasks. Denial is a dominant defense mechanism. Flattening of affect and withdrawal from challenging situations occurs.
V Moderate-severe cognitive decline (early dementia)	Patient can no longer survive without assistance. During interview, patient unable to recall major, relevant aspects of his current life—e.g., address or telephone number of many years' standing, the names of close family members (such as grandchildren) or the name of the high school or college from which they graduated. Frequently some disorientation to time (date, day of the week, season, etc.) or to place. An educated person may have difficulty counting backward from 40 by 4's or from 20 by 2's. Persons at this stage retain knowledge of many major facts about themselves and others. They invariably know their own names and generally know the names of their spouses and children. They require no assistance with toileting or eating, but may have difficulty choosing proper clothing to wear.
VI Severe cognitive decline (middle dementia)	Many patients at this stage occasionally forget the name of the spouse on whom they are entirely dependent for survival. Will be largely unaware of all recent events and experiences in their lives. Retain some knowledge of their past lives, but this is very sketchy. Generally unaware of their surroundings, the year, the season, etc. May have difficulty counting from 10 both backward and (sometimes) forward.

	Will require some assistance with activities of daily living (e.g., may become incontinent). Will require assistance with travel but occasionally will display ability to find familiar locations. Diurnal rhythm frequently disturbed. Almost always recall their own names. Frequently continue to be able to distinguish from unfamiliar people in their environment. Personality and emotional changes occur; these are quite variable, and include (a) delusional behavior (e.g., patient may accuse spouse of being an imposter, may talk to imaginary figures, or to their own reflections in the mirror); (b) obsessive symptoms appear—the demented person may continually repeat simple cleaning activities; (c) anxiety symptoms, agitation, and even previously nonexistent violent behavior may occur; (d) cognitive abulia occurs (loss of willpower because an individual cannot carry a thought long enough to determine a purposeful course of action).
VII Very severe cognitive decline (late dementia)	All verbal abilities are lost. Frequently there is no speech at all, only grunting. Incontinent of urine, requires assistance with toileting and feeding. Loses basic psychomotor skills (e.g., the ability to walk). It appears the brain is no longer able to tell the body what to do. Generalized and cortical neurological signs and symptoms are frequently present.

Reisberg, B., Ferris, S.H., Leon, M.J., and Cook, T. The Global Deterioration Scale for the Assessment of Primary Degenerative Dementia. *American Journal of Psychiatry* 139: 1136–1139, 1992.

PARTS OF THE BRAIN
AFFECTED BY ALZHEIMER'S

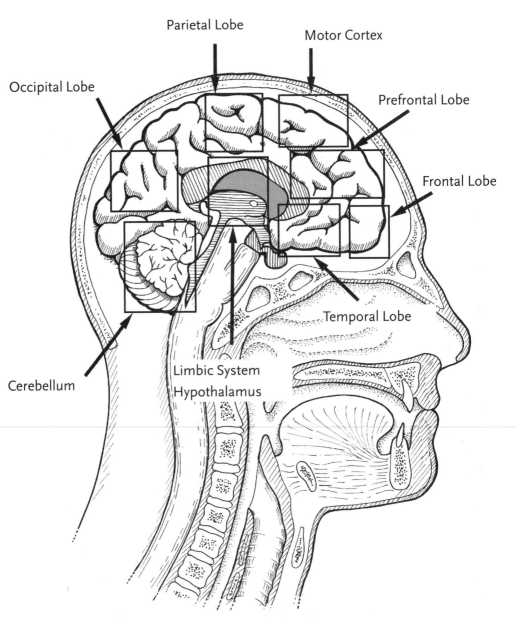

Parietal Lobe

Motor Cortex

Occipital Lobe

Prefrontal Lobe

Frontal Lobe

Temporal Lobe

Cerebellum

Limbic System
Hypothalamus

FIGURE 5-1

5

The Clinical Course of Alzheimer's Disease

I think, therefore I am.
—René Descartes

The Gentlecare system emphasizes the need for family members and professional caregivers to understand the nature of the diseases experienced by the people in their care. Each dementing disease has its own progression, which produces its own sequence of behaviors. I'll use Alzheimer's disease to illustrate the course of dementia, because it is the dementing disease seen most often. It affects every area of the brain, and so illustrates all the problems associated with any of the dementias, such as vascular illness, Parkinson's disease, chronic alcoholism, and others. Understanding the pathology of Alzheimer's disease helps caregivers and family members to understand behaviors caused by any of the dementing illnesses.

What follows in this chapter is an explanation of the effects that Alzheimer's disease has on brain tissue, and consequently on brain function and behavior.

First Signs: Damage to the Limbic System

In Alzheimer's disease, the first nerve cells to die are those in the area deep within the brain known as the *limbic system*. The limbic system is responsible for memory and emotional control. Memory processing

LIMBIC SYSTEM
Damage

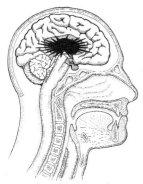

FIGURE 5-2

may take place throughout the whole brain, but certain areas within and bordering the limbic system, particularly the hippocampus, appear to be vital to memory. Control of sexuality is also thought to be located there.

As this area of the brain becomes filled with the characteristic tangles and plaques of Alzheimer's disease, memories of the recent past fade and the memory processing function becomes compromised. Over time, more long-standing memories will fade.

As the limbic system dies, affected people give evidence of emotional instability. They experience rapid changes of mood, alternating between a flat affect and euphoria. They are unable to control their anxiety, and switch rapidly from states of fearfulness to restlessness to irritability to aggressiveness—eventually lapsing into helplessness. At this point in the disease process, the following behaviors arise:

- People will act fearful and anxious.
- They may act depressed and suspicious.
- They are certainly terrified and frustrated.
- They may have verbal outbursts.
- They are agitated.
- They engage in seemingly purposeless activity, wandering to and fro, trying to make sense of what is happening to them.
- They are unable to retain the meaning of written words after reading.
- They misplace objects and then become suspicious that others may be taking or hiding things from them.
- They may be sexually active.

To build a prosthesis for people with these problems, caregivers need to be understanding, supportive, and provide information as often as necessary—as often as the afflicted person requests it. The person with dementia needs therapy for depression and/or anxiety. All stresses on the patient, and demands or expectations placed on them, must be modified. Life activities need to be simplified. The family needs education and assistance in terms of sexual issues.

Damage Spreads to the Parietal Area

Damage eventually spreads upward to the parietal area of the cortex. The *parietal lobe* is the center for spatial perception, sensory integration, and concentration. As this area of the brain becomes affected, people with Alzheimer's lose the ability to recognize places, objects, and people (faces). At this stage:

- They easily become disoriented and lost.
- They begin to lose the ability to recognize familiar sensory stimuli, a condition called *agnosia*.
- They have problems identifying objects in terms of their function.
- They begin to have problems identifying people—especially those of a different generation, or people they do not see often (called *visual agnosia*). Families need to understand why the person may not recognize them.
- They may experience imaginary visual images (hallucinations).
- One in ten people with dementia will have grand mal or petit mal seizures.
- They lose the ability to concentrate or focus. This means a person with Alzheimer's disease will have trouble maintaining attention and will be very easily distracted. Noises or activity in the environment can interfere with the person's ability to listen, process information, and perform a given activity. At this point in the disease, stress of any kind is toxic. This is a critical deficit.
- As spatial perception declines, they begin to lose the ability to locate certain parts of the body. Activities like grooming, or following directions in exercise groups, become difficult.
- Deteriorating hand skills often makes it difficult for them to carry out activities of daily living, such as crafts, cooking, and so on. This is the beginning of what is called *constructional apraxia*.
- They begin to experience deterioration in speech organization. The person with dementia has difficulty interpreting symbols, and thus cannot benefit from signs or notes. As a result, driving (for example) becomes dangerous.
- They have difficulty with syntax (the rules governing the arrange-

PARIETAL LOBE
Damage

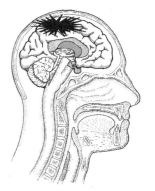

FIGURE 5-3

ment of words in sentences). These problems are referred to as *auditory agnosia.*

- They have problems in touch interpretation (*tactile agnosia*); they can't identify an object unless they can see it. Care needs to be taken with sharp objects.

To build a prosthesis for people with these problems, caregivers must assist the person by "grounding" them and helping them to focus and concentrate. This is accomplished by reducing stress, noise, glare, confusion, and rush in the living environment. The person's tasks and environment are simplified. Good wayfinding cues are needed, such as written cues, pictures, and familiar objects. All the person's senses need to be involved for orientation. Desired activities can be mimed to "kick-start" tasks. Figure/ground distinctions need to be emphasized so the person can recognize objects. Family members and care staff need help to understand the stage of dementia, which will improve their effectiveness.

TEMPORAL LOBE
Damage

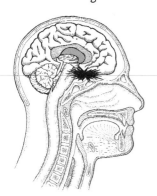

FIGURE 5-4

Damage Continues: Involvement of the Temporal Lobe

The disease next attacks the *temporal lobe,* the area of the brain just beneath the temple. The temporal lobe is the center of speech and language control, and is also responsible for time awareness.

At this point in the disease process the person with Alzheimer's must cope with yet another devastating loss as they experience problems with communication. Communication is what makes us uniquely human—it is the way we reach out to one another, make our wishes known, and give voice to our thoughts and feelings. Once a person loses the ability to communicate she slips into a subhuman limbo and begins to lose control of her life. Others speak for her, make decisions for her, determine her needs and wishes as they see fit. The person with dementia becomes invisible.

People with temporal lobe damage demonstrate the following deficits:

- They forget names, even those of close family members.
- They have problems finding the right word to express what they mean, and may say "no" for "yes" or "purse" for "nurse" (this is called *anomia*).
- They ask questions repeatedly, seeking information they can't retain.
- They cannot string ideas together, and may lose their train of thought in mid-sentence (the phenomenon of the dangling sentence, e.g., "I would like to . . ." is called *abulia*). They may get up to go somewhere and forget where they are going. (All of us do this from time to time. It does not mean we have dementia!)
- They may develop *Broca's aphasia,* in which people speak haltingly or telegraphically because of difficulties in word-finding ("Doctor . . . going . . . coming . . . who . . .") or substitute a word for an entirely different one ("I don't like carburetors" rather than "I don't like cauliflower").
- They may repeat the same meaningless sound or word over and over, echo sounds (*echopraxia*), or speak gibberish or "word salad" that is difficult to understand (a symptom of *Wernicke's aphasia*): "I don't want to burn myself. I found myself. I was gone. I have to go back again. It's the same thing. I can't . . . figure. . . ."
- They may have total *expressive/receptive aphasia,* in which people lose all sense of the meaning of words. Aphasia presents many problems: it may affect the production of written and spoken language, compromising both the person's ability to communicate, and the ability to acquire information from signs, messages, or notes. A person may become mute due to fear of making a mistake in speech. Language comprehension may be affected, leaving the person unable to understand what people are saying. This problem is compounded when many different people provide care in a noisy environment.

As time awareness becomes affected, the person slowly slips into a time warp. The present becomes confused; the person cannot look forward to the future; and past memories can be accessed only with help.

Seasons become meaningless. The normal cycle of the day becomes confused. People in this situation:

- repeatedly ask for assistance with time orientation, such as "Is it time yet?"; "What time is dinner?"; "Am I late for...?"; "What day is it?"; "When is supper?"; "I have to get to work"; "I must get the children off to school";
- have decreased knowledge of current events;
- can't remember personal history accurately (but may have "memory remnants");
- have impaired ability to travel or handle money; and
- begin to have problems performing complex tasks that require sequencing, use of equipment or supplies, or involvement with people (e.g., personal care activities, cooking, gardening, driving, etc.).

At this stage, the person with dementia denies that she is having problems. The following is a common scenario:

A 75-year-old wife comes in to visit her husband in a nursing home. The 80-year-old man looks at her and says, "Who are you?" or "Hello, Mother." He can't see himself as married to this elderly person, because due to loss of memory about recent times, he may think of himself as a 30- or 40-year-old!

The old man finds himself living in a time warp because memory of recent events has been destroyed. He can't be brought back to the present with prompts and reasoning, because the part of his brain that handles the sense of "the present"—his memory and awareness of time—has been destroyed and can no longer function. In his mind, he is living at some point in time in his past life. Clues to just where in time he is can be gained by listening to his conversation:

Let's suppose the man's wife is accompanied by their 30-year-old daughter. The man calls her by his wife's name. (The daughter probably looks a great deal like her mother did at 30.) The man remembers his wife at 30, but no longer remembers her at 75. The daughter looks more like the wife he remembers!

The daughter has her 10-year-old son with her. He is greeted by the elderly man who calls him by his own son's name. The boy looks like the man's son when the old man himself was 30 years old.

This time distortion is very frustrating for everyone concerned: the family members feel they've been forgotten, and the elderly man is caught up in confusion and helplessness. The entire family (including younger members) needs help to understand the effects of dementing disease. They need to learn strategies to help them connect with their husband/father/grandfather, instead of arguing with him about which year it is, or embarrassing him about his loss of memory, or not visiting because they are not recognized.

GENTLECARE Best Practice

MINDTRIP is a technique whereby the professional caregiver helps the family to travel back in time to the period in time preoccupying the person with dementia, so that they may talk about pleasant news and happenings *in that time frame.*

Gentlecare uses several techniques to help families communicate effectively with their loved ones. For instance, the family is taught the MINDTRIP technique. People learn to ask, "What's the point in time that my father is talking about due to the disease process?"; and then they learn how to talk about pleasant news and events of that time period. The person experiencing dementia can join in the conversation because it involves long-term memory, which may still be intact.

I find that children, in particular, enjoy using this strategy. I compare their grandfather's behavior to that of someone from a science fiction episode who has experienced time travel. Once they have that image, they immediately relate to the effects of the disease, and take up their appropriate roles as caregivers and supporters.

For example, compare this frustrating conversation with the following conversation:

Father: "How is the mother?"

Daughter: "Whose mother, yours or mine?"

Father: "The mother."

Daughter: "Well, your mother is dead, for heaven's sake! And my mother is buried in Edmonton!"

Father: "The mother's dead?"

Daughter: "Of course, both our mothers are dead."

Father (mournfully): "Nobody told me the mother was dead."

Sometimes you have to look really hard at the person with dementia and realize they are doing the very best they can.

Here's the same conversation using the Gentlecare Mindtrip strategy:

Father: "How's the mother?"

Daughter: "You are thinking of mother. She was someone special, wasn't she? Remember the wonderful pies she used to bake, and the rabbit stew?"

Gradually, by evoking old and pleasant memories, it's possible to draw people with Alzheimer's disease into conversations in which they *can* participate because the subject of the conversation does not involve damaged areas of the brain. The unhappy subject of death is avoided.

To build a prosthesis for people with these problems, caregivers need to apply superb and effective communication skills. Communicating with someone afflicted with dementia is exhausting and time-consuming, but may be one of the most potent therapies. The following are effective strategies:

- Avoid abstractions. Instead of saying, "He said...." try, "The doctor said...."
- Avoid questions. Questions imply a performance requirement in the form of a response. Due to language disintegration, this can be very frightening to the afflicted person. Instead, supply information. If it's necessary to ask questions, ask only one at a time. Al-

GLOSSARY

ABULIA	The inability to hold a thought long enough to complete an action or sentence.
AGNOSIA	The inability to recognize familiar stimuli (visual, auditory, tactile, etc.).
ANOMIA	The inability to recall the correct word or phrase to identify an object.
APHASIA	A deficit or loss of ability to express oneself by speech or writing; or to read or understand the speech of others.
APRAXIA	The inability to carry out skilled and purposeful movement—to make the body do what the mind wants it to.
ECHOLALIA	The meaningless repetition by a person of words addressed to him.
WORD SALAD	A jumble of seemingly meaningless words and phrases containing small bits of meaningful communication.
PERSEVERATION	The repetition of actions and/or sounds.

FIGURE 5-5

ways wait for the response...leave time for the response. Keep the person with dementia talking and involved. Avoid noisy groups, malls, big family or social gatherings—the environment is too confusing. Praise the person frequently (and praise yourself).

• Use lots of non-verbal communication: hugs, kids, pets, touch, dancing, walking, hair brushing, nail care, flowers, aromas, perfume, lovely textures.

• Use the Mindtrip strategy. Family members should learn communication strategies, and staff can practice this with them.

The damage described thus far happens as Alzheimer's destroys the limbic system, the parietal lobe, and the temporal lobe during stages 1 through 4 of the disease (as described in Reisberg's Global Deterioration Scale).

Transition between Stages IV and V

The next period, the transition between stages IV and V, is a very stressful time for both the person with dementia and family caregivers. During this time, the afflicted person has memory loss, decreased language skills, decreased wayfinding ability, and diminished recognition of places, objects, and people. There may also be psychiatric problems, and there will likely be emotional instability.

The caregiver is likely exhausted, possibly physically ill, and probably socially isolated, anxious, and burned out. Frequently, all of these factors come together to create a crisis. It is not unusual at this point in the disease for families to decide that 24-hour care is required. The person with dementia is, at this stage, probably functioning at approximately the developmental level of an eight-year-old.

Damage to the Occipital Lobe

OCCIPITAL LOBE
Damage

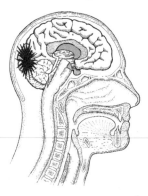

FIGURE 5-6

As Stage V approaches, the disease moves to the back of the brain, where the occipital and parietal lobes meet. The *occipital lobe* and the *visual cortex* are the areas responsible for visual processing and visual significance. Damage in this area presents afflicted people with many problems:

- They lose their peripheral vision; they can now see only straight ahead. They will not be aware of objects or people to the side. They will not see a glass on a side table or someone sitting next to them.
- They lose the ability to look up, and their gaze is directed downward. They can miss signs or pictures or objects that are placed too high. They also tend to run into people or objects in their path.
- They lose the ability to focus on, or track, a moving object like a ball. This can be very frightening. It becomes impossible for them to watch and understand television, or identify staff members who move too quickly.
- They become very obsessive, and may repeat a motion over and over again.

- They often have the delusion that their spouse is unfaithful, or that "This is not my house."
- Their agitation increases.
- They engage in "rummaging" activity, which can be very disruptive to others but can provide them many hours of pleasing activity.
- As anxiety levels escalate, they wander occasionally about, making physical threats to people they encounter or verbal outbursts.
- They are disoriented in three spheres: time, place, and person.
- There may be personality changes, emotional upheavals, which under stress can lead to "violent behavior" or catastrophic reactions.
- There is a marked loss of willpower. Their consequent unwillingness to participate in activities may be misinterpreted as indicating poor motivation or noncompliance.
- They begin to suffer from cognitive abulia: they can't hold an idea long enough to complete an intended action.
- They may experience nausea or a general feeling of malaise.
- They lose the ability to read.

At this stage, the person with dementia is now functioning at approximately the developmental level of a five- to seven-year-old. To build a prosthesis for people with these problems, it is critical to reduce stress, glare, noise, and rush. It is helpful to lower pictures and important objects. Pictures should be substituted for written information. In care facilities, it is useful to remove carts and cleaning equipment from pathways. Television sets should be moved into areas where cognitively alert residents can enjoy them. Staff should be trained to slow down and converse with each person with dementia. In Gentlecare, this is called the Personal Therapy Concept. Staff should also be trained to use the Gift of Legacy concept as a means of orienting people with dementia. This concept involves everyone who comes in contact with the person afflicted giving them personal information about themselves; for instance: "Good morning, Mr. Smith. I understand you used to be the principal at Oak Street Elementary?"

MOTOR CORTEX
Damage

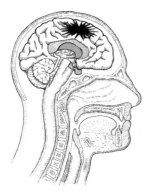

FIGURE 5-7

Damage to the Motor Area

As the illness progresses into approximately Stage VI, damage moves from the visual cortex across the top of the brain to the motor area. The *motor cortex* is the area of the brain responsible for motor function, and damage to this area leads to the following difficulties:

- The person has problems initiating and following through with movements such as eating. This condition is known as *apraxia,* the inability to initiate purposeful movement to make the body do what the mind wants it to do.
- The person may experience problems with swallowing (*dysphagia*).
- Gait, posture, and motor planning are affected.
- The person has trouble getting up from a seated position because of the inability to organize body movements.
- There may be symptoms of rigidity, due to decreased amounts of the neurotransmitter dopamine, often due to prescription of neuroleptic drugs.
- The person leans to the side, leans forward, or pulls backward, shuffles, leans forward with knees bent, and has problems lifting the feet. He may exhibit *hypotonia* (muscle weakness).
- Balance is compromised.
- The person may experience *hyperkinesis* (a feeling of restlessness, with the need to move about).
- There may be muscle cramping.
- The person at this stage may show *hypermetamorphosis* (a fascination with small objects). People with hypermetamorphosis may worry at or pick at a spot or tiny object such as a design in clothing or upholstery, or eat buttons or jewelry parts.
- In later stages, the person may curl into a fetal position.

To build a prosthesis for people with these problems, caregivers must safety-proof the physical environment, getting rid of shiny, slippery surfaces, or surfaces with too much texture or pile. It helps if the afflicted person wears good footwear.

When assisting the person to walk, stand close beside and take a firm hold on the forearm for support. Never walk backward, holding out your arms to the person. This does not afford sufficient steady support. Do not try to walk behind the person being assisted; if you cannot be seen or heard, the person may not like being touched, or held, or propelled forward.

At this stage, the use of physical restraints should be avoided. Instead, try preparing a variety of seating locations, and change from one to another during the course of the day. Limit the size of the space within which the person moves, to reduce environmental stimuli.

In Gentlecare, "soft rooms" are used for people in this stage of disease. These are small, lovely rooms with carpeting, soft furniture (often modular) with pillows, and interesting objects. Such spaces allow people to move about freely and safely, and be comforted by the ambiance.

Damage to the Occipital Region Continues

Damage to the *occipital* region continues, causing increased visual impairment. The afflicted person can now distinguish only contrasts; consequently, if caregivers wear white or pastels (the usual colors of institutional uniforms) the person has difficulty seeing them, and may resist treatment or care, especially at night. The person may not be able to distinguish a white toilet standing on a light-colored floor, and may therefore tend to use clearly defined objects (planters or dust bins) as toilets instead.

The person begins to suffer from *mind blindness,* and is unable to distinguish night from day. This results in wakefulness at night (with a need for support at that time) and also in a desire to nap during the day.

MORE OCCIPITAL LOBE
Damage

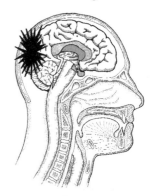

FIGURE 5-8

Damage to the Limbic System Continues

As Stage VI progresses, the limbic system, including the *hypothalamus,* is destroyed completely. The hypothalamus is the area of the brain responsible for control of temperature, thirst, and appetite. As a result:
- People may feel cold deep in their bones, or be uncomfortably hot.
- Thirst can be extreme.
- They have an enormous appetite, partly because, due to memory

MORE LIMBIC SYSTEM
Damage

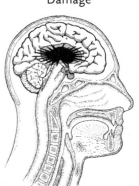

FIGURE 5-9

loss, they do not remember when they last ate. Often, they will eat anything, even if the substance is toxic or disgusting, since their sense of taste and smell has been destroyed.

- They are unaware of recent events and their surroundings.
- There may be evidence of personality and emotional changes, which can cause a variety of challenging behaviors whenever the person is stressed.

To build a prosthesis for people with these problems, caregivers must develop:

- a hydration program offering the person six to eight cups of water each day. It is important to monitor liquid intake, as the affected person may require assistance with drinking.
- a means of keeping the person's body temperature at a comfortable level. It is necessary to experiment to find the appropriate room temperature and clothing needed.
- a means of monitoring food intake, due to a condition known as *pica* (a tendency to eat anything at all, including harmful substances).

PREFRONTAL AREA
Damage

Damage to the Prefrontal Area

As Stage VI continues, the *prefrontal* area of the brain is damaged, which causes further motor planning problems. Concurrently, damage to the visual cortex continues, and more visual changes occur. The person is affected by severe apraxia, and is unable to make the body do what they want it to, or what caregivers would like it to do. The person cannot follow directions.

Visual changes continue, and now include the problem of *visual field neglect* (inability to be aware of one side of the visual field, usually the left side). This means that at this stage the person with dementia may not be aware of food or drinks placed on one side of their food tray, or of people standing outside their field of vision.

To build a prosthesis for people with these problems, caregivers as-

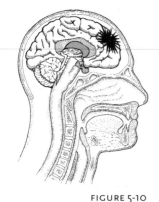

FIGURE 5-10

sist the person by "kick-starting" movement, and offering further help only as required. Directions must be given slowly and clearly, using mimed gestures and verbal prompts. The person's attention must be directed to the neglected side of the body, and items should be placed directly in the line of vision. At meals, the plate should be turned around so the person becomes aware of food on the neglected side.

At this point, the person is functioning at a developmental level of a child between four and five years of age.

Damage to the Frontal Lobe

As the disease progresses to the end of Stage VI, *frontal lobe* damage occurs. At this stage of the disease, the frontal lobe slowly ceases functioning. The critical functions of cognition (thought formation, reasoning, judgment, abstract thinking, and social consciousness) are lost.

FRONTAL LOBE
Damage

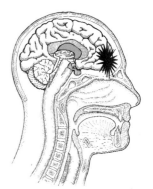

FIGURE 5-11

The disease causes the affected person to become totally focused on personal needs, no longer able to feel concern for or be aware of others. People in this stage of dementia demand instant gratification. They are uninhibited in all their actions, including sexual activity. Because memory has been lost, the afflicted person does not have the benefit of past experience, and therefore cannot anticipate the consequences of behavior. In consequence, people with dementia have diminished social judgment.

To build a prosthesis for people with these problems, caregivers must offer the kind of care given to a tiny child. They are now functioning at a developmental level equal to that of a child between two and three years of age. People at this stage should not be integrated with other client populations. Care is offered at a sensory level: touch, massage, supervised visits of children and pets, rocking, wrapping, crooning, and spiritual care.

These people must be relieved of responsibility for their actions. Both staff and family benefit from education about the effects of the disease, particularly with respect to sexual activity.

Damage to the Cerebellum

Finally, *subcortical* damage occurs. The subcortex (*hind brain,* or *cerebellum*) controls the vital involuntary body systems: the heart, lungs, diaphragm, digestive system, and some coordination and balance functions. The body begins to shut down, and death is not far off:

- The body fails to thrive, no matter what interventions are undertaken.
- The person experiences irreversible weight loss as the body metabolism burns fat. This stage is very difficult for the families who worry that the person is starving to death, and wonder if artificial feeding would help.
- The involuntary systems of the body begin to fail.
- It is not unusual for a person with Alzheimer's disease to die of a secondary infection, such as a lung or bladder infection.
- Sensory areas continue to be affected. The person will process things such as positive or negative, warm or cold, sweet or sour, dry or wet, pleasant or frightening.

CEREBELLUM
Damage

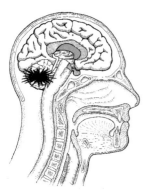

FIGURE 5-12

The person is now functioning at a developmental level equal to that of a child between the ages of 4–12 weeks and 15 months. The prosthesis at this stage consists of total care, just as one would provide for a baby. Good hydration programs, massage, wrapping, rocking, and comforting strategies are recommended.

The role of family is critical, so a good deal of effort is directed at helping the family through this stage. Family members often take comfort in being able to "do something" for their loved one: they can play music or read aloud favorite pieces such as poems and prayers. Massage and hair, hand, and foot care is soothing as well. Sometimes favorite pets are comforting.

The family needs to be supported to stay with the person as death nears. Family presence seems to provide a powerful source of comfort for the dying person at a sensory level. It is important to provide a room where the family can rest and get refreshments. A designated staff liaison is very effective in supporting family members. Staff members

CORRESPONDENCE OF STAGES IN ALZHEIMER'S DISEASE TO FUNCTIONAL AGES		
Stage i Stage ii	Not discernible	Functions as an adult
Stage iii	Deficits in employment skills	Functions as a young adult
Stage iv	Requires help with complex tasks	8 years to adolescence
Stage v	Moderately severe dementia	5 to 7 years
Stage vi	Severe—requires assistance with self-care	24 months to 5 years
Stage vii	Very severe dementia— requires total assistance	4 to 12 weeks to 15 months

FIGURE 5-13

also need support at this critical time of loss. Everyone must live the reality of Alzheimer's disease, while celebrating the memory of the afflicted person.

6

Violence and Aggression: Learned Behavior

Chimera (ki-'mir-a)—*an imaginary monster compounded of incongruous parts, an illusion, fabrication of the mind, something existing only as the product of unrestrained imagination.*

Violence is the chimera of dementia. Like the fire-breathing monster of Greek mythology, violence swirls through dementia literature and practice: violence carried out by elders against one another, violence done to staff, violence acted out against families—and heartrending violence in the form of invasive practices imposed on sick, elderly people.

Why has violence become so prominent and pervasive an element in health care systems devoted to the care of the elderly? Why has attention been focused on the belligerent, angry behavior of afflicted people, rather than on the nature of the diseases or the context of care? Is elder care merely a microcosm of society as a whole, or are we in health care experiencing an aberration?

Families are aghast when they hear language that is totally out of character coming from the lips of someone they love; or when their mother or father turns on them in an ugly rage; or when they hear their loved ones described as aggressive or dangerous by professional staff.

It is claimed that violence perpetuated by elderly people against staff are increasing in incidence and severity. A very large part of the agenda of elder care concerns itself with the management of violent behavior. Texts, journals, courses, behavioral strategies, investigating committees, labor agreements, specialized equipment, and repressive sanctions have developed as a result of this preoccupation. In some cases, the residential units for people with dementia are referred to as "behavior wards," "locked units," or "management areas," as if the environment were dedicated to containing some dangerous animal. The myth that violence is an inevitable outcome of dementia has flourished to the point where more attention is invested in documenting perceived abusive behavior than in developing care programs to prevent it. Based on the perception that people with dementia are dangerous or violent, a locked area becomes a "lockdown," and the people who live within it are imprisoned by that perception, rather than by the limitations of their illness.

Isolation and immobilization contribute to frustration, fear, and aggression.

I FOUND A MAN IN HIS LATE 50s *lying flat on his back in a reclined geriatric chair. My attention was drawn to him because beside the chair was an IV pole—somewhat unusual equipment for a dementia care area! His wrists were manacled to the chair at his sides, as were his ankles. A feeding tube led out of his stomach and he was catheterized. When I leaned close to him he said, "Please help me die."*

I asked the staff why such extreme measures had been taken. I learned that the man was in the early stages of Alzheimer's disease. He was confused and angry about his hospitalization, and determined to go to his construction company site. He had made an attempt to do so, and was physically restrained and returned to his room, where, in frustration, he lashed out at staff members. They called for backup, and his response was to fight even harder. Staff members were injured in the fracas. The restraint, feeding, and elimination measures had been applied as a result of his resistance.

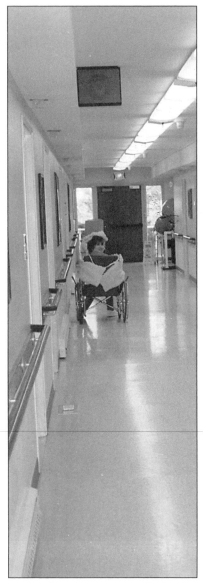

Unfamiliar environments filled with glare, rush, and strangers create terror.

Why the Violence?

As we have seen, dementing illnesses such as Alzheimer's disease assail the emotional centers of control during the earliest stages of the disease. As damage continues, the ability to interpret external stimuli, to tolerate stress, to communicate, and finally to use reason and judgment is lost. From the onset of Alzheimer's disease, afflicted people lose the ability to manage life's challenges. The emotional controls that healthy people take for granted are absent. The social mores that direct our lives are eroded. The cognitive process that permits us to figure out solutions to problems or deal with other people has been destroyed. People who can no longer handle ordinary situations become frightened.

Then we place these terrified people into psychiatric hospitals, units for the physically disabled, chronic care institutions, or "holding units" in medical/surgical facilities. Should we be surprised when they react aggressively to the stress inherent in those situations? Should we, in fact, categorize their behavior as aggression at all, or should we understand that in their fear and frustration, they react with the only behavior available to them: resistance?

Resistance can easily evolve into aggression. Even the tiniest, mildest old lady will fight like a tiger if she perceives herself to be cornered and in danger. And if such a person feels repeatedly threatened by the stresses of her surroundings, her normal response whenever she encounters the same stresses may well be to become assaultive. Let us try to imagine how she feels.

How would you feel if you were sitting in your room and a complete stranger of the opposite sex came up to insist that you get undressed and have a bath in a public room? How would you respond if someone unknown woke you up at night and insisted that you go to the bathroom accompanied by that person? What would you do if you found yourself locked in a strange place with dozens of other sick people, and were told that this was your home? Of course you would be enraged in any of these situations and the resistance that they provoke begins to sound appropriate, given the circumstances!

Turning Things Around

I was once asked to work with two men who were "violent" at wake-up time each morning. Upon investigation, I found that staff on the evening shift awakened the people with dementia at 4:30 every morning, and did their grooming and dressing.

"Why so early?" I inquired.

"Oh, to get them ready."

"Ready for what?!"

"Well, just ready."

It turned out that this practice gave the day staff an early start on the day's work, making it possible to have everyone ready for breakfast at 7:30 A.M. The two gentlemen in question clearly resisted being awakened from a deep sleep, and proceeded to swear at and hit anyone who tried to force them to get up. Medication had been prescribed to control the violent behavior.

We decided to try a different strategy: let them sleep in and wake up naturally. This notion initially met with a great deal of resistance:

"They'll sleep all day."

"We'll never get our work done."

"They'll miss breakfast."

A choice all of us would like to exercise!

As it turned out, when staff went about their work but left the two men to sleep in, they woke up naturally around 7:00 A.M., were able to manage most of their own grooming, and were among the first to show up in the dining room.

The Gentlecare strategy of choice in this case was to allow a flexible routine around wake-up and meal times. Setting that strategy in place involved:

- communicating with all staff about the implications of the new plan;

- assessing the impact of change on each department or work group;
- planning for any necessary schedule changes, and finding solutions for any problems such changes might create;
- ensuring that all staff knew what to do and what not to do in the new circumstances;
- developing alternate menus and eating locations;
- trying out the plan;
- evaluating results;
- identifying and making any necessary changes to the plan; and finally
- celebrating the changes in functioning!

It is not because things are difficult that we do not dare. It is because we do not dare that they are difficult.

—SENECA

The institution where those two gentlemen live has now implemented the "relaxed breakfast" for all residents. When the idea of doing so was first broached, staff in many areas expressed great anxiety:

"How will everything get done on time?"

"How will we keep track of medications?"

"Will we have to reschedule activities?"

Three weeks after implementing the new flexible routines, staff comments sounded like this:

"This is great!"

"The dining room is operating very well; in fact, clean-up is happening a few minutes earlier than usual!"

"The residents are calmer."

"Residents are often awake and usually getting ready on their own by the time we get there to help them."

As well, one gentleman who previously required total care now manages his own self-care and is on a walking program. One lady who had always required total care now sleeps in and gets her own toast and coffee in the dayroom.

Comments from the residents were also positive:

"I love being able to snuggle back into bed for a while before breakfast."

"I'm much more relaxed and I sleep better knowing I don't have to get up."

"I love having toast and tea when I'm properly awake. I love mornings now!"

Buoyed by the positive results, staff members at the facility are eager to try new ways of delivering care. They are relaxed, proud of their accomplishments, and find they can do the same amount of work in a shorter period of time than was previously required. Residents are functioning at a higher level of competency, and everyone feels pleased.

It should be noted that these changes happened because everyone decided to make them happen.

The Context of Violence

Linear and Lateral Thinking

Violence must be considered within the context of issues such as:
- the nature of the person's disease;
- the extent of dysfunction;
- the level of stress/fatigue/anxiety of all parties;
- the degree to which the person understands what's being done to him;
- the number of people involved;
- staff attitudes and approaches; and
- the environmental context.

Our current health care system is *linear*. It is structured to respond to crisis defensively, rather than to understand and avoid crises. For example, suppose the problem was that a person with dementia struck out at a caregiver during personal care. A caregiver using a linear approach to the problem would document the incident, and give the person a psychoactive medication to calm him down. The person would then become comatose, and would thus be easier to groom and dress.

A linear care plan acts quickly and dramatically, but has terrible long-term effects. Facing the same problem, a caregiver using *lateral* thinking would:
- ask why the patient had struck out;

Violence does not equal dementia. Violence results from the effects of dementia.

Try substituting the word terror for aggression.

- want to know who was involved in the interaction;
- find out what was going on in the environment;
- ask if the person understood the procedure;
- consider the necessity for the procedure;
- ask if the person had received an "energy boost" (a drink or some food) before undertaking the task;
- want to know if the person had been allowed to rest between stages of the task;
- ask whether a different plan of approach had been tried, and tried again; and
- ask if different people had tried to help.

Staff in one facility wore lapel buttons that read: "Have you been hurt today?"

This kind of plan takes longer to implement, but it solves the problem instead of masking it, and prevents the development of long-range, costly problems. However, non-linear or system thinking is anything but easy. It involves a real commitment on the part of everyone offering care to understand and empathize with the person, rather than judge or condemn. It comes from a place of love—not fear.

Some will argue that non-linear planning is too time-consuming, but experience shows that in the long run, this is simply not true. Such strategies help the afflicted person to improve function; they support family caregivers, make it easier for professional caregivers, and make care itself less expensive.

It is wonderful what a different view we take of the same event four and twenty hours after it has happened.

—SIDNEY SMITH, ENGLISH CLERGYMAN 1771

ONCE UPON A TIME *I filmed a 56-year-old man who had Alzheimer's disease. He had been a very successful business executive, and was part of a lovely family. The disease had tragically devastated large portions of his speech centers, but with support and care, the essential human being behind the disease could be reached. During the course of the disease, this man reacted violently to stress in his environment, and was hospitalized.*

Thirteen months later I saw this same man again. Perceived as dangerous and agitated, he was receiving large doses of antipsychotic medication. He was restrained in a geriatric chair. His head hung on his chest. He was drooling and asleep. He was "too ill" to participate in any activity.

I sat and talked with him about his part in the film we had done together. I told him that the interview he did with me had helped people like himself all across the country. Thinking he was asleep, I got up to leave, but realized he was crying. He said, very carefully, very painfully, "I tried...we tried, Moyra."

Supporters of linear or closed systems look at such a person and see a middle-aged, physically fit man, agitated and anxious. They perceive danger. They know their perception is real because in fact, under stress this person had been violent. Chemical restraint is the obvious, easiest, fastest, and most widely practiced response to his behavior. Linear thinking localizes the problem in the person with dementia. The problem is "fixed" by altering his ability to function. But is it?

This is an example of empty hand syndrome—people engaged in no activity, often for up to 12 hours each day.

Supporters of a participatory system (or lateral approach) look at the same person and see someone whose dynamic, independent personality has been severely stressed by being placed in an environment that—from his perspective—tried to take control of his life. Supporters of such a participatory approach would find the root of the problem in the poor fit between the individual's personality/life experience and the environment in which he found himself. They would seek to resolve the problem by assessing the person's functional level and finding safe areas of personal autonomy for him; by making sure he understood why certain procedures were necessary; by relaxing schedules and rules where possible; and by changing other social and environmental factors to support his personality and remaining skills.

The bottom line in eliminating the sense of violence surrounding dementia is that if change is to occur, the change must happen within the agents of the system. We must change the system of health care because the person with dementia can't.

There are four common elements in the present model of dementia care that magnify the phenomenon of violent behavior. All four also contribute to accelerated dysfunction, excessive disability, and rising health care costs. They are externalizing the problem; misuse of medication; the power of inappropriate language to shape inappropriate action; and the misuse of restraint. Each of these elements is discussed below.

Externalizing the Problem

The assumption in most care facilities is that violence is an expected and enduring aspect of the workplace. If you work with people who have Alzheimer's disease, chances are you will get punched or kicked or bitten. Consequently, staff members take turns or draw lots to see who is unlucky enough to have to "do" Mr. X today. Staff members work in pairs (or three- or five-person teams) to give Mr. X a bath or to change his clothes.

Man did not weave the web of life, he is merely a strand in it. Whatever he does to the web, he does to himself.

—CHIEF SEATTLE

Furthermore, the approach to violence in health care traditionally has not been focused on seeking the reasons for its occurrence, but rather on finding ways to manage it or reduce the impact of assaults on staff. In current practice, surveys and staff abuse recording tools focus on such issues as:

- staff fitness;
- effective alarm systems;
- patients' history of assault;
- identifying potentially assaultive behavior toward each staff member;
- procedures for reporting assaults to the administration and to the police;
- legal penalties;
- support for assaulted staff;
- restraint procedures;
- job satisfaction issues; and
- physical/mental exhaustion of staff.

But, as the philosopher Wheeler observed, to understand anything in nature we must cross out the old word *observer* and put in place the new word *participant*. To comment on a person's behavior, therefore, is really to comment on the nature of one's own interaction with the sick person. A report of violence is in itself an admission of failure on our part as caregivers to meet one or more of the specific needs of a person in our care, whether that need is for more information, a slower pace, calm and quiet, or a hug.

> *From physics to psychology, every department of science is realizing more and more that to observe the world is to participate in it, and that as frustrating as this may first seem to be, it is the most important clue to all further knowledge.*
>
> —ALLAN BATES

At the same time, it must be recognized that failure to meet the needs of people with dementia does not mean that caregivers are stupid, cruel, or uncaring. It simply means that they must try something else, or try one more time. We must try to understand the disease more clearly; try to put ourselves in the other person's shoes; try talking about the problem with another caregiver or the person's spouse. There is something we must do differently. We must find out what that something is and do it differently until the person with dementia is comfortable.

Violence can't be isolated from its context, or from ourselves as participants in the context. Staff abuse is not a patient problem—it is a system problem. To reduce the violence shown by persons with dementia, we must dare to examine and understand the whole system that operates where we work. Conscious participation is necessary. We must understand not only ourselves, but also the systems we create and perpetuate. We must evaluate our actions and the systems we operate, in relation to those who need our help. Jung referred to this process as acceptance. We cannot change anything unless we accept it. Condemnation does not liberate us from our problems, it only creates new ones.

In the example on page 61, we see violence exchanged for dependency. Acceptance, on the other hand, opens and releases our creativity to find new solutions, to find and help the person who still exists behind the disease.

CHAPTER
SIX

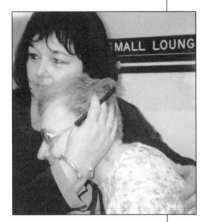

Sometimes a shoulder to lean on comes in handy.

Please listen carefully, and try to hear what

I am not saying

what I would like to be able to say.

What for survival, I need

to say, but I can't say.

Each time you are kind,

and gentle, and encouraging,

Each time you try to understand because you really care,

My heart grows wings

very feeble wings, but wings.

I want you to know how

important

you are to me.

Who am I?

You may wonder.

I am someone you know very well

For I am every man you meet

I am every woman.

I am you.

—Author Unknown

Misuse of Medication

In many care facilities, aggressive behavior is controlled by the widespread use of chemical substances that were designed for other purposes: antipsychotics, antidepressants, and anti-anxiety/hypnotic drugs. People with dementing illness are sedated with these medications after catastrophic behavior has occurred, or in anticipation of future violence.

The use of drugs to restrain a person with dementia is perhaps the most serious chemical threat to safety and well-being in the long-term care environment—though that threat to safety is often unconscious and unintended.

I REMEMBER DISCUSSING the situation of a tiny woman patient. She had hit out at a staff member who had approached her abruptly from the side (by his own admission). The woman had been given Ativan, to quiet her down. That morning she hung in her restraint vest in her wheelchair in deep sleep. After lunch she was finally put to bed, as no one had been able to wake her. Just before dinner, I chanced by her room and found her still asleep.

When I inquired about her, I discovered that the afternoon staff, upon reading about the violent incident of the previous day, had given her another prescription of Ativan "as a preventive measure." It was another two days before this woman was able to eat her food by herself.

The principal strategy of quality dementia care is to assess and maintain levels of function not yet destroyed by disease. When demented people are given medication for purposes other than prescribed treatment, vital remaining functions are blotted out—not by the disease, but by medical intervention. This results in the person feeling more confused, frustrated, and vulnerable than ever, and leads inevitably to an escalation of belligerence and terror.

Medication used for restraint has a multitude of harmful effects on elderly people:
- loss of personal volition
- confusion
- heart rate change
- depression
- tardive dyskinesia
- agitation
- bladder problems
- sedation
- postural hypotension
- anxiety
- slurred speech
- stiffness

IT MUST BE EMPHASIZED THAT THE ABOVE COMMENTS REFER TO MEDICATION USED FOR RESTRAINT PURPOSES ONLY, NOT TO DRUGS USED HONESTLY AS TREATMENT MODALITIES.

It should be understood by everyone who cares about people with dementia that while there have been some encouraging preliminary results reported on drugs that help somewhat in early stage dementia only, no drug in current use ameliorates the effects of dementia. Many drugs, in fact, exacerbate the effects of Alzheimer's disease or related dementias. Nevertheless, medication is often given in the guise of treatment to calm the person down, to reduce anxiety or catastrophic behavior, or to reduce violence.

Families generally know very little about pharmaceutical treatment, and are reluctant to question the use of medication to control behavior. Many believe they cannot question the prescription of psychotropic (mood altering) medication. And yet families are frontline advocates; they must become informed and courageous enough to be able to ask: How is this drug going to change the course of dementia in my family member? Sometimes medications prescribed for other medical conditions suffered by persons with dementia can be harmful too. This is especially true if the side effects of the prescription are attributed to dementia, rather than to the drugs being given. This issue is a factor in a significant number of cases when prescriptions are not reviewed regularly nor adjusted according to the person's current health status.

The most important consideration for appropriate psychoactive medication usage is whether any drug is needed at all.

—JAMES W. COOPER, UNIV. OF GEORGIA NURSING HOMES

HE LAY CURLED UP *on his side sleeping soundly, and gave no response as his wife gently touched his hair and spoke to him. His caregivers reported that he slept most of the time and was very resistant to personal care. When we reviewed his care plan, I learned that he suffered from Parkinson's disease and took five medications daily for that disease.*

This therapy plan had been developed several years ago when he weighed 150 lbs. and was very active. His current weight had slipped to a point that concerned everyone, and he was involved in almost no physical activity.

IMPASSE

I placed my darling in a nursing home
With a special ward for folk like he.
He was welcomed and we both responded thankfully!
We felt a part of this community: it seemed a caring place.
On the ninth day my love was expelled
As "dangerous to residents and staff."
They notified me that he had been in restraints:
He was not wanted there! I was aghast!
Another place made room for him somehow to my relief:
Otherwise he would have been sent to a mental hospital!
I later found he had been over-medicated the last three days
With drugs that crazy him. For me it was disaster!
How could they ignore me, his caregiver
And the hospital staff who had known him for years?
A nursing home must be a caring place:
Its staff must have an endless store of empathy and love,
Plus training in "no restraints and minimal medication"
Techniques—that experts now espouse.
All who would care for the Alzheimer's victim must share
A true acceptance of this unique person who has dementia.
Only then can we treat him as we would want for ourselves.
A huge compelling and complex prescription—but possible!
For my love I need a caring place that loves enough
To ignore restraints and drugs—so over-used
One that can accept serenely
The fear and anger and confusion
That can occur in any Alzheimer's victim—
Where can I find this place in our imperfect world?

—Gil Ludeman

It was suggested that his medication be reviewed in terms of his current health status. As a result, three medications given for Parkinson's disease were discontinued. To date there have been significant— even remarkable—changes in his level of functioning. He is now able to sit up and feed himself, enjoy his wife's visits, go out for drives, and visit his home. Nothing changed in this man's dementia or Parkinson's disease. Only his medical treatment was altered.

Use of psychotropic medication in dementia care should be considered an absolute last line of defense, to be used only after every other conceivable intervention has been tried and failed, and preferably not then either.

Inappropriate Language Shapes Inappropriate Action

Language is not neutral—it plays an active part in shaping what we think of things and people. A large part of the difficulty we have in accepting the person with dementia is caused by the way language is used in our health care system.

LANGUAGE VERSUS EXPERIENCE

The relationship between language and experience is often misunderstood. Language actually defines experience for us by reason of its formal completeness, and because of our unconscious projection of its implicit expectations into the field of experience.

—Edward Sapir,
Conceptual Categories in Primitive Languages

Labels abound in dementia care, and most of them are negative: dirty old man, spitter, aggressive, feeder, problem patient, and vegetative are only a few examples. Labels pin behavior on individuals, irrespective of context or the role of others. Placing a negative label on someone suggests that the labeled individual is acting with malicious intent, premeditation, and/or in order to control the behavior of others.

Careful study of the pathology of dementing illnesses demonstrates the impossibility of any of those intentions.

The language we use has the power to change the emotional intent of what we say. For example, the Latin prefix *dis-* means apart, asunder, away, or having a negative or reversing force. It is used in the construction of such common words as disability, disbelief, dishearten, or dislike. In the vocabulary of dementia care, *dis-* appears in such words as disoriented or dysfunctional. Disorient, for example, means to cause to lose one's way (the strange streets disoriented him); to confuse by removing or obscuring something that has guided the person, group, or culture such as customs or moral standards (society has been disoriented by changing values); and in psychiatry, to cause to lose perception of time, place, or one's personal identity. The use of the word disorient clearly describes the terror and confusion of old people as their cognitive ability slowly and inexorably declines.

The Latin prefix *mal-*, on the other hand, means bad, wrongful, ill. It is commonly used in such words as malfunction, malcontent, maladroit, and maladjusted. In dementia care, a new word has been coined (not found in the dictionary): *maloriented*. This word is used to describe people who are oriented but not happily so, people who are "unhappy" because they need to resolve past emotional issues and unresolved conflicts. When such made-up language is used to describe elders who experience psychiatric and/or dementing illnesses, the implication is that it is their responsibility to change their bad behavior, and therefore that the onus to do so rests with them. Language imposes this burden on those who have little or no control over their behavior.

People afflicted with a dementing illness can never be reoriented to time, place, or person, because of the progressive nature of their disease. With help, their state of disorientation can be supported, and its side effects can be ameliorated. With support, a person with dementing disease will be less fearful, less frustrated, less confused, and less angry, but not less disoriented.

The language we use shapes the way we think about, approach, plan for, and ultimately care for people with dementia. And not only is our thinking influenced by these labels—so is the thinking of everyone to

If thought corrupts language, language also corrupts thought.

—GEORGE ORWELL

Sticks and stones are hard on bones Aimed with an angry art: Words can sting like anything And silence breaks the heart.

—ANONYMOUS

whom we talk about the person with dementia. Spouses frequently talk to me about their violent husbands. When I ask, "What gives you the idea that your husband is violent?" they reply, "I was told he was." When I ask what their own impression is, they often say, "You know, Moyra, my husband never ever acted this way until he got sick. It's so unlike him." Labels impede effective dementia care—and they are cruel.

Restraint as a Metaphor for Failure

The use of restraint on elderly people living in health care facilities is so pervasive that it cries out to be examined: What is the rationale for this phenomenon?

There has been a great reluctance on the part of policy makers in the care of the elderly to acknowledge and address the issue of cognitive impairment in those in residential care facilities. Traditionally, people living in facilities have been expected to understand the procedures associated with illness and care, and to comply with staff requests—in fact, to be appreciative of their services. As the population of residential care facilities has changed, however, more and more of those in care are people who lack the reasoning and judgment to accept care. Many are, in fact, resistant to care and unwilling to comply with staff directions.

Rather than attempting to understand and adapt to the needs of such people, health care services have opted to make cognitively impaired elderly people comply with expected behavioral norms—even though such people lack the cognitive ability to do so!

In some large psychiatric hospitals, restraint devices are part of the daily linen distribution: patients are restrained, as part of the program. When complaints are received in such situations, staff are bewildered: the use of restraints has become so normal that they don't understand what the fuss is all about.

What's the easiest way to ensure that mobile, resistant, non-compliant people suffering from dementing illnesses conform to norms of

POSTURE IN RESTRAINT-RELATED DEATHS

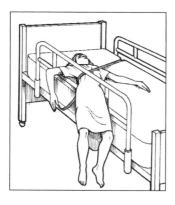
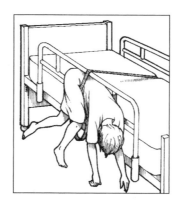
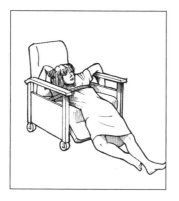
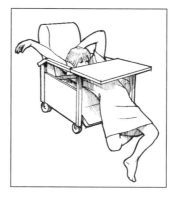

FIGURE 6-1

Drawings by Robert English, adapted from originals by Elizabeth Dempsey. Used with permission of Biomedical Graphic Communication Department at the University of Minnesota, from *The Gerontologist,* Vol. 32, No. 6, 762–766, December 1992.

behavior? The answer is the use of restraints—physical, chemical, environmental, and psychological. Tying up, drugging, and threatening vulnerable elderly people—under the guise of providing health care—truly represents the ultimate failure of the system. To change such practices, we must understand what they are and their consequences, and we must create alternatives.

Physical Restraints

A physical restraint is any physical or mechanical device, material, or equipment adjacent to the person's body that restricts movement or normal function of the body, and which the individual cannot remove. Examples of physical restraints are:

- vests or shirts
- ankle cuffs
- groin/pelvic straps
- wheelchairs
- lock-down food trays
- bed tables
- wrist straps
- sheets
- abdominal belts
- wall hooks
- mitts
- bed rails
- "Geri-chairs" (geriatric chairs, recliners)
- elevated chairs/soft chairs, such as bean bag chairs
- "paired cuffing" to another person

Environmental Restraints

An environmental restraint is any structure or impediment which is built into the environment in order to limit or restrict personal mobility and the exercise of will. Examples of environmental restraints are:

- maze/look-alike corridors
- seclusion rooms
- shiny floors
- large open spaces
- circular corridors
- isolation
- fences
- alarm systems
- doors, locked doors, and alarmed doors
- confusing areas, such as a complicated route to the outdoors
- sensors on beds or chairs attached to people and triggered when they move

> ## EFFECTS OF MEDICATION USED FOR RESTRAINT PURPOSES
>
> - confusion
> - slurred speech
> - bladder problems
> - sedation
> - dizziness
> - heart rate change
> - depression
> - agitation
> - blurred vision
> - constipation
> - drooling/dry mouth
> - stiffness
> - tardive dyskinesia (involuntary movement)
> - postural hypotension (inability to maintain body posture)
> - anxiety
> - and more...

FIGURE 6-2

Chemical Restraints

Chemical restraints are any medications given to control mood, mental status, or behavior, that have no therapeutic benefit. Such restraints include:

- mood-altering medication
- psychoactive drugs
- tranquilizers and sedatives

Psychological Restraints

Psychological restraints are threats or verbal requirements that restrict a person's freedom of movement or will. These include:

- warnings
- threats
- withdrawal of privileges
- requests (from a position of power)

I VISITED A VERY QUIET *dementia unit some years ago. Every single person sat quietly in their chair. No one except staff moved around the unit. This was so unusual that at first I suspected chemical restraint, but a review of the charts indicated only normal use of medication. As*

I passed a bedroom a tiny lady who had been peering out scuttled back to the chair beside her bed. When I went to talk to her she appeared very anxious and frightened, and asked, "Am I going to be allowed to come out today?"

Restraints may be imposed for purposes of discipline, for convenience, or because of low staffing levels. They in no way contribute to the treatment or performance ability of a person with dementia. A number of restraints may be used in combination, compounding the risk of damage to people.

Safety Devices versus Restraints

Physical restraints should be clearly differentiated from safety devices. Restraints are used to restrict movement. Safety or rehabilitative devices, on the other hand, enhance the person's functional ability and safety. Examples of safety devices are padded lap belts on wheelchairs that allow the person to move about safely and independently; and a chest harness that allows a person with weak back muscles or postural dysfunction to remain upright in a functional position. Such devices are individually prescribed, and adapted to the individual's specific requirements. They are checked regularly, and adjusted as the person's condition changes. Most improve the person's level of function and are welcomed by the person wearing them.

On occasion, family members actually request the use of restraints, or support staff members in using restraints—usually because they are worried about fractures, or because they are afraid that if their family member doesn't comply with regulations, he will be discharged or transferred to a psychiatric institution.

Common Arguments for the Use of Restraint

The use of restraint as a means of managing people with dementia is not without its proponents. Many of the arguments in favor of restraint use essentially focus on organizational issues. It is argued that restraints:

DESTRUCTIVE EFFECTS
OF RESTRAINTS

- loss of personal freedom and will
- loss of bone mass, weakened bone structure
- decrease in muscle function/strength/mass
- deterioration of skin tissue, ulcers, pressure sores
- lower extremity swelling
- changes in metabolism
- loss of balance, falls
- increase in incontinence and elimination problems
- loss of independent toileting
- sensory deprivation
- psychiatric disorders
- depressed psychological status
- decrease in social behavior/interaction
- increased problems with sleep patterns
- gastrointestinal stress
- decreased interest in eating
- loss of energy
- increased dependency, learned helplessness
- emotional disorders, withdrawal
- increased agitation
- angry, belligerent, or combative behavior
- stress to staff, families, others
- injuries
- muscle contractions
- death

FIGURE 6-3

- provide answers to safety concerns;
- can compensate for inadequate numbers or levels of staff;
- minimize fear of liability due to falls;
- compensate for lack of adequate or appropriate environments;
- substitute for lack of secure perimeters in buildings, such as fences and alarmed doors;

- solve the problems that arise when people with different levels of cognitive functioning share accommodations; and
- prevent confrontation between afflicted people or between people and staff, which leave bruises and therefore raise questions of abuse.

A Word on Wheelchairs

The only thing necessary for evil to triumph is for good men to do nothing.

—EDMOND BURKE

Wheelchairs are a North American disease! Elderly people, especially those living within institutions, often spend their lives in wheelchairs.

Wheelchairs were originally designed as necessary equipment for seriously paralyzed or paraplegic patients. Eventually, people began to use them to move elderly people quickly from point A to point B. The problem arises when wheelchairs become an elderly person's home. As a rule, wheelchairs do not have good seating: the person's spine is not supported, and over time, this causes acute discomfort and pain. Elderly people often lack the muscle strength to change or adjust their sitting position—especially if a restraint device is used in combination with a wheelchair.

Wheelchairs have evolved into restraints.

Wheelchairs are often placed in front of blaring television sets, grouped in front of nursing stations, or lined up in busy hallways—with the ostensible objective of stimulating their occupants. Elderly people only rarely have the necessary muscle power to move themselves to a more comfortable, quiet location. Thus, ironically, a rehabilitative device designed to improve function and mobility has evolved into a restraint, and in fact is often the cause of dysfunction.

If a wheelchair is to act as a prosthetic device, it should be individually designed to meet a person's needs. Wheelchairs are not interchangeable! If a wheelchair is assigned, it should be carefully prescribed in terms of size, design, seating, and adaptations by a professional staff member knowledgeable in this field. Beware of wide chairs that provide no support for tiny women, or regular or narrow chairs that pinch or rub larger men. Wheelchairs should always provide support for the legs and feet.

Avoid the use of plexiglass tables with people experiencing dementia. It is very disconcerting to have an obstacle that cannot be properly perceived (a clear table) between the upper and lower part of one's body. Similarly, objects that float without obvious support are very confusing. Avoid attaching so-called sensory stimulating objects such as busy boards to table tops on a permanent basis.

THE FOLLOWING ARE SOME SUGGESTIONS FOR STRATEGIES THAT CAN BE USED AS ALTERNATIVES TO RESTRAINT:

- Assessment of the person with dementia by an interdisciplinary team, including the family, identifies the person's strengths and weaknesses as well as lifelong habits, daily routines, attitudes, memory capability, disease status, activity interests, and family dynamics. Information on the medical profile is critical.

- Assessment is ongoing. Persons with dementia require an individualized care plan that guides everyone in their contact with the affected person. Such a care plan must be communicated to everyone—all staff, family, volunteers, and support people.

- The care plan includes direction for approaches to the person, communication requirements, ideas for meaningful activity, ways to support the family structure, assistance necessary for management of self-care, spiritual requirements, movement programs, and any special environmental requirements.

- Environmental adaptation includes silent alarms; secured perimeters; enhanced lighting; reduced glare; comfortable furniture; indoor/outdoor access; effective signage and wayfinding cues; interesting objects/points of interest; warm, mid-range colors, especially in staff clothing; effective figure/ground contrast; small social spaces free of noise and confusion; normal, home-like ambiance; and reduced use of alarms, announcement systems, and call bells.

- Attention is given to physical needs such as hunger, thirst, movement, toileting, pain, cold, and heat.

- Attention is given to psychological needs such as fear, anxiety, lone-

Do unto others as if you were the other.

liness, lack of support, hallucinations, delusions, confusion, disorientation, and memory loss.

- Staffing and family/volunteer levels are appropriate to the needs of people with dementia, throughout a complete 24-hour period, as is the case with any other medical specialty.
- There is flexibility in routines and schedules to allow for the progress of disease and personal needs, reduction of stress, rush, and schedule rigidity in favor of performance, activity, and interaction.
- In acute care settings, staff are trained in the care of people with dementia.
- In medical situations where intravenous equipment, dressings, or other medical material is required, it is helpful to organize teams of family members and volunteers to sit with the person with dementia through the crisis. Practices similar to those used in palliative care are most effective.
- "Soft" or "comfort" rooms which are secured should be available for people who wake during the night. Mattresses or beds low to the floor help eliminate the need for restraint.
- Development of programs and environments that support rather than challenge vulnerable individuals also help eliminate the need for restraint. These include points of interest; interesting objects, things to touch, to do; familiar, relevant activities that focus on one step, repetitive actions using old memory and former skills; focus on movement such as walking indoors and outdoors, dancing, work activity, use of volunteers, students, young people, families to assist with walking (all movement should be charted); relaxation and stress-reducing activities such as children's visits/pets, massage/bathing/manicures, one-on-one visiting; socialization programs in tiny groups of one to three people that promote fun, competency, former life activities, family connections; family conversations and specific music, or prayers, stories, etc. on tape, using Walkman or small sound systems; areas designed indoors and outdoors for safe movement; and all staff, volunteers, and families engage in validation, reminiscing, and general family communication.

It is important to note that many people feel these ideas are idealistic or unrealistic in the economic climate of today's health care system. Nevertheless, it should be stressed that there are facilities all over North America and Europe that are restraint-free and practice this type of prosthetic care successfully with no increase in funding. The secret to the elimination of all types of restraint in the elderly is simple: individualized therapeutic care.

The philosophy of Gentlecare is one we can all embrace with ease when afflicted people are compliant and co-operative. It is easy to care for, respect, give control to, or communicate with the archetypal elderly man and woman: those who enjoy our company, are appreciative of service, and whose faces light up when they see us coming. It is easy to care for people when nothing is required of us except to move through a routine task that makes no demands on our cognition or creativity.

Dementia is the ultimate restraint.

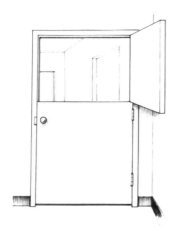

The Dutch door is one of the least harmful restraint measures that allows full movement within a restricted area, and facilitates removal of a person in case of fire or emergency. This comfortable safe space allows people who can't ambulate safely to move and exercise.

FIGURE 6-4

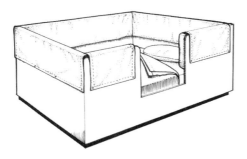

Bed adaptation courtesy of Riverview Care Center, Washington, U.S.A.

FIGURE 6-5

CHAPTER
SIX

The hard part comes when we are required to honor our philosophical ideals when we are working with those who, because of illness, neither appreciate nor agree to our presence in their life. When the people we care for are resistant or show catastrophic behavior, then it becomes all too easy to forget our high-minded resolve and succumb to the seduction of old practices. It becomes easier to reach for chemical restraint than to talk the person out of distress; easier to transfer them out of our jurisdiction; easier to see the person as dangerous or violent, or someone so unpleasant as to be undeserving of our care and attention.

In those circumstances, eliminating undesirable behaviors and approaches becomes more difficult. And when inappropriate practices such as the use of restraint on elderly persons are entrenched in the system of health care, the task becomes monumental. For example, decision-making about the use of restraint can be beyond the control of individual caregivers, as it is almost always ordered by a physician, based on the information given him by care providers.

Caregivers correctly say the system has to change, because we can't do it alone. And that's true—but we are part of the system, and we can take part in changing the attitudes, assumptions, language, and approaches that underlie and support the use of restraint.

Ethical and Legal Issues

The practice of using restraints in dementia care facilities is increasingly coming under public scrutiny because it raises complex ethical and legal questions. For example, restraints are most often used on elderly persons, many of whom cannot express opinions due to cognitive impairment. But all persons, regardless of age, have the right to be free of physical and chemical restraint and (within reasonable limits) to enjoy autonomy, regardless of their level of cognition.

Restraint of any kind can be applied only on a medical order from a physician. When such orders are imposed for purposes of convenience, rather than because they are required to treat medical symptoms, the act calls into question the *Hippocratic oath* which commits a physician to do no harm.

As concern regarding the use of physical and chemical restraint increases, and the practices of applying such restraint come under regulation, a word of caution is necessary. It is far easier to disguise drug therapy as a medical strategy than it is to claim that physical restraint is a medical necessity. We must therefore all be vigilant in seeing that there is no further proliferation in the use of mood-altering drugs to control behavior in the elderly. We must also see that the use of psychologically punitive tactics does not escalate.

Family caregivers are often uninformed, misinformed, frightened, or simply not sufficiently assertive to advocate on behalf of their family members. They often feel, and are encouraged to feel, that there is no alternative to the use of restraint. But there is! Working together, we can ensure that elderly persons become truly liberated from restraint of any kind. Health care practitioners and family carers all over the world are beginning to say, "The time has come for change!"

GENTLECARE 12-POINT ACTION PLAN FOR ELIMINATING USE OF RESTRAINTS FOR PERSONS WITH DEMENTING ILLNESS

1. EDUCATE ALL STAFF and family caregivers in the process of dementing illness, the behavior caused by the disease process, and the effects of chemical and physical restraint.

2. REVIEW THE LIVING SPACE of the person with dementia. Create a safe, secure, comfortable area, however small, in which the person can move about freely.

3. REVIEW YOUR PROGRAMS to ensure that there are interesting, beautiful objects available for the person with dementia to touch, move, enjoy, and interact with. Use music, pets, books, pictures, flowers, old jewelry, stuffed toys, purses, briefcases, mops, dusters, brooms, rummage opportunities, pillows, afghans, cards, folding towels, different sized boxes, etc. Make the environment feel like home.

4. ASSESS ONE PERSON AT A TIME—review all medication. Consider discontinuing any medication that does not have a therapeutic effect on the person receiving it. Consider dosage, length of time administered, reasons for giving each medication, circumstances under which medication was given or order requested, and by whom it was requested. Review circumstances before medication use and effects of medication on the person's level of function for at least two days following use of the medication. Review patterns of staff practice. Who uses medication? Who uses alternate strategies? Record findings.

5. ONE PERSON AT A TIME—review type or combination of physical restraint being used. Review length of time person is under restraint. Review practice of adjusting or checking restraint: How often? By whom? Were observations recorded? Was person asked about comfort level? Were non-verbal communications noted and recorded? How often was person released from restraint, and allowed to, or assisted to, move about freely? Were effects of restraint recorded such as anxiety, crying, withdrawal, angry frustrated behavior, hitting, swearing, throwing objects, yelling, skin abrasions, pressure marks, leg swelling, bruising, incontinence, dehydration, skin rash, banging, rocking movements, etc.? How much staff time was used monitoring restraint?

6. ONE PERSON AT A TIME—under supervision release person from restraint and place in safe, secure, quiet, comfortable area. Observe and

FIGURE 6-6

record reactions. Begin by providing ongoing assistance with move-ment and balance, interaction with others. Observe and protect against exhaustion and overexertion. After a period of movement, place person in deep comfortable chair. Consider use of safety device in terms of a padded lap belt until person adjusts to freedom of move-ment. Once safety and functional assessment is completed, provide person with appropriate seating and movement area. Observe and record carefully for at least one week, and work with all staff groups/ shifts. Once a review is completed, move to #7.

7. REMOVE THIS ONE PERSON'S PHYSICAL RESTRAINT(S) FROM THE UNIT OR WARD TO AN AREA OF THE FACILITY WHERE IT CANNOT BE ACCESSED AGAIN...EVER!

8. DOCUMENT NEW CARE STRATEGY and communicate to all care staff/families/volunteers. Emphasize that this new strategy is a treat-ment developed by the team, and is not subject to adaptation by any one staff without consultation and approval of the whole interdiscipli-nary team. Implement the requirement that any staff using restraint for the person under review must document all alternate strategies tried prior to the use of restraint, and the particular circumstances that war-ranted the action of re-introducing restraint.

9. FOR EVERY NEW PERSON who walks into the facility or care unit, avoid the use of both chemical and physical restraint, and HELP KEEP THEM WALKING for the duration of the disease.

10. It is recognized that SOME PERSONS WILL BE SO DEBILITATED OR EXCESSIVELY DISABLED that some form of safety device is necessary to assist with posture and comfort. For each of these persons, review their seating and functional requirements. Use an absolute minimum of adaptive equipment or furniture to ensure their comfort and safety. Ensure that they have interesting objects within their reach. Change their positions and location frequently.

11. TRAIN FAMILY CAREGIVERS, VOLUNTEERS, STUDENTS, AND PEO-PLE FROM COMMUNITY ORGANIZATIONS in appropriate ways to assist with indoor and outdoor walking programs and bedside sitting programs.

12. ADAPT BEDROOMS by lowering beds, or using low beds, placing safety mats around the bed, using one safety rail padded with pillows, placing one edge of bed against the wall to increase security. Consider the use of Dutch doors, or gates to limit exhaustion and exposure to the complex and demanding facility when the person with dementia can no longer manage.

Part Two

ASSESSMENT IN DEMENTIA CARE

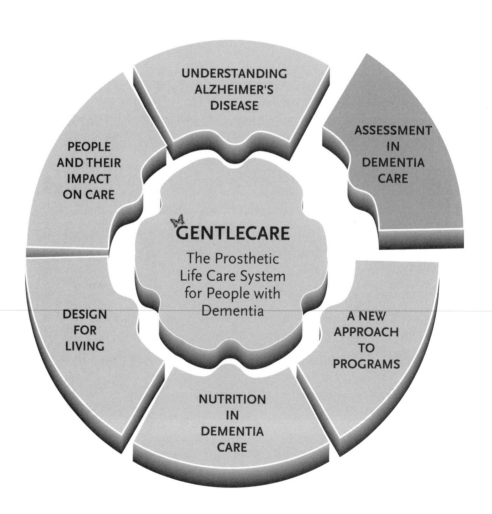

7

Assessment: The Missing Link in Dementia Care

He was a man, take him for all in all,
I shall not look upon his like again.
—William Shakespeare

ASSESSMENT: An Introduction

Once the disease process has been identified, the next important step in care is a review of the client's current level of abilities and deficits. Most elderly clients in the health care system today are coping with three significant challenges. First and most prevalent are the physiological problems inherent with aging. All body systems are affected and they slowly begin to break down as we age. The second problem is the onset of mental illness. Elderly people are faced with changes in competency, environment, and life-style, as well as lost relationships and the death of family members and friends. Symptoms of mental illness begin to appear. Depression, the mental illness most commonly experienced by elders, is estimated to affect as many as three out of every four clients under care. Unfortunately, the effects of depression and other mental illnesses are often assumed to be a normal part of the aging process, and consequently elders may not be properly diagnosed or effectively treated. The third problem, which is reaching epidemic levels, is dementia. Progressive neurological illnesses such as

Alzheimer's disease are so destructive that it is easy to lose the essential human being in the devastation. As people are robbed of their cognition and lose their ability to communicate, their behavior may become irrational. They slowly slip from the role of mother, father, wife, husband, neighbor, and friend toward a state of helplessness. And, as we have seen, dementia can destroy caregivers as well, sentencing them to lives of exhaustion, grief, and poor health.

Gentlecare's signature response to the issues of aging, dementia, and mental health problems is the design and application of a "Prosthesis of Care" for each afflicted individual. As we have noted, the prosthesis is a device, program, or strategy offered by a professional or family caregiver to help protect the client's remaining abilities and compensate for losses the person may be experiencing. The foundation of each prosthesis is a current and accurate assessment of the client's level of dysfunction with special emphasis placed on the client's remaining abilities and wellness. In Gentlecare, we refer to these remaining abilities as the person's wellness quotient.

The dementia client's initial and most significant loss is that of access to cognition and memory. The Gentlecare process provided by the carer substitutes a "mental prosthesis" for these losses in cognitive capacity. What makes this process both challenging and remarkable is that we, as carers, actually substitute our thinking for the losses of our client. We become his memory! We become her hearing aid! We become his wheelchair! It is important to remember that significant parts of the client's brain continue to function. In spite of this, many caregivers assume that the client cannot function at all. If this happens we lose the person to the disease.

Today we cannot stop the relentless progress of Alzheimer's disease and other dementing diseases, but we can do a great deal to optimize the parts of the person's brain that are not yet affected. In addition, we can apply the prosthesis of care to replace the parts that have been destroyed. The challenge for the caregiver is to determine how much of the person's brain remains intact: What does the person feel? What can the person do? What help would he ask for if he could think clearly enough to articulate his current needs? The answers to these and other questions will be revealed if we carry out a careful, multifaceted assessment.

A proper assessment will reveal that many elderly people have several and sometimes many concurrent physical and mental problems. Assessors who expect one set of symptoms to account for the person's overall behavior are frequently disappointed. Mental illness will often be matched with physical symptoms, and physical illness may appear with mental disturbances. To gain accurate information about a client it is necessary to assess the whole person.

Quality care can be achieved if the findings of a full and complete assessment are used to help construct the necessary prosthesis of care. Such an evaluation is indispensable in a valid treatment plan.

The overall purpose of an assessment is to determine:
- how to build a care plan.
- the health status of the person in care.
- the links between diagnoses, behaviors, and social roles.
- The degree to which help is being provided.
- if iatrogenic issues are affecting the client in a negative way. If so, these issues must be addressed.
- if alterations in the care need to be made at this point.

There are many factors that can complicate the assessment process. The number and variety of available tools is so large that selecting the most appropriate is difficult and frequently discouraging. Most of the standard tools for carrying out functional assessments have evolved from rehabilitation practice and are not ideally suited for assessing people with dementing illness. These tools must be modified if they are to work effectively for dementia clients.

Some organizations prefer to develop their own assessment tools which can lead to subjective testing and biased results. Government health agencies may require the use of specific assessment tools and procedures.

Sometimes these complexities, coupled with the high workload, cause staff to move assessment down the priority list. Under pressure, it is easier and faster for care staff to respond as they customarily have,

Whenever two people meet there are really six present. There is each man as he sees himself, each man as the other person sees him, and each man as he really is.

—WILLIAM JAMES

The cornerstone of good treatment is assessment.

rather than to provide the specialized care dictated by the person's assessment.

It is important to resist the impulse to fix the problem before it has been assessed. Experience and intuition are important qualities to bring to the assessment process, but objectivity, consistency, and standardization of the assessment methods are essential if we hope to maximize our help to the client. Yesterday's way of working is giving way to a care model centered on an individual prosthesis of care designed to meets the needs of the individual client.

This prosthesis of care is a system of intervention and support custom-designed for each individual. It allows caregivers to provide care that compensates for the person's deficits and helps to preserve the client's wellness quotient (existing abilities) for as long as possible.

ASSESSMENT: Perspectives

A client's function can be perceived in several ways. For example, function can be determined:

- at an organ level: i.e., how has the disease affected the person's brain? This assessment perspective would be of interest to the family physician or a neurological specialist.
- at a personal level: i.e., how has the disease affected the person's ability to perform a certain function or task? This perspective is of primary interest to the care provider.
- at a social level: i.e., does the disease prevent the person from carrying out social activities or life responsibilities? This perspective is of primary interest to family members.

Each of these perspectives gives rise to different interpretations, and consequently different types of interventions (see Figure 7-1).

When caring for the elderly, it is important to remember that assessment observations must be current because most diseases associated with aging are progressive. In Gentlecare facilities, the goal is to complete a thorough assessment of each resident upon admission and then conduct a comprehensive reassessment at regular intervals.

With this information we can plan appropriate interventions, mobilize resources, and build an individualized prosthesis of care.

	ORGAN LEVEL	PERSON LEVEL	SOCIAL LEVEL
	PATHOLOGY	BEHAVIORAL	ROLE
CONDITION	Anatomical, physiological, mental, psychological deficits	Performance deficits within the environment	Environmental and social deficits influenced by values, norms, policies
KEY TERMS	Impairment (organic dysfunction)	Disability (difficulty with tasks)	Handicap (social disadvantage)
ANALYSIS	Diagnostic descriptions (Alzheimer's disease)	Behavioral or performance descriptions ("violent")	Role descriptions ("Dad can't drive anymore")
	PHYSICIAN	CARE PROVIDER	FAMILY

FIGURE 7-1

Effective assessment requires not only a formal periodic review of the client but also a continuous gathering of information from observations and comments made by everyone who has contact with the client. The information from the neurologist who pinpoints brain pathology, the housekeeper who notices an elderly lady talking to herself at a bathroom mirror, the food service worker who observes a man ignoring food on one side of his plate, the care aide who correctly identifies signs of depression, the volunteer who discovers that a mute gentleman loves to sing...every piece of information contributes to the puzzle that is the current, but ever-changing, condition of each person in care. The continuous inflow of information helps with the refinement of the prosthesis of care for that client.

It is important to remember that dementia is not a disease. It is a group of symptoms, signs, and problems that can be caused by a num-

Everything that we see is a shadow cast by that which we do not see.

—MARTIN LUTHER KING

ber of different individual diseases, and, sometimes, by several diseases at once. Since the path taken by each dementia client is unique, it is important to determine which disease, or diseases, is/are causing the dementia. Therefore, in the first phase of assessment, answers to the following questions are sought:

- Which diseases are causing the problem?
- Is the disease acute or chronic?
- Can the client benefit from treatment?
- Is it possible that the person's behavior is being caused by physiological factors other than the disease? (noise, rush, crowds, fear, etc., all defined as Iatrogenic Factors)
- Is it possible that the person's behavior is being caused by depression or another psychiatric illness?

No assessment measures have value at all, unless the results are communicated to the staff and family caregivers who are actually delivering care.

It is not uncommon for a person with a dementing illness, such as Alzheimer's disease, to also present with psychiatric problems. Depression is the most common psychiatric problem seen in dementia clients. It is marked by changes in appetite, altered sleeping patterns, loss of interest in and enjoyment of life, increased general fatigue, feelings of worthlessness, and thoughts of suicide. Fortunately, depression is one of the most treatable of all the psychological disorders.

Other major psychiatric symptoms that often accompany Alzheimer's disease are paranoid delusions ("Someone is spying on me," "Someone has stolen my money"); misidentification (mistaking the caregiver for someone else or believing people seen on television are real—i.e., the client feels a character on television is real and in the room with them); and hallucinatory experiences, both auditory and visual (the person may converse with an imaginary person, see snakes in the bathtub, or imagine burglars are climbing in the window).

Hallucinations are imaginary, sensory feelings. Delusions are imaginary or distorted thoughts.

I VIVIDLY REMEMBER *the first time I became aware that my father was hallucinating. Usually all of the family slept like logs at night, having kept up with Dad all day. However, one night I heard strange sounds and when I investigated I found my father in an absolute*

*frenzy, moving furniture out onto the lawn. He was sweating and ex-
hausted from his efforts, and the whole place was in chaos.*

*When I asked him what was the matter, he looked at me in panic
and said, "Can't you see the house is on fire; there is fire everywhere.
We must get everything out!" His absolute terror left me no doubt that
he was surrounded by a circle of fire.*

GENTLECARE Best Practice

If appropriate, tell the person with dementia frequently
that he/she is loved and needed; that the caregiver
understands and will always be there. Remember that the
person may suffer from memory loss and need to hear
these loving words over and over again.

The symptoms of severe depression can closely imitate the symptoms
of Alzheimer's disease. Because of this, depression is often referred to
as "pseudo dementia." More women than men appear to be affected,
and a woman is especially likely to be depressed if there has been a history of mood disorders in her family.

It is critical that staff members recognize the signs of depression
when and if they appear in their dementia clients. In the early stages of
the disease, the client is frequently overcome with grief and anxiety because of gradual but continuous loss of function. Care providers who
understand the client's behavior, and who support and reassure them
that they will not be abandoned, can be very effective in relieving the
person's emotional anxiety. The observations of staff are important
contributions toward the proper diagnosis and treatment of depression
of dementia clients.

In Gentlecare, information sheets are designed as a resource for
care providers. These sheets list the important elements of prevalent

diseases that clients may be experiencing. Care providers are encouraged to develop these information sheets as an education tool.

The following is an example:

UNDERSTANDING DEPRESSION

Before a diagnosis of clinical depression is confirmed, at least four of the following symptoms must be present every day for a period of at least two weeks (Diagnostic and Statistical Manual of Mental Disorders, IV):

- loss of interest or pleasure in activities or pastimes;
- sad, blue, hopeless, down-in-the-dumps, irritable;
- mood is prominent and persistent;
- poor appetite/weight loss or increased appetite/weight gain;
- insomnia or hypersomnia;
- psychomotor agitation or retardation of movement;
- loss of energy/fatigue;
- feeling of worthlessness, self-reproach, guilt;
- complaints about ability to think or concentrate;
- indecisiveness; and
- recurrent thoughts of death/suicide.

Gentlecare staff and family members are encouraged to value observations and comments of other staff members and family members. Because dementing and aging illnesses are progressive, who better to comment on changes in the client than the people who see and speak with them daily?

Levels of Assessment

There are many general and specific assessment tools available in the health care field. Gentlecare does not promote the use of any one set of tools for the assessment of elderly and/or dementia clients, but rather values and incorporates the use of information from all possible sources. See Figure 7-2.

```
┌─────────────────────────────────────────────────────────────┐
│                  LEVELS OF ASSESSMENT                         │
│                                                               │
│   LEVEL 1    General awareness                                │
│                                                               │
│   LEVEL 2    Observational and anecdotal recording           │
│                                                               │
│   LEVEL 3    Basic assessment of person's ability to perform  │
│              daily living activities                          │
│                                                               │
│   LEVEL 4    Assessment instruments to be administered and    │
│              interpreted by skilled professionals             │
│                                                               │
│   LEVEL 5    Specialized dementia rating scales to pinpoint   │
│              specific areas of dysfunction administered by    │
│              skilled professionals                            │
│                                                               │
└─────────────────────────────────────────────────────────────┘
```

FIGURE 7-2

Level 1: General Awareness

In order to make this almost continuous flow of information about the client as useful as possible, Gentlecare supports the use of the 7 W's of Functional Assessment and Dementia M-P-A^5-C-T. These two tools help organize anecdotal and observational information and prevent important information from being lost.

THE 7 W'S OF FUNCTIONAL ASSESSMENT

- What can the person do?
- What does the person do?
- How does he or she do it?
- Which parts of the task is the person unable to do?
- Why is he or she unable to do them?
- Where does he or she perform best?
- When does he or she perform best?

(*Doing Things*, by Jitka M. Zgola, Johns Hopkins University Press)

DEMENTIA M-P-A^5-C-T

- **(M)Memory**—a person with dementia loses the ability to recall information that has just been made available, and short-term memory progressively declines. Long-term memory is retained long into the disease process and can be used to help compen-

More often than not, symptoms of disease will manifest themselves in functional performance (i.e., the person's ability to do things). Even though non-medical interventions will not stop the disease process, they will alleviate a lot of distress for the individual, his family, and caretakers. Thus symptoms are reduced.

—ALIX MCGINITY,
OCCUPATIONAL
THERAPIST

sate for short-term memory deficits. As short-term memory continues to fail it often triggers bouts of anxiety. These troublesome periods may be eased and perhaps eliminated if the caregiver is able to move the client's attention smoothly from the present to the past. This technique (talking about the past instead of the present) is known as distraction.

• **(P)Perception**—people with dementia lose the ability to interpret sensory information. They have problems perceiving directions, distance, and the relationship between external objects and their own bodies. They fail to recognize how one body part relates to another.

• **(A)Agnosia**—people with dementia lose the ability to recognize familiar sensations.

• **(A)Anomia**—dementia destroys the ability to recall the word or phrase that identifies a familiar object.

• **(A)Aphasia**—a person with dementia may experience a deficit or total loss of ability to speak, understand speech, to write, or to read.

• **(A)Apraxia**—dementing illnesses can destroy a person's ability to carry out skilled and purposeful movements—to make the body do what the mind wants it to do.

• **(A)Abulia**—a person with dementia may be unable to hold a thought long enough to complete an action or a communication.

• **(C)Communication**—a person with dementia is afraid of making mistakes, losing a train of thought, and not finding the correct word to express feelings or meaning. Conversation may come out as a "word salad" or jumble of words: "I don't want to burn myself. I found myself. I was gone. I have to go back again. It's the same thing. I can't figure."

• **(T)Thought processing**—people with dementia can't process new information, interpret external events, use reason or judgment, or think abstractly. They cannot problem-solve, initiate thinking, focus, or concentrate. Thus, they are extremely vulnerable in new learning situations.

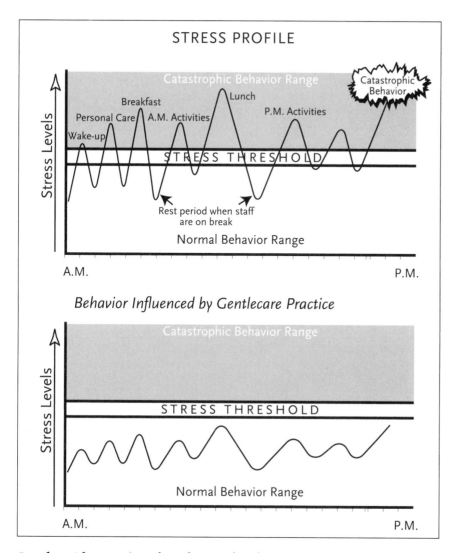

STRESS PROFILE

FIGURE 7-3

Level 2: Observational and Anecdotal Recording

Gentlecare uses two additional tools to help staff members, families, and volunteers organize their anecdotal information about stress and behavior exhibited by clients.

1. The Stress Profile is based on the work of Geri Hall, (see Fig.7-3) and developed as an assessment tool by Moyra Jones Resources Ltd. With a well-developed stress profile you will know what types of activities cause stress. The challenge is to remove the client from the stressful situation or remove the source of stress. For example, the

breakfast period may be stressful for a client. His stress profile tells you that he is bothered by noise, so your first move is to reduce some of the noise around his breakfast.

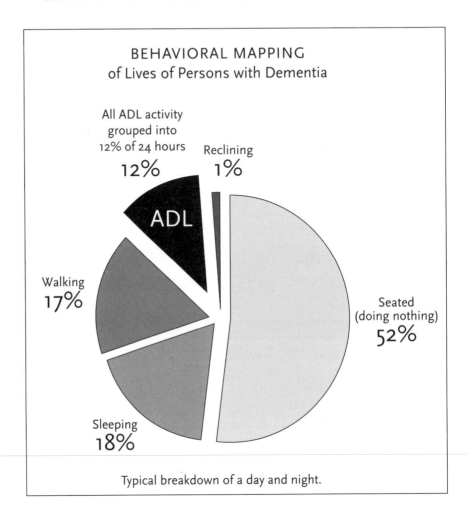

BEHAVIORAL MAPPING
of Lives of Persons with Dementia

All ADL activity grouped into 12% of 24 hours
12%

Reclining
1%

ADL

Seated
(doing nothing)
52%

Walking
17%

Sleeping
18%

Typical breakdown of a day and night.

FIGURE 7-4

2. A technique called Behavior Mapping (see Fig.7-4) involves observing an individual with dementing illness for 24 hours. Observed behaviors are then divided into categories (sleep, activity, walking, rest, etc.) which can be plotted on a graph to show the client's activity level over the period. This information helps care staff understand the daily pattern of the people whose lives they manage. With this information staff can develop and schedule programs that have a good chance of working for the client.

Level 3: Basic Assessment of Person's Ability to Perform Activities of Daily Living

How can we measure a client's ability to perform tasks, the most important of which are labeled Activities of Daily Living (ADL)? There are many instruments available for assessing ADL which are usually administered by skilled professionals. The Katz Index of ADL is an example (see Figure 7-5). The information on the client's current level of function must be interpreted and displayed in a way that will prove helpful to and usable by care providers and family members.

THE KATZ INDEX OF ADL

INDEX OF INDEPENDENCE IN ACTIVITIES OF DAILY LIVING

The Index of Independence in Activities of Daily Living is based on an evaluation of the functional independence of patients in bathing, dressing, going to toilet, transferring, continence, and feeding. Specific definitions of functional independence and dependence appear below the index.

A Independent in feeding, continence, transferring, going to toilet, dressing, and bathing.

B Independent in all but one of these functions.

C Independent in all but bathing, and one additional function.

D Independent in all but bathing, dressing, and one additional function.

E Independent in all but bathing, dressing, going to toilet, and one additional function.

F Independent in all but bathing, dressing, going to toilet, transferring, and one additional function.

G Dependent in all six functions.

Other Dependent in at least two functions, but not classifiable as C, D, E, or F.

Independence means without supervision, direction, or active personal assistance, except as specifically noted. This is based on actual status and not on ability. A patient who refuses to perform a function is considered as not performing the function, even though he/she is deemed able.

FIGURE 7-5

Katz Index con't.

Activity	Independent	Dependent
Bathing (sponge, shower, or tub)	Assistance only in bathing a single part (such as back or disabled extremity) or bathes self completely.	Assistance in bathing more than one part of body; assistance in getting in or out of tub or does not bathe self.
Dressing	Gets clothes from closet and drawers; puts on clothes, outer garments, braces; manages fasteners: act of tying shoes is excluded.	Does not dress self or remains partly undressed.
Going to Toilet	Gets to toilet; gets on and off toilet; arranges clothes; cleans organs of excretion (may manage own bedpan used at night only and may or may not be using mechanical support).	Uses bedpan or commode or receives assistance in getting to and using toilet.
Transfer	Moves in and out of bed independently and moves in and out of chair independently (may or may not be using mechanical supports).	Assistance in moving in or out of bed and/or chair; does not perform any transfers.
Continence	Urination and defecation entirely self-controlled.	Partial or total incontinence in urination or defecation; partial or total control by enemas, catheters, or regulated use of urinals and/or bedpans.
Feeding	Gets food from plate or its equivalent into mouth (precutting of meat and preparation of food, such as buttering bread, are excluded from evaluation).	Assistance in act of feeding; does not eat at all or parental feeding.

FIGURE 7-5

EVALUATION FORM

Name_____ Date of Evaluation_____

For each area of functioning listed below, check description that applies.
The word "assistance" means supervision, direction, or personal assistance.

Bathing—either sponge bath, tub bath, or shower.

☐ Receives no assistance (gets in and out of tub by self if tub is usual means of bathing).

☐ Receives assistance in bathing only one part of the body (such as back or leg).

☐ Receives assistance in bathing more than one part of the body (or not bathed).

Dressing—gets clothes from closets and drawers: includes underclothes, outer garments, and using fasteners (including braces if worn).

☐ Gets clothes and gets completely dressed without assistance.

☐ Gets clothes and gets dressed without assistance except for assistance in tying shoes.

☐ Receives assistance in getting clothes or in getting dressed, or stays partly or completely undressed.

Toileting—going to the "toilet room" for bowel and urine elimination; cleaning self after elimination, and arranging clothes.

☐ Goes to "toilet room," cleans self, and arranges clothes without assistance (may use object such as cane, walker, or wheelchair and may manage night bedpan or commode, emptying same in morning).

☐ Receives assistance in going to "toilet room" or in cleansing self or arranging clothes after elimination or in use of night bedpan or commode.

☐ Doesn't go to room termed "toilet" for the elimination process.

Transfer

☐ Moves in and out of bed as well as in and out of chair without assistance (may be using object for support, such as cane or walker).

☐ Moves in or out of bed or chair with assistance.

☐ Doesn't get out of bed.

Continence

☐ Controls urination and bowel movements completely by self.

☐ Has occasional "accidents."

☐ Supervision helps keep urine or bowel control; catheter is used, or is incontinent.

Feeding

☐ Feeds self without assistance.

☐ Feeds self except for getting assistance in cutting meat or buttering bread.

☐ Receives assistance in feeding or is fed partly or completely by using tubes or intravenous fluids.

FIGURE 7-5

AN OLD GENTLEMAN *and his wife had returned to the young neurol-*
ogist's office for a regular checkup. As the doctor entered the office, the
gentleman began the visit by saying, "Listen, Sonny, two and two are
six, and that's all I want to hear about that!"

Level 4: Assessment Instruments and

Level 5: Specialized dementia rating scales to pinpoint specific
areas of dysfunction are designed to be administered and
interpreted by skilled professionals.

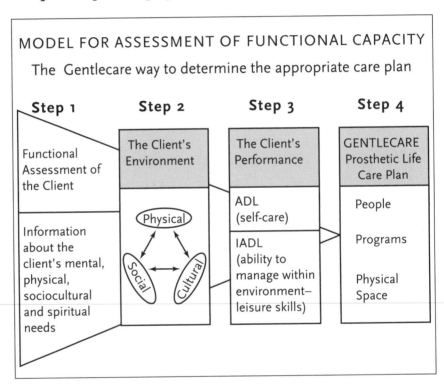

MODEL FOR ASSESSMENT OF FUNCTIONAL CAPACITY

The Gentlecare way to determine the appropriate care plan

Step 1	Step 2	Step 3	Step 4
Functional Assessment of the Client	The Client's Environment	The Client's Performance	GENTLECARE Prosthetic Life Care Plan
Information about the client's mental, physical, sociocultural and spiritual needs	Physical Social Cultural	ADL (self-care) IADL (ability to manage within environment– leisure skills)	People Programs Physical Space

FIGURE 7-6

The Gentlecare Model of Assessment

Introduction: It is not hard to imagine that the flood of information
from a number of assessment tools could easily lead to information
overload. In order to organize the assessment information in a way that
is helpful to both the client and the care providers, Gentlecare promotes the use of the four-step model (see Figure 7-6).

In **Step 1,** all of the information known about the mental, physical, socio-cultural, and spiritual aspects of the client is screened through the Step 1 filters (questions). Step 1 is about the client.

Step 2 examines the environment in which the person must live. The physical, social, and cultural aspects of this environment are assessed to explore the challenges this environment presents to the client.

Step 3 assesses the client's ability to manage his/her personal self care (the activities of daily living or ADLs: toileting, bathing, grooming, dressing, and eating.) In addition, the client's ability to manage the environment is evaluated. These skills, the Instrumental Activities of Daily Living (IADL), are usually more complex and include mobility, relationships, management of food, clothing, transportation, etc. They also include leisure skills or activities that give sheer pleasure to the clients and do not challenge them in any way (for example, stroking a visiting pet, walking in the garden, joining in a singalong of old familiar tunes.)

Thus Steps 1 to 3 provide the necessary assessment data.

Step 4 examines the prosthesis of care created for the client. The three elements that make up the prosthesis of care in Gentlecare are (1) the involvement of a variety of people, including the family, in the person's life, (2) the special programs that require the person's time and energy, and (3) the physical space in which the person's life unfolds.

Now that we have looked at an overview of the Gentlecare Model of Assessment, we are ready to assess the functioning of the client, beginning with the group of activities that make up mental capacity.

STEP 1: ASPECTS OF THE CLIENT
Step 1 Mental Component

The mental component refers to the total intellectual and emotional response of an individual to her environment (the place where she lives). A huge array of complex and interrelated aspects of mental function must be evaluated in this category.

Questions the assessor should ask:

Step 1

Functional Assessment of the Client

Information about the client's mental, physical, sociocultural and spiritual needs

Orientation

- Does the person know who he or she is?
- Does he know where he is?
- Does she lose her way?
- Is orientation to time/place/person impaired?

Cognition

There is no place like home.

Cognitive skills are determined by observing:
- problem-solving
- expressive communication
- ability to follow instructions
- memory/memory processing
- attention to detail
- ability to accept responsibility

The less competent an individual is, the more the environment accounts for his or her dysfunction.

- judgment
- reasoning
- ability to abstract
- ability to sequence
- reality orientation
- ability to communicate needs
- ability to do a simple task
- ability to understand and follow directions
- ability to recall information from minutes before
- ability to put on clothing in correct order
- understanding how to transform flour into muffins
- being centered in the here and now, as opposed to operating in another time frame.

Mood and affect

These two aspects of mental capacity refer to the person's feelings, and the appropriateness of the expression of those feelings. For example, a person may be in a state of grief and sadness (mood) due to the death of a loved one. Feelings (affect) may be expressed by withdrawing or being angry. Assessment clarifies both the level and the appropriateness of feelings.

Due to the effects of Alzheimer's disease on the limbic system the afflicted person may, from the onset of the disease, exhibit rapid shifts in moods, which can be very alarming for caregivers. Such rapid shifts in moods have given rise to the myth that people afflicted with Alzheimer's disease are unpredictable. On the contrary, behavior can be accurately predicted if the caregiver knows what signs and symptoms to look for:

- Is the person sad or withdrawn from life's activities?
- Is the person anxious? Is the degree of anxiety appropriate given the circumstances of the moment?
- How are the feelings being translated into actions?

Behavior

Behavior is a measure of all the actions taken by the client. Assessment strategies measure the appropriateness of the person's behavior and their ability to control it.

Is the person:
- hoarding or stealing?
- exhibiting behavior that bothers others?
- destroying the clothing or property of others?
- lying on someone else's bed?
- suspicious, angry, or intrusive?
- striking out at others?
- engaging in public activity that is not socially acceptable, such as undressing, masturbating, taking out dentures, or urinating?
- behaving in unpredictable or unexpected ways?

Perception

Perception refers to a person's awareness of reality and visual/spatial awareness. Brain damage in the area that controls perception the parietal lobe) may result in hallucinations. The affected person may hear imaginary voices, see visions, and experience tastes and sensations that are not real.

It is believed that significant numbers of people with dementia experience terrifying and disturbing hallucinations. Treatment for this psychiatric phenomenon is rarely offered. Frequently, the "crazy" things said or done by elderly people are a source of amusement or labeling. Neglect or exploitation of such behaviors is, of course, tantamount to abuse.

- Does the person appear to perceive things correctly?
- Can she tell the difference between someone on TV and a real person?
- Does he recognize himself in a mirror or photograph?
- Does she avoid an area of glare or shine on the floor as though it were a pool of water or a sheet of ice?
- Does he avoid walking on a dark-colored area of the floor as though it were a pit or hole?
- Does she react to patterns on walls or bed covers as though they were moving objects?
- Does he misinterpret sounds? For instance, is the noise of a branch hitting against a window interpreted by the client as an intruder? A public address announcement interpreted as a message from beyond?

Thought content

This aspect of mental function refers to:

- clarity of thinking
- appropriateness of thoughts
- organization of thinking patterns
- compulsiveness.

Compulsiveness refers to preoccupations, compulsions, rituals, and phobias that may lead to delusional thinking. People so affected may believe others are stealing their things when they have, in fact, misplaced them due to memory loss. They may feel that they have been deliberately left out of the conversation, talked about, or feel that they have not been served a meal. With little or no short-term memory, the person sees others eating, does not remember having eaten, and feels neglected or wronged. The person cannot respond to the reasoning provided by staff or a family member that he or she has, in fact just finished a meal.

It is important to remember that some real event or factual trigger may have led the person to misinterpret information, and caregivers can help by carefully examining the hallucinatory or delusional behavior of the person with dementia. Every effort should be made to remove any identified stimulant and seek psychiatric help for the client. Both lay caregivers and professional care providers need to understand that mental illness is often blended with dementing illness. Also, only the care staff and family members can observe and pass on the vital bits of information that permit medical staff to formulate appropriate treatment. Examples of critical information include:

- Does the person evade questions?
- Does his conversation indicate appropriate thinking?
- Does she feel others are out to get her?
- Does one thought logically follow another?

Emotional defense

Emotional defense refers to the use of denial or projection. From time to time I hear people with dementia labeled as "blamers." When an elderly person with dementia projects responsibility for various actions onto other people, they are using a very common emotional defense! Projection or blaming deflects attention from us to someone else. It relieves us of responsibility and/or negative attention.

- Does the person withdraw from stress, responsibilities, and expectations?
- Does he blame others for his problems?
- Does she try to deflect questions?

IMAGINE THAT YOU *are sitting in a room with your purse or briefcase. You are called to the phone and when you return your possessions are gone. What do you think? What do you say?*

The majority of us healthy normal folks say something like, "Who stole my purse?" Think about that the next time you are tempted to call an elderly dementia victim a blamer, or suspicious, or paranoid, when, due to memory loss, that person thinks their possessions have been stolen.

Reaction/adaptability

This aspect of mental function refers to a person's ability to react to the effects of their progressive disease. Some clients react in an aggressive manner while others are able to achieve a level of understanding.

At a time when they are most vulnerable, dementia clients are required to separate themselves from their familiar support systems and adapt to living in a new "home" that is full of strangers. At the same time, they are expected to have and use excellent wayfinding and participatory skills, and to have the ability to assimilate a vast array of new rules, regulations, and schedules. A deficit in this aspect of cognition (reaction/adaptability) would present any of us with formidable problems. The piling on of a second or third dysfunction will often cause the client to break down. Caregivers need to ask these questions:

- Does the person withdraw?
- Does he follow instruction? Can he?
- Does she follow others' lead?
- Does the person seem frustrated, angry, agitated, or helpless?
- Does he use compensatory behavior to overcome his disabilities, such as walking, talking randomly, clinging to others, asking repeated questions, hiding, exhibiting catastrophic behavior?

Body image

Some clients have difficulty with their perception of their own body. Others have problems accurately matching their appearance with their age. Does the person see only one-half of his body?

- Does she recognize herself in a mirror or photograph?
- Does he perceive himself as younger than he is?

YOU HAVE PROBABLY *heard the story of the old lady who was shown a current picture of herself.*

"Who is that?" she asked.

"It is you."

"No!"

"Yes, it is."

"Well, I sure was a lot older then than I am now!"

Step 1 Physical Component

The physical component of assessment refers to a person's ability to move the body freely and purposefully through space—indoors and outdoors, day or night. In addition, physical capability includes the sensory functions of the body (hearing, sight, speech, smell and touch).

Range of movement

This aspect of function remains relatively healthy and intact throughout the course of dementia if the person is not restrained in a wheelchair or geriatric chair, in a bed, by drugs, or in any other way.

Care staff should focus on how a lack of full range of movement affects function.

Questions the assessor should ask:
- Does the person have the appropriate range of movement in upper arms and shoulders, hips, and ankles to perform necessary activities?
- Can she put on and take off personal clothing?
- Can he brush his own hair?
- Can she raise her arms high enough to reach food on her tray?
- Can he move from chair to standing or standing to his bed unassisted or with minimal assistance?
- Can she cleanse herself after toileting?

Strength and muscle tone

Does the client have sufficient muscle strength to perform functional tasks for the duration of the task, i.e., reaching, climbing, feeding oneself, brushing or combing hair, and so on?

Coordination/balance/involuntary movements

- Has the person's balance been affected by immobilization and/or medication?
- Does the person's body exhibit tremors on initiating activity, after sustained activity, or while at rest?

Endurance

- Are activities appropriate to the person's ability, strength, and interest?
- Does the person show signs of fatigue or stress?
- Has the activity ever resulted in catastrophic behavior?
- How long has the person engaged in an activity?
- Have rest breaks been scheduled and implemented?

Sensation

This aspect of physical function refers to abilities and limitations or disturbances in:

- **Touch:** Is the client overly sensitive to touch during care?
- **Pain:** Pain is subjective! See Figure 7-7. The belief that older people do not suffer as much pain as younger people has not been validated. Pain is often a precursor to noncompliance with or resistance to care.

Paying attention to pain helps prevent it. Offer a cup of tea, a massage, or a warm blanket.

Pain exists when the person says they have pain.

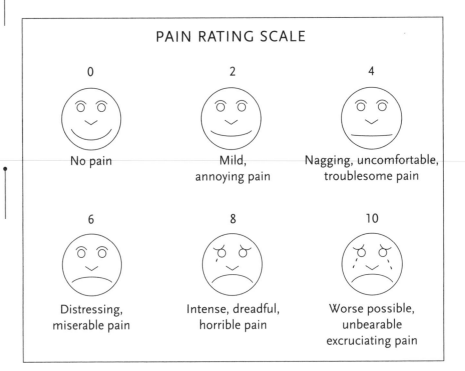

PAIN RATING SCALE

0 — No pain

2 — Mild, annoying pain

4 — Nagging, uncomfortable, troublesome pain

6 — Distressing, miserable pain

8 — Intense, dreadful, horrible pain

10 — Worse possible, unbearable excruciating pain

FIGURE 7-7

- **Sensitivity to pressure:** People with dementia often sit in wheelchairs for 12 hours a day. Wheelchairs provide very poor support for elders and their use frequently results in skin breakdown at pressure points. Also, elders have difficulty changing their position in bed and in wheelchairs and need assistance to change position frequently.
- **Vision:** People with dementia experience significant real and imaginary distortions in vision. Prescriptions for glasses should be checked frequently and glasses should be kept clean.
- **Hearing:** Distortions in hearing cause many problems for the older individual, often forcing them to miss out on important information and on many of life's pleasures. Clients should be helped to use their hearing aids as long as possible.
- **Taste:** Control centers are located in the sensory cortex and in the tongue. Caregivers should note that the taste of food is enhanced when taken with liquids. Good mouth care and a variety of liquids, including water, will contribute greatly to the pleasure of eating. This strategy is recommended to combat the condition of dry mouth caused by medication, heated rooms, and the lack of easy access to water.
- **Vibration:** Refers to unceasing movement within the body which clients find unpleasant.
- **Proprioception:** Refers to awareness of the position of one's body.
- **Kinesthesis:** Refers to the sensation of movement, and the state of tension in the muscles and joints. People with dementia have a need to move and this urge causes great anguish when the client is restrained.
- **Stereognosis:** Refers to the ability to determine the shape and weight of an object by touching or lifting it.
- **Appearance:** Refers to issues such as deformity, swelling, and skin markings.

Step 1 Socio-Cultural Component

Social interaction skills

This refers to the ability to interact with others and engage in various social activities, using socially acceptable behaviors. There is a common myth that people experiencing dementing illness keep their social skills until the end. Not so! Dementia results in loss of social interaction skills such as communication, sharing of space and equipment, sharing of the group leader, and the observance of socially acceptable behavior. Participation, particularly in large social groups, is enormously challenging for anyone experiencing dementing illness. The fact that elderly people with dementia try to react appropriately and get along with strangers speaks more of their decency and spirit than of their social skills. They just try very hard to fit in. When it all becomes too stressful, they may react with? catastrophic behaviors. The care team needs to ask these questions:

- Can this person manage within a group activity?
- Can she engage appropriately in social intimacy?
- Does he fit in with a group in terms of social behaviors?
- Does she become upset, angry, anxious, or nervous near groups of people or at family gatherings?
- Can she share support systems (staff members, for instance) with other people?

Involvement in community

This refers to the ability and opportunity to continue to carry out social roles and involvement in community activities (church, golf, driving, family gatherings, etc.). We must be very careful about involving old people with dementia in large social events, family outings, games, and competitions. Staff and families must take care to present the person with activities appropriate to their age and the stage of their disease. The care team needs to ask these questions:

- What has been the person's involvement in the past?
- In what groups, if any, has he been active?
- Are such organizations a potential source of help for her?

I AM REMINDED of a story of a woman who, over the years, was very involved in the activities of her church. Now, due to dementing illness, her behavior was somewhat disorganized and unpredictable. She missed her contacts with former friends and associates, as well as that feeling of usefulness that came from supporting her church's community programs. Her family organized an educational program for members of her church, neighbors, family friends, and home support staff. They came together to learn about dementia and figure out ways that they could involve the woman without stressing her. Her successful return to church encouraged the congregation to begin looking at how they could help other members of their church who had similar problems.

Participation in family relationships

Does the client currently have the ability to engage in family relationships and to assume responsibility for their role within their family? One of the many tragedies of Alzheimer's disease is the phenomenon of role reversal, whereby a wife must assume her husband's former tasks and duties, or the mid-life "child" is put in the position of "parenting" the parent.

Dementia also compromises the person's ability to be involved in intimate associations in familiar ways that are comforting to both partners. We can help by assigning private space with appropriate signage and by advising all staff that the couple's privacy should be respected.

A prerequisite for these strategies should be the availability of appropriate educational resources to all staff and families.

Staff can also intervene by providing an intermediate level of intimacy which is acceptable to both the family member and the afflicted person.

Driving Issues

Another common family dilemma is the issue of who drives the car. Dementia progressively destroys the skills necessary for safe driving. Early on in the dementia process, the person may lose the ability to interpret the symbols and rules that ensure safe driving. For example, he may be confused by the stop sign, the significance of colored lights that control traffic, the numbers that indicate speed limits, and the concept of motion (e.g., the person might step out of a moving vehicle).

I REMEMBER TAKING *three elderly ladies for a leisurely drive to show them the community. One lady sat in front with me, and of the two in the back, one chattered constantly and the other was very quiet.*

Suddenly I was aware that there was no response whatever coming from the second lady and turned my head to look.

She was not in the back seat!

She had quietly opened the door of the car at a stop sign and got out!

I rushed back to find her, and there she was on the side of the street still unsteady, but unhurt, thank goodness!

You can imagine that from then on I made sure that I installed child-proof locks on the doors of any vehicle in which I transported clients.

DRIVING TIPS

- Solicit your doctor's help.
- Explain the issue to traffic control officials.
- "Misplace" the car keys.
- Make mechanical adjustments so the car will not start.
- Move the car to a location out of sight.
- Sell the car.
- Explain to the person why he cannot drive in concrete terms of vision, memory, and way-finding, or injury to others. For example, "Joe, you drove through the red light!" not "You must stop driving."
- Provide significant support and alternative tasks, or roles. For instance, the driver offers the afflicted person a map to "help with navigation."
- Arrange for others to offer lots of short car drives.
- Ensure that the substitute driver has sufficient driving skills to take over the responsibility for driving!

FIGURE 7-8

Very often one member of the family has always been the driver, most likely the husband. When the driving needs to be taken over by the spouse, she is often a more dangerous driver than the person afflicted with dementia!

The caregiver needs to assess the competency of the substitute driver and recommend a safe alternative for transportation.

Giving up the freedom and control implicit in a driver's license is a terribly difficult step.

The person is not being denied driving privileges because he is old but because the disease is destroying the skills he needs to drive safely.

Often when an explanation is given to the afflicted person about the risk to others (e.g. that they might injure or kill a child or pet), the person will voluntarily surrender the car keys and driver's license.

Social occasions

One of the most difficult issues in dementia is whether or not to involve the afflicted person in family gatherings or special occasions. Families don't want to leave anyone out, but realize how stressful weddings, birthdays, and family gatherings can be for someone with dementia. Gentlecare recommends mini-celebrations where the person currently lives, rather than large parties at home or in commercial settings.

THE BRIDE FELT *that attendance at her big wedding was going to be too much excitement for her beloved grandmother. So she arranged with the staff at the nursing home where her grandmother lived that as soon as the ceremony at the church was over, and before the big dance and dinner, she and the groom and all the wedding party would come to celebrate with "Gran" and her friends. Everyone in the facility gathered in the lounge and the bride and groom and their attendants and parents entered to the Wedding March, circled the room and presented themselves to Gran for her blessing. Then the wedding party distributed little packages of wedding cake to all the residents. Refreshments were passed around by the staff and the party left in a flurry of good wishes.*

Friendship Issues

It is important to assess the client's ability to engage in intimacy, ongoing social interaction, and relationships with persons outside of the family. Dementing illness causes problems in memory, conversation, and spontaneous behavior. It also causes some people to be more sexually active or expressive than ever before in their lives. People with dementia may forget friends, may act inappropriately, may not talk or respond when others speak to them. They may engage in sexually explicit activity with strangers. Any one of these behaviors can cause longtime friends to abandon efforts to keep in touch with a person with dementia. Lack of information that would explain the behavior can cause loss of friends at a time when they are most needed.

The friend must take up the responsibility for exchanging information, storytelling, and reminiscing, and not wait for or expect the afflicted person to participate.

Friends help at Johnson Elder Care, Washington State, USA

I WAS ONCE *approached by an accountant who told a sad story of a dear friend of his who had developed dementia. He said, "I don't go to see him anymore because he can't talk." "But you can still talk, can't you?" I protested. "Of course I can still talk," he retorted. "Are you suggesting that I just go and talk to him?"*

When I told him that was exactly what his friend needed most, he agreed to try. A few days later he called to say that they had resumed their friendship. I am not sure which of the two men was more pleased.

Care teams need to ask these questions:

• Does the person have friends from clubs and organizations or with shared hobbies who could be asked to help?

• Do visitors/friends know enough about dementia to be able to visit effectively? It is often helpful to refer them to a support group for specialized education.

• Is the client encouraged to be helpless or dependent by friends/visitors?

- Is sexual interaction appropriate and comforting?
- Does the person's sexual behavior harm anyone?

Step 1 Spiritual Component

The spiritual aspect of a person refers to a sense of the purpose of their life. In dementia care, information about a person's spirituality is usually obtained from a close family member or from the organization's chaplain.

Belief/value system

A person's belief system is the set of beliefs or values that have informed his or her life for as long as the person can remember. This value system remains with the person long into the illness. Care teams need to ask these questions:

- Who is this person? What is his religious and cultural background?
- What are her habits and routines? Her likes and dislikes? Hobbies? Interests?
- Can or does he exhibit or express a sense of purpose in life?
- What is the source of this person's energy or drive? Is this found in a family role—for instance, as expressed in concern for wife/husband/children/grandchildren? Is it expressed in terms of attachment to a former job or occupation ("I have to get out to feed my cattle"; "I have to go to the office")? Does it come from involvement in church or religious activities? (The challenge of using multipurpose rooms is that areas designated for worship should remind the person of a spiritual setting rather than a bingo hall. People with dementia often assume postures or attitudes appropriate to spiritual places if such feelings are triggered by rituals, environment or décor, ambiance, and activities.)

This completes the assessment of the individual. Now we are in a position to examine the impact of environment on the client's function.

Step 2

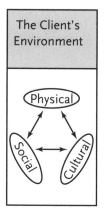

The Client's
Environment

Physical

Social

Cultural

STEP 2: THE PHYSICAL ENVIRONMENT

The person with dementia does not live in a vacuum. The living environment provided at home or in a care facility is a critical factor in the ability of a person, at whatever level of function, to live with comfort and to perform at maximum capability.

Gentlecare looks at the environment from three perspectives: the physical space, social interactions, and cultural support within the environment. All three must be assessed for their impact on the person's ability to function.

Step 2 Physical Environment

The physical environment is the physical space in which the person must live. Together with social and cultural components, it forms the context within which people live their lives. The following elements of the physical environment are critical to the development of the prosthesis of care:

Many elders with dementia live in large institutions like the state hospital pictured above. Such physical environments pose significant problems for staff who attempt to develop a residence for their clients.

Ambiance

Ambiance is the atmosphere of a person's surroundings, the feeling of a place. It is a person's experience of living in a space. Ambiance is an important aspect of the environment because it often determines a person's comfort level.

For instance, entering an elegant hotel gives an entirely different feeling than entering a neighborhood coffee shop. Elderly people with dementia appear to be significantly influenced by the ambiance within a building. Sometimes the client talks about "not belonging here" or may comment, "I can't afford a meal in such a fancy restaurant."

The Dilemma of the Locked Door

One of the most difficult dilemmas faced by family and staff is whether
or not to lock residents' rooms.

Here's the issue: When people choose a nursing home, what they
want to see most is the room—the view from the window, the curtains,
the wall colors, and the size. They may wait months for the right room.
Obviously, the choice of the room is an important decision, as it will be
the person's new home. And ambiance is an important element influ-
encing that decision.

However, when staff start having problems related to the room such
as invasion of the resident's space by another person, the knee-jerk reaction is to make the intruder stop going into the room. Once staff discover that some clients can't make judgments about ownership and
use of their room, the strategy that is often put in place is to lock all
rooms.

So what happens when we lock people out of their own personal
space, space that we have assigned? We take away control and we take
away important cueing. And we often send residents into a rage because they cannot access their own space. The minute this is done, all
therapeutic value is extinguished. Those of us who are caregivers need
to imagine how we would feel if we discovered that we had been locked
out of our "home"; locked out of the familiar and comforting personal
space where we have all our personal treasures, and where we can en-
tertain family and friends. How would we feel?

First of all, staff need to understand that people with dementia lose
the way-finding skills which help them in locating their own rooms, especially when all the rooms appear to be exactly the same.

Gentlecare has always come down on the side of keeping rooms
open, maximizing access to personal possessions. We believe in solv-
ing the problem without depriving the person of the comfort of home.

Here are some Gentlecare strategies:

1. Decorate each person's room so that it looks like, feels like, and
   smells like their own home.
2. Encourage the family to provide personal memorabilia (e.g., photo-

graphs or significant objects from the past). Gentlecare refers to this personal memorabilia as "infrastructure".

3. Develop programs that engage the individual and fill their day with interesting activities, hence distracting them from intruding on others' lives and living spaces. Left to their own devices, elders will always try to keep busy. If we don't provide them with appropriate activities, they will find something else to do: sometimes they will clean the room; sometimes they will get out their suitcases and pack for home; sometimes they will take the bed apart, or take everything out of the closet and bureau drawers. They may be enticed into other people's rooms by something that catches their fancy.

4. Help elders to use their rooms and establish ownership. For example, they can assist with or supervise the cleaning and tidying of the room; arrange their own memorabilia; make the bed (an ideal opportunity for communication between staff and client); invite a friend in for tea. People with dementia cannot do things using their own initiative. They must rely on help from everyone—professional staff, support staff, family and volunteers. We recommend a variety of familiar activities that involve work and responsibility. The personal room is the most powerful therapeutic tool we have, and the last thing we should do is to lock people out of their comfort source. This is not the solution.

The responsibility for problem-solving rests with the "people" component of the prosthesis of care. Everyone we can persuade to help us must be engaged in making the room an interesting, reassuring place for the person to be. Staff cannot do this alone. We need to identify all the people who will help us make the person's day interesting, from the caregiver who helps them make the bed to the housekeeper who helps with the dusting.

Function and activity

The essence and use of the space can make a critical contribution to the enjoyment of a client's day. The most beautiful space in the world makes no difference if it is not appropriately used or if the client does not have easy access. The client, who is unable to initiate activity, must also be helped to use the space. This is where the "people" component of the prosthesis of care is so important. The care team needs to ask these questions:

- Is this space compatible with the client's capabilities?
- Is each room clearly marked/numbered or otherwise easily identified? Is the use of each room clear to the client?
- Does the ambiance within each room encourage activity by and interaction between the clients?
- Are there lots of different things to do, interesting opportunities, beautiful objects to touch, or is everything out of reach or perhaps locked up?
- Is the noise level comfortable for the client?
- Is there sufficient light to provide good figure/ground contrast so that the clients can distinguish objects without difficulty?
- Do the activities engage the clients?
- Are all of the activities age-appropriate?

Personal Control/Comfort/Security

Physical space can provide an opportunity for individuals to feel ownership or control of some place, however small, in their residential environment. Areas should be small and comfortable, and convey a sense of peace and security. The areas should be designed to promote the gathering of small groups for social interaction or to participate in meaningful activities. Care teams need to ask these questions:

- Does each client have some private place near his bed that is easily accessible?
- Is the room decorated in a manner that makes its ownership obvious to the client?
- Is the client's room available to her at all times? (If a bedroom is locked it does not exist for a client with dementia.)

I ONCE WORKED *with a client who, instead of going to his bed by the window, frequently tried to climb into bed with the elderly gentleman whose bed was near the door. No amount of prompting, reminding, painted footsteps-on-the-floor—not even the fighting that ensued on a regular basis—was enough to change his behavior. On discussing the problem with his wife, we discovered that the bed my client had slept in all his life was positioned in his room at home exactly as his room-mate's bed was in the care facility. He thought he was climbing into the right bed.*

When we reorganized the furniture in the room so that the bed was in a similar position to his own bedroom at home, the client was able to get into the right bed.

Flexibility

Dementing illness develops over a continuum, and people with dementia will have different environmental needs over time. Environmental elements must be designed so they can be changed to meet the needs of residents at many different levels of function. Care teams need to ask these questions:

- Can the environment be changed to meet the client's changing needs?
- Are choices available, such as to stay in, go out, go to one's own room, or eat in different locations?
- Are social areas designed to encourage participation?
- Can multipurpose areas be converted for different uses, in such a way that they convey their distinct function? For example, can a room serve as a chapel/dining room/work room/living room? The short answer is yes. In Gentlecare a room must announce its function to the person with dementia. We make a room, show its current use, with the use of pictures, furniture, dishes, hutches, aromas and food displays.

Step 2 Social Environment

In the client's social environment you will find family members, facility staff, other clients, volunteers, and visitors. Assessment of the client's social environment involves evaluation of the pattern of relationships between the client and all of those people in his environment.

Keep in mind that family members, if they are participants in the client's care, are more important to the client than all other personnel. No one replaces the family!

The care team needs to ask these questions:

- Does the client have a family member or a significant other (friend, relative, person of faith) to rely on?
- Does the family member or significant person visit on a regular basis?
- Is the person a participating member of the client's care team?
- Are their visits supportive or stressful to the client?
- Does the family member understand the disease process?
- Is sufficient education and support available to the family or significant person so that they can make a meaningful contribution to the work of the care team and at the same time protect their own health?
- Does the facility provide an education center with current books, videos, and pamphlets? (This is an excellent volunteer assignment.)

Availability of help

The Reisberg Reverse Order of Development theory (see Chapter 4 Figure 4-3) suggests that clients are approximately 5–7 years of age functionally at the time they require institutional care. Consequently, the provision of care must be evaluated from the perspective of the person with dementia and not from the perspective of the caregiver(s). The elderly person with dementia should be regarded as an adult who, because of disease, is functioning in a childlike manner.

The care team needs to ask these questions:

- Does the person feel supported as we might support a child in a similarly frightening situation?
- Is someone available to address this person's anxiety, fear, frustration, and loneliness?
- Does the person live with large groups of people, with no provision for privacy during the whole 24-hour period?

Availability of companionship

Most people with dementia are separated from life partners, friends, and family. It is not surprising that they often mistake other residents for their spouses or friends. Gentlecare recommends a careful assessment of the lack of or need for human companionship. This provides the basis for developing a plan to carefully match people who might bond and feel comfortable together. The care team needs to ask these questions:

- Is someone presently available to meet the needs of the person with dementia?
- Does her spouse need assistance in reaching out to her?
- Do they need a private space or opportunity to be alone together?
- Does the person have visitors?
- Is his room companion-appropriate?
- Are roommates carefully selected and monitored? Often it is appropriate for staff to be available to help negotiate sharing of space.
- Do activities and the environment bring people together naturally?
- Does the person receive mail or gifts?
- Does the person have a special buddy among the other residents?
- Is sexual activity comforting or problematic?
- Is there any stress, abuse, or anxiety associated with the sexual relationship?
- Is the family comfortable with the sexual relationship?

I REMEMBER DISCUSSING *a man's sexual behavior at a team conference. Staff members were reporting how inappropriate, aggressive, disgusting, and unacceptable this man's behavior was. The team was considering medication, transfer, restraint, etc.*

One staff member asked whether the man and his wife ever had an opportunity for intimate relations. The team decided to talk with the spouse. Once the spouse and her husband were provided with some appropriate privacy, the man presented the staff with no further sexual behavior problems.

Friends and other support people

People with dementia slowly lose their place in their family and in their community. Gentlecare-trained staff try to create a "mini-community" within the health care system. It is important to give clients a sense of belonging and a feeling of security. The care team needs to ask these questions:

- Is there a feeling of community within the facility? Are people encouraged to do things with others?
- Is there a volunteer system in place at the facility?
- Are friends encouraged to visit? Is sufficient education and support available to the these friends so that they can make a meaningful contribution as members of the care team?
- Do members of the person's spiritual community, former business, or social groups visit?
- Are staff encouraged, as they provide care, to talk with clients about their friends and associates?

Staff as support

Staff members need to understand that clients who have no visitors see their contact with staff not merely as a pleasant part of the day, but as a critical lifeline. Since there is currently no medical treatment for Alzheimer's disease, the only effective intervention is individual therapeutic assistance, and staff members provide this therapy. Job descriptions should clearly state that supportive clinical assistance to the client is paramount. The execution of other tasks should not rank ahead of "being there" for clients who need emotional care. The care team needs to ask these questions:

- Are staff chosen because of their passion, knowledge, and skills in working with people suffering from dementia?
- Are staff encouraged to take the time necessary to support the needs of the client?
- Do the policies and procedures of the facility clearly rank personal support over tasks such as charting, meetings, bed-making or cleaning?
- Are ways of supporting clients' needs discussed in team rounds and interdisciplinary meetings?
- Is a state of anxiety, frustration, anger, or loneliness in a client viewed as a medical emergency, comparable to pain or hemorrhaging? Is there recognition of the need for immediate application of stress-reducing therapy?

No one replaces the family!

Step 2: The Cultural Environment

The cultural aspect of the environment refers to the system of beliefs, ideals, customs, and values inherent in the structure of the organization, facility, or program. The cultural environment has a powerful effect on the state of well-being of people; it can be a force that permeates and gives meaning to life. It is an element that is vitally important to elderly people because it reinforces significant life experiences, and affects their social conduct. The culture of an organization, therefore, can be a powerful therapeutic tool, because over-learned skills are retained long after other abilities are lost.

Some facilities are built and operated by a particular community for members of that community. These will be totally infused with elements of their culture, to the benefit of clients and staff alike. However, facilities frequently treat clients from different social, cultural, and religious backgrounds. The challenge is to enhance the support of these various elements without alienating any individual client in the process.

> I REMEMBER *an elderly man who could scarcely walk unassisted, and who was pretty much confined to a wheelchair, which he hated. The wheelchair seemed to represent his worst fears about helplessness and dependency.*
>
> *Since there was no physical reason why this gentleman could not walk, we decided to try a strategy: we played recordings of military marches at the time that he was expected to go to the dining room. To our delight, he straightened to his full height and marched smartly off to the dining room. This strategy worked even better when we as staff joined in, and encouraged a small squad to form for the man to lead.*

Ability to be interested in others, family, and community

Despite the devastation of dementing illness, most people continue to respond at some level to family issues. In searching for therapeutic modalities to help reach people experiencing dementia, family issues can frequently be used. Sometimes interest can be extended to the community—for example, in terms of the person's former involvement in the spiritual community, a service organization, or a community project like a ball team. The assessment process needs to explore these avenues as possible sources of therapy.

Expectations regarding work

The work ethic is alive and well in elderly people with dementia. The loss of a meaningful role as a productive citizen is devastating for most of them. Work-related activities may therefore be one of the most potent therapeutic tools we can use to help them. Reminiscing about work, or confirming their successes as workers, always elicits interest and, occasionally, joy.

It is important to be clear about the use of work as therapy: Work activities organized for elderly people as therapy are separate and different from the work done by staff, even if they involve similar tools and supplies. No elderly person with dementia "doing some work" is in competition with a staff member. Employees' jobs are not at risk because work therapy is used.

Expectations on how to behave

Elderly people hold very strong views on how people should behave—both in terms of their own actions, and with respect to the behavior of others. For example, consider the issue of bathing an elderly woman. In that woman's culture, it is probably unthinkable to undress in front of another person, let alone a stranger! To bathe nude in a large room, with a number of strange people coming and going, is beyond their belief. To have one or more people (possibly including a male) assist with the bath is intolerable. Is it any wonder that bathing becomes one of the most difficult tasks to accomplish?

Clothing provides another example of potential culture shock. Elderly people grew up at a time when a distinctive dress code was prescribed for specific occasions. One never went certain places without a hat. One wore gloves on such-and-such an occasion. Women never wore pants. Ties and jackets were worn at all times except in the privacy of one's own home, or if engaged in physical labor. Nurses wore starched caps, perhaps with veils. A "lady" never appeared in public without being appropriately dressed.

The astonishment of elders over current dress codes can only be imagined! What must they think when they see us work in jeans, gym clothes, or shorts and T-shirts, and perhaps a baseball cap? Do they recognize us in our roles as nurses and therapists? Or do they see us as their children? Could this cultural disparity account for their resistance when we ask them to perform certain tasks? Do they feel uncomfortable, inappropriately dressed, or out of place when they perceive themselves to be in the wrong clothing for events such as dinner or a church service?

Activities requiring participation for acceptance

Elderly people have strong cultural conventions about:
- people doing their share;
- people paying their way in cash;
- people complying with standards, rules, regulations;
- people participating in church or community groups/activities;
- allowing others to go first;
- not taking credit for accomplishments;
- deferring to others;
- being invited to social gatherings; and
- waiting to be asked specifically to participate in any activity.

ONCE UPON A TIME *I came upon an elderly lady sitting alone in her room. Everyone else was participating in a birthday party. When I asked her why she wasn't joining in, she said, "Oh, my dear, someone is having a party but I am not one of the invited guests."*

It is not unusual for elderly people to refuse to attend a church service because they have no money to put in the collection or to refuse to eat in the dining room because they feel that they cannot pay the bill. These are deeply embedded attitudes and practices that need to be

taken into account during assessment, since they may provide an explanation for certain reactions.

Personal remedies or approaches to sickness and disability

Older people often approach the management of illness in ways very
different from the ones we take for granted. Some elderly people have
never taken medication; they may view it as poison and taking it as
substance abuse. Some believe that a regular walk, morning and/or
evening, keeps them healthy, but this is sometimes misconstrued by
caregivers as "wandering," or even "eloping." Some don't eat if they feel
sick, following the old adage, "Feed a cold, starve a fever." Many elderly
people have been raised to believe that one simply endures adversity,
never complaining, never expecting any intervention. During the assessment process or while evaluating problematic behavior, it is helpful to keep these cultural attitudes and practices in mind. They can
often give important clues about the person's reaction.

Spiritual Issues

Spirituality, whatever its cultural manifestation, has played a major role
in the lives of most elderly people. Many elders have also had a close association to the land and its creatures, and have been taught to respect
music and books as symbols of our cultural heritage. Some have strong
beliefs in luck, fate, or predestination. Assessment procedures should
explore this aspect of the client's environment.

For professional caregivers, the religious beliefs of the client should
not matter. The staff member's responsibility is to support whichever
spiritual beliefs give the client comfort.

One woman, who was extremely resistant to being bathed, relaxed
and enjoyed her bath when we sang her favorite hymns during her
bath. The focus on a spiritual practice appeared to change the context
sufficiently to reduce her anxiety. Joining in a familiar activity (hymn-
singing) created a bond between her and the staff member that allowed
her to accept help with this intimate routine.

Of course, people with dementia must be protected from overzealous religious proselytizers. Gentlecare has found that a thorough assessment, consultation with the family, and careful listening to the person's views leads to therapeutic support of the individual's spirituality.

A LAY VOLUNTEER *minister once told me of a woman in a total care hospital who was in utter despair. She was anxious, depressed, and in tears every time the volunteer saw her. When asked what the matter was, she said, "I am so lonely, no one visits. My family is gone and I am surrounded by strangers."*

The volunteer suggested that the woman had one friend who was always available to her—her God—when she was frightened, when she was alone, in the middle of the night, whenever. If she called, God would be there to comfort her. I remember visiting this woman myself, and being amazed at the reassurance she derived from her faith. It certainly surpassed the value of any activity we had thought of in interdisciplinary conferences!

LANGUAGE

Language is often a barrier when spiritual dialogue is attempted, especially when people do not share the same set of beliefs or points of reference. Words like "blessing" or "forgiveness" are laden with various meanings, depending on one's religious background. Professionals can respectfully join a person in their care in using such words, without divulging or imposing their own religious views—for instance, "I can see the meaning of this blessing for you." Speaking someone's language often provides deep comfort in ways that are most needed. —Adapted from Lustbader & Hooyrian,

Taking Care of Aging Family Members
Courtesy of Helen A. Bache

STEP 3: ASSESSING THE CLIENT'S PERFORMANCE

Evaluating the performance of the person with dementia to perform Activities of Daily Living (ADLs) and Instrumental Activities of Daily Living (IADLs) is critical because these are the fundamental skills of independent daily life. There are five ADLs: toileting, bathing, dressing, grooming, and eating. IADLs are more complex tasks that involve equipment, the use of supplies, and interaction with other people. Travel, meal preparation, cleaning, laundry, shopping, and talking on the telephone are examples of IADLs.

Most of us take the performance of both ADLs and IADLs for granted. We are not likely to consider how we do the activity until our ability is compromised in some way. At those times we may become conscious of the sequence of events involved in the activities or the use of equipment, or how we move parts of our body to accomplish a task.

When a person begins to lose cognitive function due to a dementing illness, ADLs and IADLs become demanding, exhausting routines that consume large amounts of time and energy and result in an immediate loss of control and a dent in one's dignity. The simple task of taking off one's socks becomes impossible due to apraxia. The everyday task of phoning a friend becomes a formidable job when one is unable to remember a telephone number or how to dial. People can't make their bodies carry out the purposeful movements that their minds know are necessary. The most private activity, going to the bathroom, becomes a nightmare. One must try to find the correct spot, attempt to unfasten and remove clothing, figure out where to find toilet paper, and remember to cleanse oneself.

When assessing ADL skills, we not only evaluate a person's ability to do the activity, but also whether, in the context of daily life, the person actually performs the activity. (For instance, a person may be able to successfully operate a stove but when alone may be afraid to use it.)

The level of performance of all ADLs can be significantly influenced by the condition of the environment in which they are being practiced. For example:

Step 3

The Client's Performance
ADL (self-care)
IADL (ability to manage within environment— leisure skills)

"Activities" are tasks that engage a person's time and energy.

• If the entrance to the bathroom is obscured, the person with dementia cannot carry out the ADL of toileting.
• If a shy person is asked to eat in a large, crowded dining room, he may refuse to go in.
• If a person normally eats with chopsticks but is offered only a fork, she may refuse to eat.

Are the activities we design meaningful for the people performing them? This is the litmus test for all activity programs in dementia care.

Leisure activities are components of life that are free from responsibility, work, and self-care. They frequently take place within the context of social occasions, recreational events, or time spent with family and friends. On occasion, activities can be viewed as work, undertaken by a group for the fun of it (for example, fruit picking, making bread or jam, garden maintenance, house-cleaning, or quilting).

Leisure activities for people with dementia should be age-appropriate and stress-free. Leisure activities should not require people to do things they can no longer do, nor require them to interact with large groups of people. Whenever possible, leisure activities should involve people who offer support.

The ADL Assessment Process

Dementing illness causes the afflicted person to depend on the goodwill and kindness of others for help with very personal tasks. And therein lies the challenge for both the afflicted person and the caregiver. The most critical component in dementia care is the "offer" of the right amount of assistance. Too little assistance can leave the afflicted person floundering and stressed, and too much assistance can be diminishing and frustrating. Like the bear family's porridge, assistance has to be "just right!"

The big question is how much help to provide, in what areas, at what times, and in what form that will give the dementia client the necessary "leg up" to perform daily living activities without feeling overburdened by the very help being offered.

In Gentlecare, an appropriate ADL prosthesis is constructed on the basis of the assessment of the person's dysfunction and their remaining capabilities. Cognitively impaired people are often assumed to be unable to do anything, when in fact they may be unable to initiate a task but be quite able to carry it out once started. They should be regarded as people who have significant functional dependency and require specific help with aspects of their personal care.

Questions to be asked in identifying ADL problems:

Determine the nature of the problem

- Is it due to memory loss?
- Is it a problem with interpretive skills?
- Is it due to visual or perceptual dysfunction?
- Is it a question of finding the appropriate place to perform the activity?
- Is it a sequencing issue?
- Is it a problem of rush, noise, confusion, stress, or some other iatrogenic factor?

Performance is the key word in functional assessment. What can the person do? What does the person do?

Determine the frequency of the difficulty

- Does it occur rarely? Why?
- Does it occur occasionally? In what circumstances?
- Does it occur frequently? What time of day? Who is involved?

Determine how much help is required

- Does a little help make it possible for the person to do the task?
- Is some help required at the beginning of the activity?
- Does the person need considerable assistance to carry out the task successfully?

Determine which prompts or help work

- Prompts can be verbal: "The bathroom is this way, Mrs. Smith."
- Prompts can be mimed. Pretend to wash your hands. The afflicted person may be able to mimic your action.
- Prompts can be physical. Walk with the person to the toilet. Put the person's arm into the correct armhole of the sweater or jacket.
- Prompts can be a combination of other prompts. The object is to recognize the specific deficits the person is experiencing and support the remaining skill of each individual. No one standard method of care will meet the needs of all people. Assistance must be personalized.

In Gentlecare we refer to prompts that work for the afflicted person as "Gentlecare tips." These "tips" are posted above his bed, in the bathroom, and wherever ADLs might take place. ADL tasks must be sequenced so the parts of the activity the person can do are separated from the parts they can't do, or can accomplish only with a prompt or assistance. For example, if a person stands in front of a sink with a toothbrush and toothpaste at hand, but does not brush his teeth, you might assume that the person can't brush his teeth. If you assume that he can't brush and do it for him, any skill he has for part or all of the task, will soon be lost, and he will be evermore dependent on others for clean teeth. Maybe he can brush, and needs only a "start prompt" to get him going. If this is the case, the person retains both skills and dignity, and the helper saves time by not having to carry out the task. If the afflicted person responds positively to the "start prompt" but is unable to complete all components of the task in spite of getting additional prompts, the helper offers a prosthesis of help by doing just those bits of the task that the person finds difficult or impossible to do. Once again, both parties win.

Assistance must be personalized. Gentlecare tips help caregivers to assist with activities of daily living.

Here are some ideas for providing effective help with basic self-care activities to cognitively impaired people:

Prepare for the task
- Have appropriate information.
- Prepare supplies and equipment and space.
- Have a contingency plan.
- Organize other help if needed.
- Allow appropriate time.

Prepare the person
- Establish visual contact.
- Attract attention by touch.
- Establish your role as a caregiver.
- Explain the task to be accomplished.
- Get agreement to accept your help.

Assist the person through the task
- Watch for signs of stress and be ready with stress-reducing strate-

gies such as information, laughter, rest, a hot beverage, or finger foods
- Celebrate the accomplishment with praise and encouragement.

I WAS ONCE ASKED to work with a woman who, though very compliant in every way, was very difficult to assist with dressing in the morning. When I asked if anyone could help her successfully, one care aide said, "Yes. When I put her stockings and shoes on before she gets out of bed, I have no problem. If I put her bare feet on the floor, she resists all my help from then on." This procedure may have reflected a life-long habit; in any event, once this ADL prosthesis was identified and posted as a Gentlecare tip, the staff experienced no further difficulties in helping the woman with ADL.

STEP 4: DESIGNING A PROSTHESIS OF CARE

No assessment measure, no matter how good, has any value at all unless the results are communicated to the staff and the family caregivers who are actually delivering care. If assessment data is relegated to a medical chart, and not used directly in care planning and delivery, the individual staff or family member will approach the care process in the way felt to be most appropriate. Most often, the result of this approach is over-helping, which leads to helplessness and learned dependency. Alternatively, the caregivers may not offer enough care. This approach forces the person with dementia to attempt tasks that can no longer be performed, and may trigger catastrophic behavior.

Information must be communicated to staff on all shifts and to any staff member, volunteer, or family member who might interact with the elderly person with dementing illness. Remember that dementia clients need support 24 hours a day. Care plans that work only during the day and are disregarded at other times have no place in dementia care. Consequently, care cannot be planned or delivered effectively on an eight-hour shift basis. Information should not be withheld by some staff members and selectively "leaked" at care conferences or during

Step 4

GENTLECARE Prosthetic Life Care Plan
People
Programs
Physical Space

times of crisis. Assessment data must inform the way dementia care is delivered in every aspect of the person's life; this is critical to construction of an appropriate prosthesis of care. The importance of "seamless" or "borderless" care across all shifts cannot be overemphasized. The practice of having three different shifts singing from three different songbooks is devastating for people with dementing illness. It also promotes accelerated tension, competition, and scapegoating among staff. It results in the waste of creative energy and general loss of focus in delivery of care. The Gentlecare strategy recommends rotating staff members through all shifts for orientation purposes, to improve awareness of care issues, respect for individuals, and understanding of all aspects of dementia care. The need for respect and understanding of the client is illustrated by the following scenario:

> A STAFF MEMBER *reports that a person is exhibiting "violent" behavior", and medication is often prescribed on the basis of such a report. When the staff member is asked to explain the context of the person's behavior, the response is often a comment like, "When I approached Mr. B. he just lashed out at me!" At this point a team member will usually explain that this behavior probably occurred because Mr. B. has lost his peripheral vision, which meant that he could not see anyone approaching from the side. He was probably frightened or felt threatened by the sudden appearance of a person in front of him, which produced a predictable defensive response.*

Unfortunately, the correct information frequently comes too late. Functional assessment data, appropriately communicated to all staff, family, and volunteers, can do much to prevent disturbing events and avoid stress and fear for both the client and the staff. It is also important to remember that in the development of care plans, the assessment data used must be relatively current, since many diseases of dementia are progressive, and a person's condition can change from day to day. The goal of facilities that practice Gentlecare is to have a thorough assessment of every person as soon as possible and then to carry out reassessment on a regular basis.

A person's ADL status is dynamic. As staff members become more skilled in assessment procedures, evaluation of ADL status can occur more frequently and efficiently. As staff members become more proficient at exchanging information, the care process becomes more creative and interesting.

Gentlecare magic begins to happen!

A NEW APPROACH TO PROGRAMS

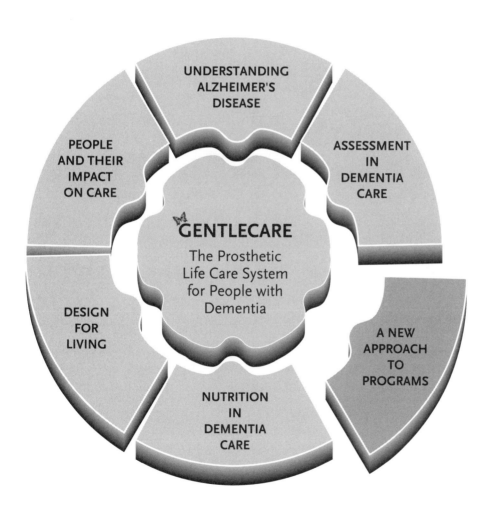

UNDERSTANDING
ALZHEIMER'S
DISEASE

ASSESSMENT
IN
DEMENTIA
CARE

PEOPLE
AND THEIR
IMPACT
ON CARE

GENTLECARE
The Prosthetic
Life Care System
for People with
Dementia

DESIGN
FOR
LIVING

A NEW
APPROACH
TO
PROGRAMS

NUTRITION
IN
DEMENTIA
CARE

8

Synergic Programs: Building the Prosthesis

You cannot create memory,
but you can create an experience
that is as powerful as memory.

Programming may be the most misunderstood aspect of dementia care. It is certainly the most neglected. Traditionally the program in gerontological care has referred to the various activities organized by recreation or activities personnel. Incredible offerings of every imaginable leisure and recreational activity are organized to give older people pleasure, exercise, educational, and social opportunities.

However, when people are not engaged in leisure activities there is no emphasis on program. Meal times are not considered part of the program; preparation for the day is not part of the program; interactions with care staff are not part of the program; scheduling isn't part of the program, nor is medical care, bath time, or any other activity of daily life. Critical aspects of the person's life care are not considered to be "program." Gentlecare considers any activity the person engages in, from wake-up to sleep, to be part of their program.

The reactions of different people to activity programs can vary tremendously. I recall one elderly man suffering from dementia who, with tears in his eyes, told me, "I feel like a trained monkey." On the other hand, a cognitively alert older man said to me, "If I had known old age would be so much fun I'd have gotten old sooner."

What accounts for these dramatically different reactions to activity programming? I believe the answer lies in an understanding of the pathology surrounding the diseases that afflict older people.

In health care services designed for elderly people, there is a tendency to regard all the people as belonging to a homogeneous group, and gerontological health care services are essentially group focused. Although at the medical level there is acknowledgment of the difference between, for example, someone who has had a heart attack and someone with Alzheimer's disease, at the operational level people with these two medical problems are provided virtually identical care. People dealing with these two distinctly different health care problems may share a room, eat meals in the same dining area, be cared for by the same staff with no specialized training in the effects of either condition, be subjected to the same routines and schedules, and be expected to engage in the same activity programs.

No other area of health care services operates this way! The care offered a teenager with cancer varies dramatically from the services provided to a youth with schizophrenia. An adult having a baby is cared for differently than an adult of the same age experiencing breast cancer. Even within physical health care categories, different types of services are offered by differently qualified staff members.

However, when we offer health care services to elderly people, the focus is on managing large groups of people as equally and routinely as possible. The individual whose needs differ from the norm is frequently considered problematic. And more likely than not, that person is experiencing a disease that inflicts cognitive impairment on its victim.

Different People, Different Needs

Cognitively alert older people who need assistance with accommodation, meals, and management of their physical illnesses are often able to explore new undertakings, learn new skills, make new friends, even travel, as they may never have before in their lives. Many become very skilled in the production of crafts, entering contests and preparing articles for sale at bazaars and in gift shops. It is not unusual for staff and clients in care facilities to spend months preparing for an elaborate fund-raising event. Often the walls in health care facilities are decorated with beautiful crafts, and some older people can make pin money by selling their creations.

Conversely, people experiencing dementing illness need help just to stay alive, to manage the most basic self-care functions, and to cope with the challenges of interacting with others in a strange and frightening environment. People with dementing illness don't fit in. They can't do things. They mess up our carefully crafted schedules and routines. They are untidy. They break things or take them apart, and they eat the plants! They resist being told what to do, and when to do it. They don't act like old people are expected to.

An elderly gentleman who has attained the chronological age of seventy-eight may in fact be able to operate only at the developmental age of seven. Does this affect his ability to participate in general daily routines and programs? You bet it does! The different needs of people in care must inform the type of programs we build to help them through the rest of their lives.

Unfortunately, as the epidemic of progressive dementing illness has swept through long-term health care services, very little change has occurred in programming to accommodate differences in functioning. At best, people suffering from dementia have been accommodated on the periphery of programs; at worst, they are made to take part in programs designed for cognitively alert elders, and are expected to perform at levels well beyond their remaining capabilities. Often they are banished, or medicated, due to "unacceptable" behavior. But most often there is no place for them at all in these intensive activities, and they

Monthly activity calendar.

are condemned to sit—doing nothing—for extended periods of time, or to walk aimlessly in empty corridors.

Survey data and experience indicates that 90 percent of all activities/recreational resources are utilized by a minority of the residents (between 10 to 30 percent) in any care facility. These people are cognitively alert, physically disabled elders who are assertive, articulate, and often hold positions of power on resident councils. They have developed a high skill level in some craft or are accustomed to social activities such as card games, bus trips, bingos, happy hours, etc. They are without doubt favorites of the staff, as they are interesting, communicative, and productive people. They also have obvious physical illnesses that can be observed.

On the other hand, 60 to 70 percent of the population in any long-term care facility is made up of people who are no longer capable of productive complex work. They are difficult to communicate with, cannot advocate for themselves, are distractible, messy, disruptive, and capable of becoming very upset, even abusive, when involved in group activities. And all this is particularly exasperating because they don't look sick!

There are many factors that contribute to this unequal situation:

- Health care services for the elderly are group focused. Staffing levels are not set to accommodate individualized interventions.
- Staff employed for recreational/leisure activities are often hired because they excel at some sport or craft. Few have specific current training about dementing illness or are aware of the deficits it causes in elderly people. Consequently, activity programs tend to either challenge elders inappropriately or infantilize them.
- Boards of directors, administrators, families, and members of the public enjoy the decorations, elaborate activity schedules, annual bazaars, and seasonal activities that are part of the recreational program at most care facilities. They like to see residents doing "normal" things, like dances and bingos. Consequently, there is a great deal of external pressure on activities staff to continue to carry out the same type of programs they have organized for years.
- Working with cognitively alert elders is thought to be easier than

Frequently, when we offer health care services to elderly people, the focus is on managing large groups of people as equally and routinely as possible.

trying to involve people afflicted with dementia. There is a bias toward providing programs for high-level functioning people at the
expense of those who have more difficulty performing effectively.

- There is a perception that people experiencing dementia can't do
anything—so why bother? This perception has led to a generalized
practice of tokenism: some activities have been identified as good
for people with Alzheimer's disease. These include exercise circles,
walking, singing, simple crafts, assisting staff to bake, reality-orien-
tation groups, ball toss, and coloring. In truth, many of these activities are not only inappropriate for people with deficits caused by
dementing illnesses, they may indeed be damaging.

- Cognitively alert people who are cared for inappropriately say so!
They appear in the administrator's office; they petition the resident
council; and they complain to staff in no uncertain terms. On the
other hand, cognitively impaired elders, deprived of language and
reasoning skills, endure, withdraw, or "act out."

- The nihilistic perception that people experiencing dementia can't
do anything leads to the practice of abandoning them to hours of inactivity.

- It is common practice to observe an activity schedule for people
with dementia that might include an exercise circle at 10:30–
10:45 A.M., a music group from 2:30–3:00 P.M., and possibly early
evening volunteer entertainment. With that kind of schedule, a person with dementia may have only an hour or two of activity each 24-
hour day.

- Higher-functioning elders with dementia may be included in special event meals, large birthday parties, barbecues, or group outings. They are allowed to participate in such activities as long as
they do not cause problems by exhibiting "socially unacceptable"
behavior. But such activities are almost always outside the range of
things that people with dementia are able to manage.

- Social programs are often offered in special care units for dementia;
however, staff who conduct these programs are frequently located
in other areas of the health care facility and must travel to the unit to
provide services. They usually have a variety of other responsibili-

The different needs of people in gerontology care must inform the type of programs we build to help them through the rest of their lives.

ties, and are rarely able to attend interdisciplinary team conferences or staff meetings. They often work with only minimal clinical information about the people they are involving in programs, and much of the operational information is anecdotal and subjective. Their work schedules frequently prevent them from participating in educational programs that might increase their knowledge about the effects of dementia. This same problem exists with staff who work in community-based programs.

This may sound like a recipe for disaster—and it is! The practices just described have major consequences:

- People with dementing illness are seriously stressed both by inappropriate challenges, on the one hand, and by lack of meaningful activity on the other. This leads to excessive dysfunction, catastrophic behavior, and escalating costs of care.
- Cognitively alert older people are terribly distressed at having to share activities with people who are dysfunctional.
- Care staff are angry and distressed at the lack of programming for residents with dementia, and at the lack of assistance offered them in "coping" with this large group of people.
- After involvement in integrated events, residents with dementia are often returned to their living quarters in a very distressed state. Frequently, staff members coming on shift are expected to manage people stressed by events that occurred during an earlier shift. For example, people with dementing illness are often involved in a bingo game or a dance that takes place outside the specially prepared dementia-care environment. On their return, they are unable to settle down and sleep, and may wander around during the night. Only too often they are medicated to reduce their anxiety and wandering. As a result, these people may be unable to participate in the following day's activity.
- Staff who are "parachuted" into a special care unit to provide programs often suffer major morale and acceptance problems. They are often not considered unit staff, nor are they seen as part of the treatment team. Other staff sometimes feel that "they get to do the

nice kinds of care," while the tough and "dirty" care is left to the regular staff. Often there is a marked lack of collegial cooperation and support: activity staff members frequently report that their programs are sabotaged by other staff who throw out, lock up, or ban supplies and equipment. The effect of these territorial and professional wars is simply devastating for elderly people who are cognitively impaired. They suffer directly from inappropriate or diminished care—but in truth, everyone suffers. Creativity is lost and the joy of working with this special population vanishes.

It must be emphasized that the problems outlined above are not people problems—they are system problems.

Concepts of Gentlecare Programs

The Gentlecare system has been designed from an entirely different perspective, based on a very different paradigm of care:

- On average, 60 to 70 percent of the people in long-term care facilities suffer from dementing illness. Only 30 to 40 percent of the population in such facilities suffer exclusively from a physical illness or a psychiatric disease. Program resources and their deployment need to reflect this reality.
- Dementia causes specific deficits in functioning, and therefore people with dementia require the use of specialized strategies and approaches that differ from those used for people with other clinical conditions.
- People experiencing dementia deserve to be involved in interesting, meaningful, comfortable, age-appropriate activity throughout their waking hours.
- A Gentlecare program consists of all activities that take place over the 24-hour day. This includes Activities of Daily Living (ADL) and Instrumental Activities of Daily Living (IADL) as well as social and leisure activities.
- All staff, family caregivers, and volunteers have a share of the responsibility for developing and implementing the program. Every-

one who comes in contact with the person with dementia is considered a potential agent for therapy or activity.

- People experiencing dementia and cognitively intact elders should not be grouped together for programs (for the most part).

- Specialized activity/recreational staff have responsibility for developing and supplying the structure (or modalities) from which the entire 24-hour program can evolve. They facilitate programs.

- Environments that stimulate activity must be specially designed and adapted for people with dementia, and be accessible to them at all times.

- The program should be person-driven, not system-driven; programs should flow from the initiatives and rhythms of people instead of being based on routines, schedules, or staffing patterns.

- Activities designed for individuals or tiny group activities involving at most two or three people are most beneficial.

- Large group events are not appropriate for people with dementia, and may be damaging.

- Activities should make use of existing levels of functioning, maximizing the person's strengths and interests. They should be failure-free.

In short, to structure a Gentlecare program for people with dementing illness, first we review the assessment information and search for the remnants of the individual behind the disease. We try to identify the power source of that person, and then we build a program based on that source of personal power.

For example, consider the portrait of two elderly women in the following scenarios. In the first case, the woman is at home and well; and in the second, she has Alzheimer's disease and lives in a conventional health care facility.

For the first scenario, imagine an elderly woman you know very well, such as your mother or grandmother, perhaps even yourself. Think about her characteristics, interests, and skills. Think about the accomplishments of her life. What does she think about? What responsibilities does she have? How does she spend her days and nights?

A healthy elderly woman.

CHAPTER
EIGHT

Elders need to be surrounded by their personal memorabilia.

Nothing gives comfort like your very own bed.

What are her first thoughts as she awakens? Perhaps she looks around her as she goes through her morning routine and thinks:

"I love that picture!"

"They sure are great kids."

"I better get moving, today is garbage pick-up."

"Sounds like the dog wants out."

"I think I'll wash those curtains today."

"Better get the kettle on."

"I had such a nice sleep but now I must get moving, washed and dressed."

"It's quite cool so I probably will need a sweater if I'm out in the garden."

"This dress has almost had it, but it's so comfy and I can change before lunch."

"Oh! That tea tastes good."

"Think I'll call Mary before I get too busy."

"Oh! There's the phone. Hi! Mary, I was just about to call you."

"I'd better straighten the bedroom before I get too involved."

"I need to think about something for lunch."

"Susie's dropping in. Maybe we could have some fresh tomato soup."

"Oh, the mail's come! I wonder what's in this parcel. Who could be sending me something?"

"Oh, it's from John! He's the best son anyone ever had. It's a picture of the family. Now where can I hang it? Over there by the window would be nice."

Now imagine this same elderly woman afflicted with Alzheimer's disease sharing a room with another woman in a care facility. What are her feelings when she first awakens? What is she thinking about? What might she want to do?

"Where am I?"

"Who are these other people?"

"Where is Bill?"

"What is it you want me to do?"

"Why are you in the bathroom with me?"

"Please leave me alone."

"I must hurry and get breakfast started."

"What do you mean I don't have to do anything?"

"Bill will be looking for his porridge."

"Bill's dead? That can't be true."

"Let me out of here!"

"This is my house and I've got to get it tidied up and breakfast on."

"Who are you?"

"Where am I?"

"Why is that other woman looking in my closet?"

"No, I don't want help dressing."

"Where's my purse?"

"I have to go home, the dog needs out."

"I have work to do today."

"Leave me alone!"

"Why are you both making me get dressed?"

An elderly woman with Alzheimer's disease.

As you can see, both women have similar impulses on awakening: they think of home, family, favorite possessions. There is a sense of pride of ownership about the space they are in, and a natural instinct to begin working on behalf of others. They share a sense of ritual, pleasure in a morning routine that is pleasing and comforting. The perception of home is pervasive. The woman who is well sees her day unfolding before her and looks forward to work, responsibility, and sharing her life with others. But the woman who has dementia feels she is in an alien space peopled by strangers, and no longer in control of her home,

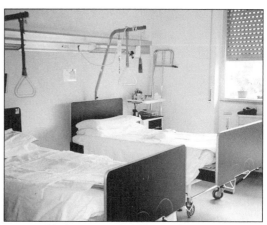

A typical bedroom in a health care facility.

her possessions, or her personal care. At the same time, she feels that her home, family, and work are in some other place, waiting for her.

These alternate perceptions are at the core of creating the Gentlecare program. If we surround people with dementia with activities or happenings that bear no relationship whatsoever to the place where they are *in their feelings,* then it is very unlikely that they will comply with our requests. And much more alarming is the possibility that they will become sicker and more dysfunctional than the disease process itself makes them (iatrogenic illness).

If the objective is to go into a room and waken, groom, and dress the person for breakfast as quickly as possible, then this can be achieved by one or two staff members focused on the task, and working against the clock. Inevitably, though, there will be side effects for the person with dementia: fear, resistance, belligerence, and ultimately, helplessness.

If, on the other hand, the objective is to make the person comfortable in spite of the disease, then it is necessary to change the focus to one of orientation, support, and empowerment. Prosthetic programming is achieved through:
- creation of a home-like environment;
- effective communication;
- reasonable pacing of activity geared to the individual's rhythm; and
- involvement of the person in the upcoming day's activities.

In a Gentlecare program, people awaken naturally and staff provides information about the day, a nutritional boost, a context for the person to look forward to, and personal affirmation. This intervention is performed slowly and gently as the person awakens.

"Good morning, Mrs. Smith. My name is Mary. I'm here to help you if you need me. It's a lovely day, and you have many things to look forward to. Here's some juice to help you wake up. At lunch time today, I think your daughter is coming to visit you. That's her picture, isn't it? What a lovely family! How proud you must be!

"I think I smell coffee! Would you like to get freshened up and dressed before you have breakfast? You know, I really enjoy our time together in the morning. You remind me of my mother."

IN THE EARLY MORNING HOURS, *Mrs. Flett experiences night-mares that are uniquely invasive, reaching all the way to her heart's core, and their subject, which she can never recollect afterward, is violent. "It's just the drugs," her doctors tell her, "a common complaint."*

In her much milder daytime dreams she drifts through scenes shabby like old backyards, dusty, with strewn trash in the flowerbeds and under piles of dead shrubbery, past streets where white-faced men and women are watering lawns choked with plantain, dandelions and creeping Charlie, lawns that because of ignorance and insufficient money are doomed never to flourish.

In the pleat of consciousness that falls between sleeping and waking she is capable of marching straight into the machinery of invention. Sketching vivid scenery. Laying out conversations, arguments. Certain phrases, remembered and invented, rattle in her afflicted head, taunting her with their rhythms and abraded meanings.

—Carol Shields,
The Stone Diaries

Perceptions that Shape Programs

The way we approach programming for people with dementia really depends on how we perceive the task, and which paradigms inform our behavior and attitudes. Depending on which map or model we use when we work with people with dementia, life becomes either very difficult for them and for caregivers or relatively comfortable.

If the map we use has as its major direction, its major roadway, the processing of a large number of people through various activities so that cleaning can be done quickly and effectively, and the organization can be tidy and orderly, then our approach to programming will be focused on organization, speed, and cleanliness. Following such a map, we would divide the workload between a night and a day shift staff. Night shift staff would wake, groom, and dress people starting as early as 4:30 A.M. in order to reduce the amount of work for the day shift. This is a system-oriented paradigm.

CHAPTER
EIGHT

Perception can be challenged by this visual puzzle:

Do you see a woman?
How old is she?
What does she look like?
What is she wearing?
What are her roles in life?

Did you see a young woman?

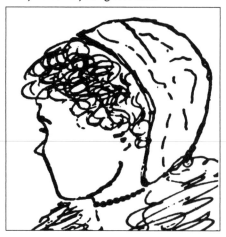

Or was she elderly?

When you look at the drawing of the woman in Figure 8.1, were you "right"? In the case of perceptions, there is no right or wrong. Each individual perceives the world in his or her own unique way. It is only in the organization of perceptions with the goal of taking action that we must consider the opinions and needs of others.

FIGURE 8-1

PARADIGM

The word paradigm comes from the Greek. It was originally a scientific term, but is more commonly used today to mean a model,
theory, perception, assumption, or frame of reference. In the
more general sense, it's the way we "see" the world, in terms of
perceiving, understanding, and interpreting it.

—Stephen R. Covey,
7 Habits of Highly Effective People

However, if the objective of our efforts is to provide the best care
possible for elderly people who have lost their life bearings due to illness, then our behavior and attitudes must be focused on their reality,
needs, and activities that comfort and support them. This is a person-
oriented paradigm.

There are some who will say, "Oh, all that's fine and dandy, but how
are we going to get the work done?" There will be those who say, "We'll
need a lot more staff to do things that way," and there will be many who
say, "It can't be done." But the truth is, we can develop and implement
a different kind of programming for people with dementia, without increasing care costs.

Each of us has many maps in our head. Some are maps of the way
things are. Some are maps of the way we would like things to be. The
challenge Gentlecare presents is this: to examine our assumptions
about the way things are, and trust ourselves enough to experiment
with change. Here is a wonderful story about assumptions:

*Is my red your red or
is your red my blue?*

TWO BATTLESHIPS ASSIGNED *to the training squadron had been at
sea on maneuvers in heavy weather for several days. I was serving on
the lead battleship and was on watch on the bridge as night fell. The
visibility was poor with patchy fog, so the captain remained on the
bridge keeping an eye on all activities.*

*Shortly after dark, the lookout on the wing of the bridge reported,
"Light, bearing on the starboard bow."*

"Is it steady or moving astern?" the captain called out.

*Lookout replied, "Steady, captain," which meant we were on a
dangerous collision course with that ship.*

157 CHAPTER
EIGHT

The captain then called to the signalman, "Signal that ship: 'We are on a collision course, advise you change course 20 degrees.'"

Back came a signal, "Advisable for you to change course 20 degrees."

The captain said, "Send: 'I'm a captain, change course 20 degrees.'"

"I'm a seaman second-class," came the reply. "You had better change course 20 degrees."

By that time the captain was furious. He spat out, "Send: 'I'm a battleship. Change course 20 degrees.'"

Back came the flashing light, "I'm a lighthouse."

We changed course.

The Impact of Assumptions on Care Programs

We all do not have to have the same reality but we can respect another's. It can be interesting to enter the world of someone we have judged to be irrational and see what there is to learn.

—DEBORAH DUDA,
COMING HOME

Many assumptions inform the way we practice health care. Some urge us to "medicalize" people with dementia: that is, to deal with "inappropriate" behaviors by giving them drugs. Some say that because of cognitive dysfunction, victims of dementia can't do anything—or perhaps it doesn't matter if they do nothing.

Such assumptions have enormous potential to affect the lives of people struggling with these horrendous diseases. If people assume that disoriented people are children—rather than childlike adults—they will offer them children's coloring books or building blocks as activities, labeled as sensory stimulation. Such activity is referred to as "sensory stim."

They will feed people with dementia in adult high chairs or at feeding tables and use bibs. They will engage in a variety of infantilizing activities, including the use of language that diminishes elderly people.

They will do these things not because they are bad, wrong, or cruel, but rather because of their assumptions about cognitively diminished people: they are children, rather than elders whose abilities are reduced but whose feelings remain intact.

And if they make that assumption, and they are the kind of people who believe that exercise is good for both body and soul, they might have people suffering from dementia play circle games, ball toss, or group exercise. In Gentlecare we do not offer this type of activity for several reasons:

- Ball toss and/or circle games are not age-appropriate activities. Elders do not generally engage in such activity in our society, especially in their living rooms!
- Catching and throwing activities require hand/eye coordination and perceptual ability beyond the scope of people experiencing Alzheimer's disease. Such activity challenges them to perform in ways that are stressful and frightening.
- Circle exercises and games require new learning, the ability to follow directions, and mirroring—skills diminished by dementia.

In Gentlecare, effective physical exercise is achieved through indoor or outdoor walks, dancing, and working—all activities that maximize existing function, use old familiar skills, and reduce stress.

A WOMAN SHARED *a funny story about her father who has dementia. The old gentleman had been encouraged to join in a ball-toss game. He had fumbled the ball the first few times it was thrown to him, and watched in exasperation as it rolled away, eluding his grasp. Finally when he did get a good hold on it, he said, "Oh sh--!" and threw it with all his might across the room.*

Of course, I've become notorious for my views on toss-and-catch activity for people experiencing the effects of dementing illness. This type of activity becomes acceptable to me only if the person is in the early stages of dementia, and is tossing a ball back and forth with a small child!

Some people perceive older people as having old-fashioned hand skills and the desire to do things properly, achieving an end product such as a craft. Based on those perceptions, they might offer people with dementia a craft activity—even though a staff member or volunteer would have to do most of the work, and the activity might have little or no meaning for the elderly person.

In Gentlecare, an activity or program is not something nice, extra, or something to keep people busy. An activity is the essence of the lives of cognitively impaired people. Activity is their life—as it is ours! Therefore, when we design activities for people with dementia, we ask the following questions:

- Who are these people?
- What are we doing to them? For them?
- Does what we are doing make sense to them?
- Does it contribute to a feeling of well-being?
- What impact does the program have on the person?
- Have we designed the best life activities possible, given the circumstances?

In the current health care paradigm, programs for people with dementia are designed to fit needs of busy professionals. Frequently we bring a sense of urgency and task-focus that shapes the lives of people in care, which actually reflects not the reality of their lives, but the pace and pressure of staff. Why, for instance, do elderly people have to get up so early in the morning when they have no responsibilities? Why do they have to eat in large crowds, and finish their meal within 15 minutes when they have nothing urgent to do?

Wake-up
All ADL
Breakfast
Work
Lunch
Work
Dinner
Work
Rest
Recreation
Sleep

FIGURE 8-2

EXAMPLE OF NORMAL LIFE ACTIVITY SCHEDULES

Let us imagine a typical work day for a health care worker on a day shift. Activities of daily living are grouped into a rush at the beginning of the day in order to prepare for work. After a brief break at noon, work resumes. After the dinner hour, either some leisure activity or more work takes place before sleep. The day is governed by four major blocks of time: work, work, recreation/work, and sleep. Grouped around these major foci are our activities of daily living.

EXAMPLE OF A HOLIDAY SCHEDULE

Let us contrast a typical working day with a holiday or day off. Wake-up time is usually much later. We have a cup of coffee, rest, and reflect on the day. Maybe we will do minimal grooming. If we dress at all, it is casually and comfortably. After another rest, we may have a late breakfast, visit with friends, or engage in some sport or exercise. This is followed by a late lunch and more rest and relaxation. Sometime in the late afternoon, we may feel a spurt of energy and bathe, get dressed, tidy up, and prepare and eat dinner. After dinner, we engage in social activities, rest, and recreation until it is time for sleep. Note that our daily self-care activities are interspersed throughout the day with rest and leisure time activities. The shape of our leisure day is dramatically different from our work day.

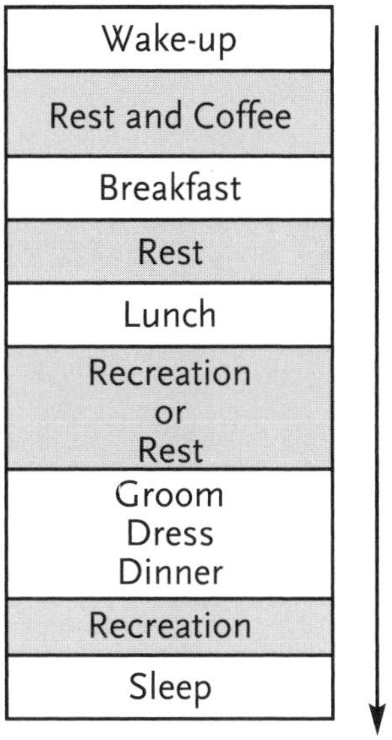

EXAMPLE OF A TYPICAL DAY OF SOMEONE WITH DEMENTIA LIVING IN A FACILITY

Let us now examine a typical day of an elderly person with dementia living in a health care facility. Morning wake-up and activities of daily living occur very early, between 4:30 and 7:00 A.M. The person is helped to get ready for breakfast at 8:00 A.M. and then sits in a dayroom, frequently engaging in null behavior until lunch time. After lunch, some ADLs may occur followed by another period of null behavior. After dinner the person is prepared for sleep. As we can see, the person's day is informed by three major blocks of time: null behavior, null behavior, and sleep. Activities of daily living are clustered in intensive periods around meal time and bracketed by long periods of inactivity.

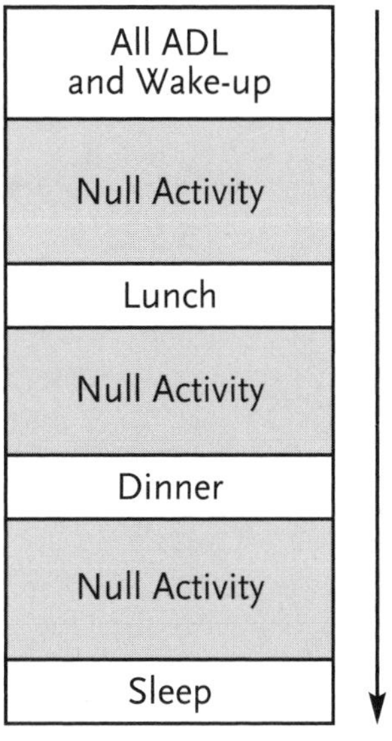

FIGURE 8-3

Null behavior is characterized by a total lack of activity or stimulation.

FIGURE 8-4

This configuration of activities closely resembles the design of a work day for health care workers, with activities of daily living clustered around large blocks of time. The person with dementia has large blocks of time arranged for them that correspond to health care workers' schedules, but because of disease and circumstances this time is usually spent in meaningless inactivity.

THE GENTLECARE DAILY SCHEDULE

The Gentlecare day has been designed to resemble a holiday or day off in the lives of healthy people. The person with dementia is cared for when they wake up naturally. Grooming and breakfast follow in a leisurely fashion. Dressing may be deferred until after breakfast and a rest, if the combination of ADLs is too exhausting for the person with dementia.

After a morning rest, Gentlecare activity in the form of walks, talks, and simulated work may take place. The person rests and relaxes before and after lunch. Afternoon Gentlecare activities such as music, family, recreation, walking, or reminiscing take place. The person rests before and after dinner, and then engages in some social activity such as music, dance, visits with family, etc. Preparation for sleep includes orientation, reminiscing, massage, bathing, family tapes, prayers, and music. Natural sleep is encouraged. The pace of the person's day is predicated on his or her ability to perform activities, not on the system's organizational requirements.

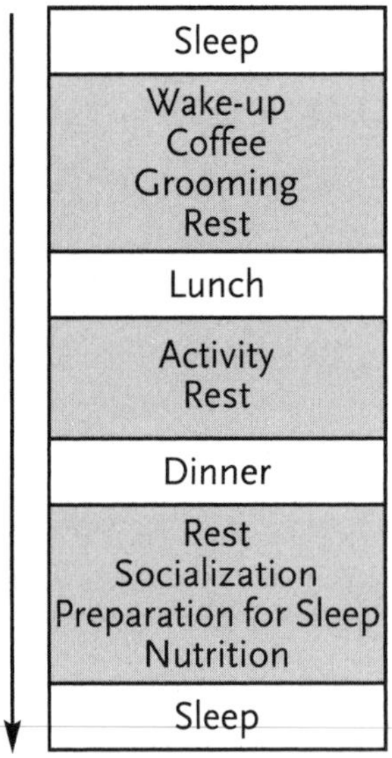

Sleep
Wake-up Coffee Grooming Rest
Lunch
Activity Rest
Dinner
Rest Socialization Preparation for Sleep Nutrition
Sleep

FIGURE 8-5

A flexible schedule such as is outlined above produces some significant outcomes:

- Cognitively impaired elders are less confused, belligerent, and frightened.
- As a result, they are able to perform more of their personal care themselves rather than requiring assistance.
- The strain on staff are dramatically reduced and fewer staff are required to support the affected person.
- The normalized schedule of activity makes it easier for families and volunteers to be part of the person's life.

This photograph illustrates the "empty hand syndrome" of elders with nothing to do.

A Day in the Life

of a Person

with Dementia

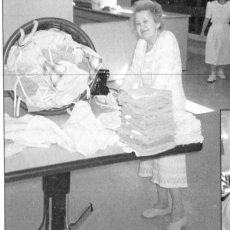

These pictures illustrate the joy of people with dementia when they are involved in meaningful activity.

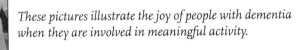

9

Gentlecare Programming

Today I was a person.
                —An elderly person

The Gentlecare program is based on a belief that activity is most effective when it is an integral part of the daily living process, rather than an "add-on," or a "take-out," or a program that is "parachuted" into a person's life.

The Gentlecare program focuses on and supports self-care activities, communication, family interaction, intimacy, relaxation and stress reduction, competency, and former life roles. Gentlecare programs avoid challenging people inappropriately, and are designed to support and indeed celebrate their existing strengths and spirit.

Gentlecare practitioners search for the essence of the individual, the residual parts of functional ability, the place of power or motivation within the person. We choose activity that resonates for the client, that interests people, makes them feel comfortable and in control of their lives to the degree that such control is possible.

ONE HOT SUMMER DAY *Michael J, my big basset hound, and I went to visit a Gentlecare facility. As soon as the elderly people saw this funny-looking dog they clustered around. Michael always provides an instant activity program. We slowly moved the dog and the group into the therapeutic garden. The staff slipped in and out of the garden, offering lemonade, encouraging an elderly lady to serve us ice cream cones, sometimes urging one or two to leave with them to "get freshened up," returning moments later with a freshly bathed elderly person. We sang some songs and talked about gardening and children.*

I noticed one gentleman on the periphery of this activity. Once or twice he peered through the window, but did not venture out to join us. I took Mike and went to ask the gentleman if he would help me walk the dog. He took the lead, and together we began to walk the perimeter of the garden. He began to talk by giving the dog lots of directions: "Come along!" "Heel, heel!" Michael doesn't pay much attention to people's notions of a walk, so there was a need for the gentleman to explain to me how the dog should have been trained.

Then he told me about a little dog who had been dear to his heart, and we talked a bit about his children.

As we neared the door to the facility, the old man stopped, looked me square in the face and said, "Today I was a person."

Normal Human Development

The model used in Gentlecare to develop effective programming is based on an awareness of normal human development, and a knowledge of how performance skills decline due to dementing illness. Figure 9.1 illustrates the process of acquiring skills through normal development, and losing those exact same skills due to brain cell damage. In normal development, a person moves from a preoccupation with basic survival needs, to participation in a family group, to development of a sense of self through life roles and accomplishments. The final stage of self-actualization (as described by Maslow) is one in which an individual operates through integration of all skills, knowledge, and experiences. He controls his life experiences.

Major catastrophes in life such as the death of a family member, job loss, or illness can cause any person to temporarily drop down this developmental scale to a lower level of preoccupation or performance. In dementing illness, however, the systematic loss of cognitive ability causes the afflicted person to lose control of life events, to become inca-

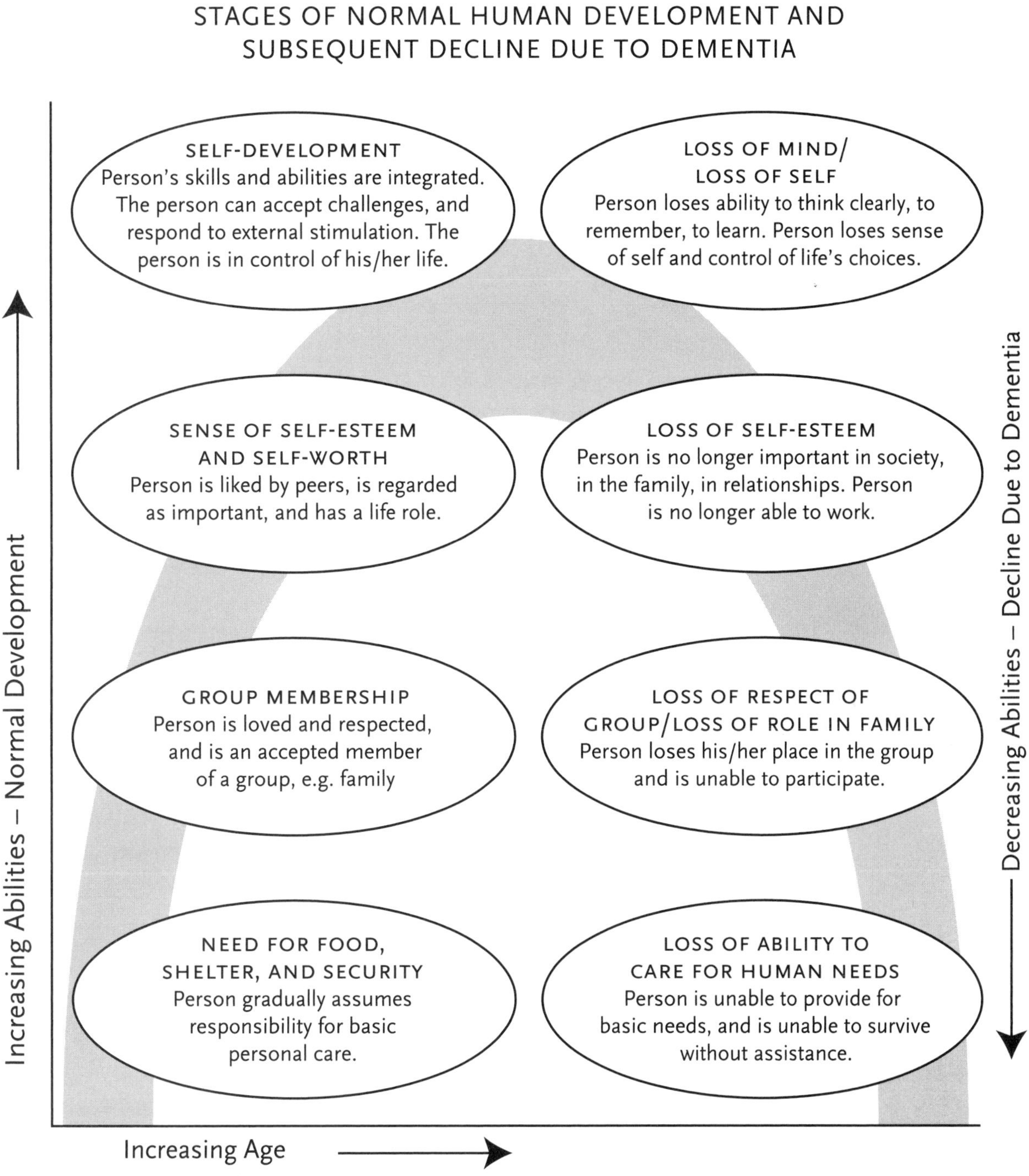

STAGES OF NORMAL HUMAN DEVELOPMENT AND SUBSEQUENT DECLINE DUE TO DEMENTIA

SELF-DEVELOPMENT
Person's skills and abilities are integrated. The person can accept challenges, and respond to external stimulation. The person is in control of his/her life.

LOSS OF MIND/ LOSS OF SELF
Person loses ability to think clearly, to remember, to learn. Person loses sense of self and control of life's choices.

SENSE OF SELF-ESTEEM AND SELF-WORTH
Person is liked by peers, is regarded as important, and has a life role.

LOSS OF SELF-ESTEEM
Person is no longer important in society, in the family, in relationships. Person is no longer able to work.

GROUP MEMBERSHIP
Person is loved and respected, and is an accepted member of a group, e.g. family

LOSS OF RESPECT OF GROUP/LOSS OF ROLE IN FAMILY
Person loses his/her place in the group and is unable to participate.

NEED FOR FOOD, SHELTER, AND SECURITY
Person gradually assumes responsibility for basic personal care.

LOSS OF ABILITY TO CARE FOR HUMAN NEEDS
Person is unable to provide for basic needs, and is unable to survive without assistance.

Increasing Abilities – Normal Development

Decreasing Abilities – Decline Due to Dementia

Increasing Age

FIGURE 9-1

pable of maintaining his life role or work situation, to be unable to fulfill family roles or responsibilities—and eventually to lose even the ability to care for basic personal needs. This decline reflects in reverse the acquisition of skills in a normal or healthy person.

The Gentlecare model of activity programming has as its goal to design and put in place an individual prosthesis of care that can support and assist the person to move up the developmental scale if possible, or to retain a place on the developmental scale for as long as possible.

Gentlecare uses the lovely adjective "synergic" to describe Gentlecare programs. "Synergic" describes increased effectiveness or achievment produced by combined action or co-operation. Synergy is fostered within all of the Gentlecare programs to combine efforts of staff, family members, and volunteers to focus their energy on the client. The goal is to enable him or her to be as independent as possible. Using accurate assessment information, individualized daily care programs are based on the highest point of competence or power of the individual. The process first identifies the current maximum functioning ability of the person—his or her personal place of power. Then the person's current deficit or lowest point of power is calculated. The area of deficiency is the part that must be compensated for by the prosthesis, which is the work of the caregiver.

In standard care of the elderly, activities occur episodically during the day, and different kinds of activities are dealt with in different ways. For instance, the person with Alzheimer's disease is assisted with activities of daily living or the activity is done to them. As a rule, these activities take place at specific times and within specific time frames. However, other necessary activities such as planned rest or time out occur only randomly and are often confused with times when nothing is happening in the person's life. Planned rest energizes people. Inactivity destroys people.

In current practice, many of the essential activities of life—movement, family, social intimacy, and communication—are sometimes specifically scheduled (for instance, as an exercise group, or reminiscing group). Family visits are modeled on hospital visits, rather than being viewed as a critical part of the person's care plan and a normal life activity.

SYNERGIC PROGRAMS

CORE ACTIVITIES	NECESSARY ACTIVITIES	ESSENTIAL ACTIVITIES	MEANINGFUL ACTIVITIES
The five activities of daily living	Activities necessary for human health	Activities essential for human interaction	Special undertakings
Toileting Grooming Bathing Dressing Eating	Natural sleep Rest/Relaxation Time out/Privacy	Communication Movement Intimacy/Touch Family/Social	Work Play Recreation

FIGURE 9-2

DETERMINING THE PROSTHESIS

The Gentlecare Prosthesis of Care, comprised of three elements—People, Programs, and Physical Space—is designed to match or compensate for the person's deficit. The person is not overhelped or underhelped.

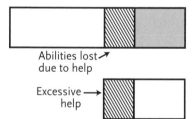

If the prosthesis is excessive, then the person will lose ability in direct proportion to the excess help.

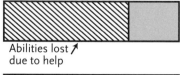

If total assistance is offered in order to make the task go more quickly the person will lose total functioning. This is referred to as iatrogenic illness (illness due to factors other than disease) or dysfunction.

Note marked increase in workload as inappropriate care is offered and client becomes helpless.

I can, therefore I am.

—SIMONE WEIL

FIGURE 9-3

Furthermore, standard care services tend to define other *meaningful activities* of life exclusively as those that utilize higher developmental skills. By definition, these are usually considered to be out of reach of people afflicted with dementia, who are rarely consulted on the subject or allowed control over their life activities. Standard care rarely sees activities such as movement, communication, family, or social interaction as principal therapies. In fact, such activities are seldom even charted.

Conversely, the Gentlecare Synergic Program regards all of these activities as critical for maintaining the optimum functioning level of the person experiencing dementia. All these activities are woven into a complex supporting fabric designed to give people with dementia the highest possible quality of life.

In Gentlecare, recognition is given to the level of energy that individuals require in order to accomplish ADLs. With proper support and prompting, many people can perform ADLs for themselves, rather than be dependent on someone else to do it for them or to them. Some ADLs such as eating and bathing can be the source of much pleasure and relaxation, if appropriately organized. Therefore the Gentlecare program emphasizes these activities, according them lots of time and thus maximizing their therapeutic value. Such activities become the central focus of the day for people with dementia. All staff work to make residents as comfortable, satisfied, and independent as possible.

It is often assumed that those cognitively impaired people who have difficulty performing ADLs are unable to do anything for themselves. On the contrary: such people should be regarded as having significant functional dependency, and needing help with specific aspects of their personal care. Care routines that do not acknowledge existing and residual functioning levels or assess deficits, that are rushed or under-staffed, contribute significantly to excessive disability.

The Gentlecare Model for Organizing Activity

Core activities are the constellation of activities related to Maslow's first building block of development: the need for food, shelter, security, and

GENTLECARE MODEL
FOR PLANNING ACTIVITIES
FOR PERSONS WITH DEMENTIA

Ascending and Reinforcing Spiral of Daily Performance

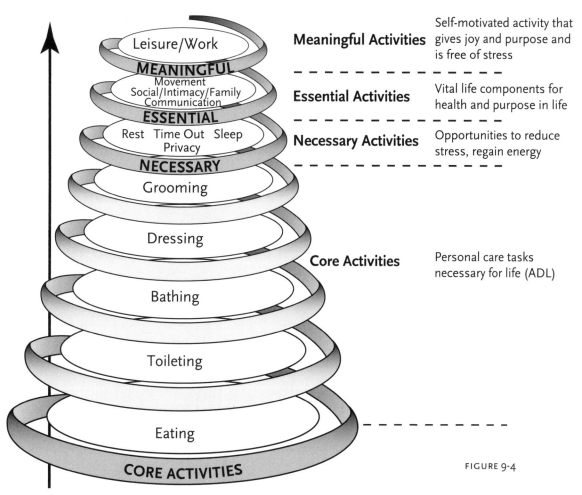

Leisure/Work

MEANINGFUL

Movement
Social/Intimacy/Family
Communication

ESSENTIAL

Rest   Time Out   Sleep
Privacy

NECESSARY

Grooming

Dressing

Bathing

Toileting

Eating

CORE ACTIVITIES

Meaningful Activities — Self-motivated activity that gives joy and purpose and is free of stress

Essential Activities — Vital life components for health and purpose in life

Necessary Activities — Opportunities to reduce stress, regain energy

Core Activities — Personal care tasks necessary for life (ADL)

FIGURE 9-4

Gentlecare aims to build on success in ascending levels of activities
so each person is able to reach the maximum level of meaningful activity.

basic personal care. In health care, these activities are referred to as Activities of Daily Living (ADLs). However, *core activities refer to the five ADLs as they are combined and integrated into a person's daily life* to enhance the person's quality of life.

For example, grooming is an ADL but in the larger sense, helping an elderly person achieve a pleasant feeling and appearance because a spouse is coming for lunch puts grooming in context, and provides the reason for carrying out the ADL in the first place. If a similar context is provided for bathing or dressing, the ADLs combine to form the core of the person's day—they provide his reason for living.

So although core activities in fact consist of ADL activities, when viewed together they form the basic context of daily living.

Necessary activities, on the other hand, are activities that all people must undertake to prepare for or provide the energy for carrying out other life activities. For the most part, people attend to necessary activities (rest, sleep, relaxation, time out, privacy) without giving them much thought. However, people with dementia must either be helped with these activities, or have them arranged for them. Health care providers must realize that these activities are absolutely necessary to prevent people with dementia from becoming overloaded, overstressed, and challenged beyond their functional abilities. Necessary activities also help give people with dementia the energy to enjoy life.

Essential activities are distinct from necessary activities—and people often ask me what the difference between the two actually is. Many people with dementia manage with only the first two activity levels: core activities and necessary activities. In Gentlecare, however, people with dementia are offered more than just ADLs and a bed to sleep in. Essential activities are the things that you and I do that connect us with other people; that allow us the joy of freedom and movement; and that offer us the pleasure of communication, whether verbal or non-verbal. These activities are superimposed on core and necessary activities to give completeness to the lives of elderly people with dementia.

Meaningful activities refers to the highest level of development in Maslow's developmental scale. These activities are special undertakings that require integration of all our cognitive, social, and functional

Excessive disability may be defined as a reversible deficit that is more disabling than the primary disability.

—DAWSON, KLINE, WIANKO, WELLS, GERIATRIC NURSING

skills. Achieving this level of development is very difficult for people with dementia. The Gentlecare program helps afflicted people achieve the highest possible level that they can. As people reach each developmental level, their success keeps them with the next new challenge. The ascending and reinforcing synergy of these programs raises people with dementia to their highest level of achievment and the highest quality of life possible.

Core Activities

Toileting

When assistance is needed for this most personal of all activities, there are problems for everyone—devastating the person requiring care, embarrassing family caregivers, and exhausting professional caregivers. The following suggestions, gathered from the personal experience of caregivers, may assist you with this difficult task. Remember to always apply the Gentlecare formula (the person/the pathology/the deficit/the prosthesis of care) to help you find creative solutions!

Organize the physical environment:
- Clear the clutter from the bathroom.
- Contrast the color of the toilet fixture with that of the floor and wall.
- Place the toilet paper in plain view by putting it on a small stool in front of the person.
- Make sure the door to the toilet is clearly differentiated from all other doors; try decorating the door with a large graphic of a toilet, painting the door a special color, or putting a small canopy over the door.
- Maintain good lighting in toilets 24 hours a day.

Plot the person's individual toileting routine:
- Consult with the person's family.
- Organize the care plan so the person is discreetly reminded, just prior to their regular elimination times, to visit a toilet.
- Support and reward successful toileting!
- Minimize reactions to problematic toileting or accidents.

Discover appropriate language to describe toileting activity:

FIGURE 9-5

CHAPTER
NINE

- Consult with the person's family.
- Make sure that everyone is informed of the correct language to be used, and that everyone uses it.
- Do not infantilize this activity through the use of language such as "diapers," "pee-pee," or "potty time"; refer to diapers as protective undergarments.

Offer appropriate assistance:
- Offer only the help required to accomplish the task.
- Practice being quiet and invisible.
- Try to place yourself to the side and behind the person's range of vision.
- To keep a person from popping up and down, try placing your hand lightly on the person's shoulder.
- DO NOT USE RESTRAINTS.
- Some facilities place a waist-high privacy screen in front of the person on the toilet.
- Try placing liners on the outside of underwear initially until the person becomes accustomed to the use of protective undergarments.
- Reassure, reassure, reassure!

Prepare caregivers (including families) for this task:
- Conduct regular in-service.
- Provide magazines for the use of those assisting in bathrooms because toileting takes time.
- Unless a person's skin condition is severely compromised, do not wake a person for toileting during the night.
- If a person needs to use the toilet at night, make sure light levels in both bedroom and bathroom are adequate and even.
- Wear mid-range colors, and make sure the person understands who you are and what you are doing.

Avoid the need for enemas or suppositories by providing good nutrition:
- If enemas are required, work in care teams: one member of the team supports, explains, and distracts while the other carries out the procedure.
- Proceed gently and slowly. Do not push through distress or fear around toileting. Try to talk the person through the procedure.
- Observe for pain and/or physical dysfunction.

GROOMING

Refers to mouth, teeth (dentures), eye, ear, hair, skin, and nose care as well as the application of cosmetics. These aspects of personal care are all too frequently neglected, avoided, or not attended to altogether.

WHEN I VISITED *my own father in hospital years and years ago, my routine was as follows: I would first embrace him; then I would wash his face and eyes, brush his hair, give him his dentures out of the top drawer of his night stand, put his collar out over his sweater, wash his hands, clean his nails, put his gold ring on—and then stand back and say, "Hi, Dad!"*

Grooming: Mouth Care

I have no magic formula to offer with respect to mouth care. It's the toughest kind of care to give. I only know it must be carried out three or five times a day if we want the person to feel good.

Ask the family carer for advice. Members of the family have often worked out effective routines or tricks for providing mouth care.

I AM ALWAYS ASKING *caregivers for tips on managing mouth care: "How do you get their dentures out? Do you have any ideas about this that work?" One care aide told me she had a foolproof strategy. She said, "I just show them what I want them to do by pulling out my own denture . . . and they always do what I do!"*

In helping the person with dementia to remove dentures, place the person's hand between yours and the denture. In other words, assist the person to take dentures out and put them in. Mime the activity. Describe what it is you want done, slowly and clearly, over and over again. Use the toothbrush and toothpaste to stimulate visual awareness of the activity you want carried out.

I ONCE WORKED *in a hospital where residents' dentures were passed out before each meal and retrieved at the end of the meal. Between meals, dentures were stored in little individual boxes at the nursing station. But dentures are meant to replace natural teeth. They are needed in the mouth for many reasons—talking, eating, and looking your best. A person in care should have teeth in the mouth during all waking hours.*

GENTLECARE **Best Practice**

Make sure each person has a "comfort bag" or satchel or briefcase. That's usually where they will put their dentures. Except for my father. He kept his in the toe of his shoe!

Ensure that dentures are identified (labeled). Dentures often fit poorly, and when they irritate the mouth, people with dementia will sometimes take them out and hide them, or throw them away.

Sometimes people will clean their own mouth and tongue if given a clean wet cloth. Remember that the tissue around the mouth (and eyes) is very fragile!

Practice distraction while you do mouth care. Reminiscing and news of family are good distractions. Or give the person something beautiful or interesting to hold in their hands.

Dentures should fit properly! If they do not, and it proves impossible to have them fixed, the person may in fact be more comfortable without them. However, it's best to keep dentures in working order as long as possible.

Skin Care

Elderly people often have dry skin, and medications, hot temperatures, and dehydration are some of the factors that contribute to the condition. Massaging hands, face, feet, and legs with lotion is a lovely, relaxing technique for making a person feel marvelous! (Family members and volunteers can often contribute to this type of activity.)

Remember to wash elderly people's hands frequently during the day. This is especially important before and after meals. Gentlecare recommends the use of hot towels, which are distributed before each meal. (Again, this is a good family and/or volunteer activity.)

Hair Care

Clean hair, well cut and cared for, makes people look and feel like themselves at their best. Families should be involved in discussions about finding the most attractive, simplest-to-care-for hairstyle; however, old styles and patterns of caring for hair must always be respected. Long hair should not be cut, nor beards or mustaches shaved off, unless there is an extremely compelling reason for doing so, and family members have been consulted.

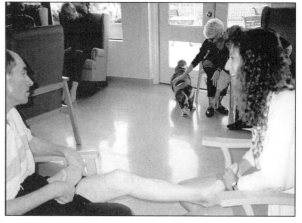

Touch is ten times more powerful than visual or auditory stimulus, whether from a friendly human, or a favorite dog.

Beauticians should be included in all dementia educational opportunities, and be given relevant clinical information about the people they serve. Brushing hair and massaging the scalp is an effective way to relax the person with dementia.

I WAS WORKING *on a dementia care unit one day brushing out an elderly lady's very long, thick hair. We had tied it up in a ponytail, and I was working out a big tangle of hair near her waist. Suddenly a staff member said, "I know how to fix that!" and took some scissors and cut off the ponytail at the point of the rubber band. With a snap of the scissors, the woman's appearance and autonomy were violated in a way the dementing illness had never been able to do.*

People should wear shower caps while bathing or using the shower, and water should never be poured over the person's head. Be considerate: do not wash a woman's hair if it has been recently styled or set. Try to schedule hair-washing so that it coordinates with visits to the beauty parlor.

ONE OF THE MOST DEVASTATING events in my life as a family care-giver occurred when I visited my father one day and discovered that his hair—which was distinctively long and luxurious—had all been cut off. Only tiny wisps of hair remained among the bald patches. He was unrecognizable!

I was told that this short "haircut" lasted longer, and eliminated the "problem" of regular haircuts. Years and years later the image of my father, looking like an inmate of a concentration camp, remains in my memory because someone thought it didn't matter what kind of haircut one gave an old man with dementia.

THE USE OF COSMETICS

The application of cosmetics should be done gently, discreetly, and in-dividually, respecting old patterns of practice. Family carers can often provide advice or pictures that can help in this respect.

JEWELRY

Jewelry is a great conversation starter. Like the Queen, many elderly women would not dream of being seen in public without their three strands of pearls! Ask family members to replace valuable pieces of jewelry with inexpensive jewelry that is similar in appearance so that people with dementia can enjoy the jewelry they have worn all their lives. Costume jewelry also makes a wonderful small gift that can be mailed to the person in a facility. Remember, old men enjoy jewelry too!

ONCE WHEN AN ASSISTANT of mine asked if he could take a picture of an elderly woman and her husband, she readily agreed but asked if he would wait outside for a moment. I thought she was going to put in her dentures, do her hair, or apply some lipstick. Instead she rum-maged around in her top drawer until she found just the right neck-lace, and then she was ready to be photographed.

Dressing

Clothing is necessary for warmth and comfort, social conformity, and expressing individuality. "Clothes make the man," so the old saying goes, and it is unfortunately true that our society judges people by what they wear. We dress up for company. We buy new clothes for important interviews or social events. Kids wear certain styles to be accepted by their preferred group of friends.

Most elderly people who experience dementia belong to a generation that practiced very strict dress codes. Women wore hats, wore their skirts a prescribed length, and did not wear slacks. Men wore shirts, ties, and jackets at all times.

So what happens to their social mores when dementia strikes? Dressing is a very complex activity requiring manipulation of a variety of articles and materials. Satisfactory dressing requires sequencing: getting underclothes on first, not last. It requires color matching, being aware of right and left, top and bottom, and having an accurate sense of body image. It requires the use of judgment in choosing clothing suitable for hot or cold weather and for indoor or outdoor wear. Socks, shoes, and gloves are worn in pairs, hats must suit the season—the list of choices is endless. So how do we help our family members and clients dress appropriately and still be as independent as possible?

I ONCE LISTENED *to a husband rant on and on about his wife's "stupidity" in not matching the colors of her shoes each morning. He said, "Every time I look at her she's walking around in one brown shoe and one black shoe! Surely to goodness she can see the difference!"*

We talked about what dementia does to one's ability to differentiate colors, and there was a long silence as he thought about the effects of this awful illness. At last he said, "You don't think it's her fault, do you?" And I said, "No, I don't." He said, "You think it's up to me," and I said, "Yes." There was another thoughtful pause, and then he said, "Well, I could just put out a pair of brown shoes, or a pair of black shoes for her, couldn't I? That should make it easier." And I agreed.

Dementia is a continuum of declining functions. It's possible—with gentle assistance—for people to wear regular clothing until they are at the stage of moderate dementia (Late Stage 4 or 5 on the Reisberg Scale). To be able to provide the kind of help that will allow this to happen, however, the caregiver must learn how the disease affects functioning, as in the case of the husband who wanted his wife to wear matching shoes. Later on, as the skill level of a person with dementia declines, it becomes necessary to modify clothing so that independence can be maintained for as long as possible. Here are some of the modifications that help extend independence:

- Choose clothing with wide necklines and wide, deep armholes.
- Eliminate fasteners wherever possible.
- Consider using sports clothing, even though the person may never have worn such clothing before. Gym suits are warm and comfortable, easy to wash, and easy to get on and off. It is also possible to layer sports clothes to accommodate the wild swings in temperature that dementia causes. Discuss these advantages with family members who may not understand why clothing changes are necessary.
- Consider using gym suits instead of pajamas at night. They are warm around the shoulders and lower back, and easy to change.
- We recommend the use of little "huggable" jackets for women. These jackets cover the shoulders and arms, and have knitted cuffs at the wrists that keep the jacket in place. One of the reasons people with dementia wander out of their rooms at night is that they feel cold; they may not think to pull up blankets around their shoulders.
- Some family members prefer to have their female relatives wear dresses. Where that is the case, Gentlecare recommends using long robes with Velcro closings in the back, for reasons of both comfort and ease in dressing. Robes also have the advantage of covering knees and legs, especially if the person is in a wheelchair or has a habit of pulling up clothing. And robes make elderly women feel special and dressed up.
- Men like to wear vests, and baggy sweaters with deep pockets to put their treasures in. They also often enjoy scarves and hats, worn indoors too.
- If the person frequently undresses in public, consider using a jumpsuit (one-piece suit of clothing) with fasteners either at the front or at the back. Jumpsuits present real challenges during toileting, however.

- Eliminate belts, buttons, linings, or any clothing construction that impedes easy dressing and undressing.
- For a slim woman, it is sometimes possible to substitute a warm undervest for a bra.
- Stretchy leggings are easier to put on than nylons or pantyhose, and are warm and comfortable. Leg warmers can be substituted for nylons and pantyhose, and are easier to put on. Above-the-knee nylons are also easier to manage than pantyhose.
- Lightweight leggings make excellent leg covers under skirts or dresses, or on their own.
- Every person who is up and about should wear shoes. Consider using sport shoes or walking shoes for footwear, rather than dress shoes. They are more stable, more comfortable, and easier to get on and off.
- Once you find a suitable kind of footwear, buy two pairs of the same shoe—it will save searching for a match.
- Beware of gym shoes with deep soles and wide rims, as they will cause an older person to stumble or trip. There are many walking shoes with narrow, neat soles.
- Do not use socks with cuffs that are elasticized or have tight ribbing; we prefer socks that fold down into a cuff. Also avoid socks with seams or ribbing on the underside. Buy one size of same-color socks, and lots of them. Socks are expendable!
- And to keep everyone happy make sure clothes are made of easily washable, non-wrinkle fabrics, and give the person in care as much choice as possible in selecting colors and accessories.

I WAS ONCE ASKED *by family caregivers to act on their behalf in presenting a problem to the facility administration. What was the problem? They felt that staff was stealing their family members' socks. I assured them I thought it unlikely that any staff member would covet old, shrunken, mismatched socks, and reminded them of how difficult it is to keep socks organized in the hospital laundry. I suggested they try to solve the problem. So they formed a sock committee!*

They pooled all their resources and purchased dozens of pairs of one-size, one-color, non-shrink socks. Members of the committee then placed three pairs of socks in each resident's drawer. They removed and organized all existing socks. Of course, everyone was enchanted and the committee received much praise for its problem-solving approach. I heard later that the family caregivers at that facility also formed an underwear committee!

When assisting with dressing identify each item of clothing for the person you are helping, not only by name, but by function: "Let's put your slacks on over your legs so you'll be nice and warm." Offer one item at a time. If you are unable to supervise the whole dressing procedure, lay clothing out in the sequence to be put on. Undo fasteners, and open up the clothing for the person who's dressing. People with dementia may have problems when trying to distinguish top clothing from bottom clothing, often mistaking an arm for a trouser leg.

If the person errs in putting clothes on in the correct sequence, attempt to assist the person to correct the error…discreetly! If you encounter any resistance, leave the clothing as it is. IT DOES NOT MATTER! Do not attempt to get the person to take the clothing off, turn it right side out, or fix it in any way. Taking off clothing that was just put on does not make sense to the person experiencing dementia. Your action only upsets the person and causes increased resistance. Later, when the moment seems appropriate, explain the clothing problem to the person. As a rule he will comply, and allow adjustments to his clothing. Alternatively, have someone else point out the difficulty. No arrangement or disarray of clothing is worth fighting over! Explain to staff members, families, VIPs, and visitors that the main goal is to keep the person with dementia feeling comfortable and in control. Occasional bizarre dress isn't important!

I REMEMBER SEEING *a staff member struggling with a man who was putting on a woman's sweater. He had one arm in the sleeve, and was determined to put that sweater on. The staff member tried just as determinedly to pull it off, explaining that it was not his sweater.*

The whole incident was escalating out of control, so I suggested we just leave him alone and watch what happened. The man marched off down the hall, pulling the very small sweater over his burly shoulders. Of course the sweater was very uncomfortable, pulling his arms back and constricting his movements, so after a few moments he pulled it off and tossed it on a chair in disgust. The staff member was then able to offer him his own sweater, and retrieve the discarded one for its proper owner.

A HEAD NURSE TOLD ME *a wonderful story of a very influential businessman with Alzheimer's disease who lived in a Gentlecare unit. It was almost impossible to get him to change his clothing until the staff devised a terrific and effective strategy for doing so.*

One of them would approach the man and ask if he had any jobs available. The man invariably said he did, but the person would have to have an interview. So the "interview" would be set just after lunch. Another staff member would then approach the man and whisper to him, "You will want to have a fresh shirt and tie when you conduct that interview, won't you?" Without a murmur, the man would agree, have a bath, get dressed, and go off to have his lunch looking like a million dollars, pride intact. And of course, after lunch he would have forgotten all about the interview!

Like any other ADL, dressing is very personal and private. The more control we can give the person—even if it is only the illusion of control—the more pleasant and comfortable the activity will be. Experiment, modify, adapt, observe; and when you find something that works, tell everyone about it. Reinforcing a person's identity and well-being by taking time over dressing will influence his whole outlook for the rest of the day and make life much more pleasant for him, his family, and those of us who provide care.

Bathing

No ADL causes more distress or controversy than bathing. The deficits of dementing illness, in and of themselves, cause people to be fearful,

If you don't insist, he won't resist.

—MARY LUCERNO,
   HEALTH EDUCATOR,
   FLORIDA

anxious, angry, and confused about bathing—and therefore resistant to it. However, my experience leads me to believe that organizational and structural issues are the root of most problems surrounding bathing.

Current bathing practices in the long-term health care system are strongly driven by the biomedical model of care and its values: cleanliness, infection control, skin care, and predictable, efficient routine. Physical care preempts all other considerations. Consider the situation of an elderly man with dementia—possibly a man who was the owner of a company, the head of a large family, and an active member of his church and community—who has been scheduled for a bath at 10:30 on a Wednesday morning. He is approached by two young women who are strangers to him (if he has met them before, he has no memory of them). They ask him to take off his clothes and sit on a moveable chair. He is then covered with a sheet and propelled down a busy hallway to a large and often cold room filled with mechanical equipment and supplies. In the company of strangers he is lowered into a tub full of water, bathed, dressed, and returned to his room.

If this man resists these activities in any way, other staff members will be called to assist in restraining him. (I have seen as many as five staff people involved in bathing one person.) If the man's resistance to bathing persists, in future he will be given medication (a chemical restraint) before each scheduled bath time.

The procedure described here occurs, with variations, over and over again in long-term care facilities. It produces physically clean people, but at what cost? The psychological trauma to the person is severe, the stress and injury to staff are significant, and the distress of family caregivers is profound.

Obviously, people need to be bathed, and health care standards of cleanliness must be maintained. The challenge is to provide comforting, relaxed, stress-free bathing experiences for people with dementia without sacrificing personal control, dignity, privacy, and pleasure. Bathing should be a pleasurable experience!

Gentlecare research into bathing practices has taken us into hundreds of facilities and home care programs serving people with dementia in Canada, the United States, and Europe. In many facilities, bath time is the highlight of the day (or evening). In others, it is utter disaster. The different outcomes appear to result from the way the activity of bathing is perceived, and the way in which it is organized.

The Gentlecare bathing process is based on the successful experiences of care providers, and supports the belief that bathing is a powerful way to provide comfort and reduce stress. The Gentlecare formula is helpful in establishing a satisfying bath time routine. It reminds us to ask ourselves, as we are about to bathe someone:

- Who is this person?
- What is the disease process?
- What deficits does he have?
- What information does behavior provide?
- What prosthesis is required?

Bathing should be a pleasurable experience.

If we consider the socio-cultural aspects of bathing for the population of elders we care for, we must remember that many people in this generation:

- did not bathe daily, possibly not even weekly or monthly;
- did not often bathe immersed in water;
- never appeared nude before strangers or other family members;
- are frightened of water; and
- are not familiar with showers, mechanical lifts, Jacuzzis, etc.

MANY YEARS AGO I WORKED *in a hospital for elderly veterans. My colleagues and I had a very difficult time persuading these old gentlemen to have weekly baths. One man told me in no uncertain terms that he bathed once a year, in the spring. On that occasion, he cut off his combination underwear, had a bath, and put on his new underwear for the coming year. No way was he going to take a bath "every five minutes!"*

With 200 reluctant bathers, the cleanliness issue was becoming so critical that we were forced to come up with a creative solution. So we introduced wrestling! Once a week we offered a program of wrestling, with beer and snacks in the auditorium. However, the price of admis-

sion was a detour through the showers. Each man was given clean clothes, nail care, a haircut, skin care, and a thorough shower. The program worked like magic, with long line-ups heading into the showers and exiting into the wrestling arena in the auditorium.

Gentlecare Guidelines for Bathing

Explain, explain, explain:

- Make sure the person with dementia understands the activity you are introducing. As we did with the veterans, give the person a reason to do what you want them to do, such as, "Your family is coming to visit"; "You'll want a bath before you get dressed up"; or "It's laundry day—I need your clothes for the washer" (this works for men).
- Avoid telling people they smell awful. This is insulting and causes elderly people who have lost their sense of smell to become defensive. Instead, use phrases like "freshening up," "feeling better," "nice and clean," "while the water's hot," "before all the water is used up," "this will help you sleep." And there's always the old standby: asking the person to help you in some way in the bathroom.
- Be sure the person understands who you are. Explain your role as a helper over and over and in a variety of ways throughout the bath. Try to blend into the activity, being as discreet as possible. Avoid giving orders or ultimatums, and listen to the tone of your own voice.

Prepare the environment:

- Bathrooms should look, feel, and smell like places where one would want to have a bath.
- Bathrooms should be warm and free of drafts.
- Limit the visual size of the room by using privacy curtains or screens.
- Avoid using the bathing area for storage of equipment and/or supplies, and thereby making it look like a warehouse.
- Remove posted literature from direct view of the client.
- Normalize the room with hanging plants, pictures, decorative towels, and bathroom objects.

- Warming closets for towels, flannel sheets, and robes adds a lovely touch. Using warm sheets at bedtime brings forth magical results.
- Ensure that the tub and toilet contrast with the floor and wall, with good figure/ground distinction. Camouflage all equipment, shelves, etc., not used by the person.

I MET AN OLD GENTLEMAN *I had helped, walking down the corridor of a facility. He was all disheveled and seemed upset. When I asked if something was the matter, he replied, "Oh! Moyra—I've just been through a car wash!"*

Post an "in-use" sign on the bathroom door, and limit traffic in and out of the room while it is in use:
- Never use the bathroom for more than one person at a time!
- While helping someone bathe, staff should not be required to address any other responsibilities, or take phone calls.
Avoid the use of mechanical equipment unless it is absolutely necessary:
- People experiencing dementia should use a regular bathtub for as long as possible.
- Avoid the use of a Jacuzzi unless the person is very comfortable with the sensation. Practice a desensitization process by having the person experience how the Jacuzzi works before using it. Remember that Jacuzzi use may not be a familiar activity for elderly people.
- Cover the inner surface of the regular tub with non-slip material.
- Use a low seat in a regular tub together with a hand-held shower-head.
- Position grab bars in the regular tub to promote maximum function. Avoid confusing the person with a maze of bars. Keep it simple but functional.

I REMEMBER WORKING *with a large man who was extremely resistant to bathing. Several staff people were always required to force him into the bath, and many of them had sustained injuries. As he hit out and screamed "Pig! Pig! Pig! Pig! Pig!" at everyone in the room, he clearly was a danger to anyone within his reach. We knew something about the bath was disturbing him and causing his violent resistance —but we didn't know what that something was.*

Always when we reach an impasse like this, it is important to examine our knowledge base. Using the Gentlecare formula, I decided to find out more about this man in order to understand his behavior. I met with the man's large, supportive family and discovered that he had been a farmer until he was hospitalized. Family members told me he was a gentle man who was always meticulous about his personal appearance and hygiene. I asked about his work, and his son told me he was a pig farmer. Hmmm...? So I asked about pig farming, and one of the things I was told was that after one killed a pig, one doused it in boiling water to remove the hairs. As the son mimed this activity for me, an image of his father tied in a chair and being lowered into the bubbling water of the Jacuzzi came vividly. Of course! Unfamiliar with a Jacuzzi and with limited vocabulary, the old gentleman had been trying desperately to tell us that we were going to scald him like a pig!

I returned to the facility with a new understanding of the person, and suggested that we offer him the opportunity to bathe in a regular tub. This he did, by himself, with a minimum of fuss or involvement by staff.

Think through the bathing process step by step to ensure that all the equipment and/or supplies needed are at hand:

- Prepare the bath area before you bring the person into the room.
- Ensure that an emergency call button is within reach of attending staff.
- If the person exhibits perceptual problems and appears not to be able to see the water, try adding food coloring to the water (use yellow, green, or blue and avoid red).
- Try placing a flannel sheet or a heavy bath towel on the inside of a regular tub to avoid skin contact with the cool, slippery surface of the tub.

- Cover seats or lifts with towels before the person sits on them.
- Cover shower seats with a large, colorful bath towel.

  Consider using bath teams:

  Some people can give beautiful baths and others can't. Choose one or two caregivers who are particularly skilled in bathing and persuasion, and make them responsible for this activity (including the ambiance of the room and assembling necessary supplies and equipment). These people can also be responsible for skin inspection and care (lotion to hands, elbows, feet, and face), nail care, and assessment of general mobility.

  Allow time for staff to assist with a relaxing, refreshing bath. Make bath time a significant treatment modality:

- Always give the person being bathed a "nutrition boost" before beginning the bath. Cheese and crackers, a peanut butter and jam sandwich, a muffin or a milk pudding, a shake or a smoothie—any of these can dramatically improve bath time.
- Avoid nudity. Always drape the person in towels throughout the bath.
- Make sure shoulders are covered.
- Place a towel over the lap.
- Some care providers use a towel that fastens around the waist or chest with Velcro and can be worn up to the point at which the person is submerged in water.
- If the person resists removal of a nightgown or pajama bottom, start the bath with the garment still on. The assisting staff can often slip the garment off without a fuss once it is wet.
- Never pour water over the head or face.
- Give lots of orienting information and encouragement.
- Always reward a successful bathing experience.

  Arrange for flexible bathing schedules:

  Some people prefer to bathe on awakening before they are dressed for the day. Others have traditionally bathed at night, before bedtime. Try to respect these lifelong habits. Determine the best time for a bath in consultation with the person, the family, and other caregivers. Make bathing a part of the individual treatment or care plan, rather than designating Wednesday or Thursday as bath day, and systematically bathing one person after another at 15-minute intervals whether they want to bathe or not. Remember that a sponge bath is always more effective than a fight over a tub bath. Sometimes it is possible to bathe only a part of the person before they stop cooperating. Never force a person to complete a bath! Do the best you can; then decide to try again at another time, or ask another caregiver to attempt to assist the person.

Consider using distractions:

- Always try to put an object between you, as assistant, and the person's body. For example, put the washcloth or showerhead in the person's hand, and then put your hand over the person's hand. This gives the illusion that the person is in control, rather than making them feel they are passively being bathed.
- Try back scrubs or massage to help the person relax into the bath before you begin bathing more intimate parts of the body.
- Give the person a drink or bite to eat at intervals during the bath.

ONE GENTLEMAN WAS IMPOSSIBLE *to bathe. I asked the staff if there was a favorite treat that he really loved. They said, yes, a bottle of beer. I said to the man, "Charlie, would you like a beer?" and he said, "Sure would!" I said, "As soon as we get you into the bathtub, I'll get a beer for you." The moment Charlie sat down in the tub I gave him his beer, which he drank with great enjoyment while we completed his bath. Now a bottle of beer signals a pleasant bath.*

Take advantage of bathing programs:

Bathing programs offered by day care services are invaluable for people living at home. Since most care in the home is provided by elderly female spouses, bathing is often exhausting and sometimes dangerous. Home support programs with access to facility bathing equipment are also an important aspect of dementia care. Often people with dementia resist having family members assist with their baths. Conversely, family carers may be the only ones who are allowed to help with bathing!

Install a mini-bath:

It is important to have regular bathtub facilities for general hygiene and relaxation, but mini-baths can reduce much of the fuss and bother associated with routine bathing. Special note: like ice cream, nobody does bathrooms better than Italians! In Italy it is common to see a mini-bath (not a bidet) located beside the toilet in each bathroom of a care facility.

Mini-bath.

A mini-bath is a small mesh chair that folds into the wall beside the toilet. Below it in the floor is a drain, and above it there is a hand-held showerhead. Each morning the person being cared for is toileted, then shifted to the bath seat for bathing. Then the person is covered with a large, warm towel, groomed, and dressed. The process is so natural and efficient that the bath is simply considered a normal part of the day. The mini-bath is also highly effective for management of toileting accidents during the day or at night. Each bathroom also offers clean and dirty linen storage in the wall adjacent to the mini-bath— a wonderful feature!

Shower chair.

Eating

Eating is so important a core activity, such a powerful means of therapy in dementia care, that in Gentlecare we have devoted three separate chapters to this topic: Chapters 11, 12, and 13 discuss the role of nutrition in dementing illness.

Necessary Activities

Natural sleep, rest, relaxation, and privacy are activities necessary for human health. As people age, their sleeping patterns change dramatically. Older people seem to benefit from

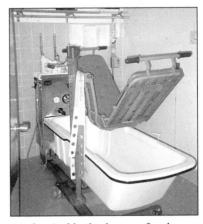
Mechanical bathtubs can often be frightening.

FIGURE 9-6

Natural sleep, rest, relaxation, and privacy are activities necessary for human health.

"power naps," and tend to sleep for shorter periods, and nap more frequently as their energy becomes depleted.

The process of living with dementia is exhausting. It is often hard to find a quiet opportunity to rest and regenerate. In addition, the dementing process causes older people to be confused between night and day (mind blindness), so they often sleep more during the day and wander around during the night.

Change in sleep patterns among elderly people is rarely considered in dementia care. It is not unusual to encounter the expectation that older people will stay in their beds for 12 hours or more—or contrariwise, stay out of their beds for 12 hours. This expectation, however convenient it may be for the system, runs counter to the knowledge that as they age, people sleep at night for shorter and shorter periods and nap more frequently during the day.

Gentlecare takes all these factors into account, arranging natural sleep periods that accommodate the older person's unique body rhythm. Programs and special quiet areas permit older people to get up in the night, receive refreshment, have socialization opportunities, and then often return to sleep.

Exhaustion and resulting catastrophic behavior is prevented by building rest opportunities into each individual's care plan. Rest is prescribed between each complex undertaking—wake-up, rest, grooming, rest, dressing, rest, breakfast, rest, etc. Opportunities are also provided for elderly people to be alone, free of demands, and to have private spaces which they control. Necessary activities organized into the life of elderly people reduces fatigue, stress, and catastrophic reactions, and gives the person energy to enjoy life.

Essential Activities

The activities of communication, movement, interaction with family, and intimacy are essential for human interaction. Dementia and standard dementia care rob elderly people of these vital life-enhancing activities. Essential activities woven into the lives of elderly people reduce stress and anxiety, and help them to enjoy life.

Communication

Communication is a human being's critical activity—it's what makes us different from other animals. Communication is a wonderful and complex activity. It involves talking and listening, and is verbal and non-verbal. Effective communication with people afflicted with dementia requires more than just talking. It requires preparation, knowledge, and new skills. But communication activities are worth the preparation since it is one of the loveliest activities you can do with elderly people. The following communication tips help us connect with elderly people:

- Establish who you are.
- Get permission to enter the person's space.
- Sit down, make eye contact.
- Focus or "ground" the person.
- Slow the pace and let the person set the pace.
- Take your time—make the time.
- Speak so the person can hear and see you.
- Be understandable and clear.
- Listen; remember that silence is golden.
- Be sensitive to feelings.
- Don't tease.
- Don't call them by "funny" names.
- Don't patronize.
- Minimize distraction.
- Use an object as an intermediary.
- Discuss whatever subject they suggest.
- Listen to the same old story as often as it is told.
- Express gratitude for the privilege, fun, experience, and honor of being there.

FIGURE 9-7

The following topics are communication strategies that work:
- "Remember when...stamps were two cents, eggs were ten cents a dozen...you bought your first car?"
- Talk about a subject through an object (perhaps something in the room).
- Don't ask questions. Give information instead.

- Don't ask, "How are you?
- Say: "You look nice/sleepy/lonesome/happy."
- "I like your sweater. It's a lovely color!"
- "Oh, I'm out of breath! Can I sit a minute with you?"
- Discuss family issues—theirs, yours, or the Queen's/famous people.
- Talk about what you saw on your way here to visit.
- Sports—especially good for men. Ask them to explain sports to you.
- Concerts/music—"I heard the loveliest _____!"
- "I would like to read to you. Would you like to listen?"
- War—medals and stories/church/prices and shopping/pets.
- The "old" days: their careers, different jobs, achievements—life review.
- Talk about dying: help them plan creatively; use your own feelings and experiences. Listen for: "I'm so tired of living. Everyone says I'm OK. I'm not OK."

Movement

Older people benefit greatly from the freedom to move indoors and outdoors spontaneously. For many this is a normal lifelong pattern of activity. Gentlecare emphasizes preparation of good walking spaces, accessible exits and entrances, and interesting activity that encourages movement through attractive settings and pleasing gardens. We emphasize music and dancing, working, playing with children, and helping activities...any activity that stimulates movement. We avoid artificial movement activities such as exercise groups that depend on staff to organize and initiate. Rather, we recommend spontaneous, ongoing familiar opportunities that elderly people can access on their own or with minimal help from volunteers, staff, or families.

As the diseases of dementia progress, many changes in motor function must be accommodated. Creative patterns of movement must be devised to maintain strength and flexibility. Gentlecare finds that familiar patterns of work often have the best chances of maintaining interest and involvement. For instance, an elderly lady will hang out laundry

ACTIVITIES RELATED TO COMMUNICATION
WHILE VISITING ELDERLY PEOPLE

- Explain and reassure them about current living arrangements.

- *If they ask*—reassure them about finances.

- Bring a bouquet of flowers and talk about them; arrange them together; look at them; hold and smell them.

- Bring a basket of objects as conversation pieces, then leave a pretty hankie, a piece of lace, a card.

- Help them write to friends and family.

- Help them record their life history.

- Bring a baby to visit.

- Bring a pet to visit.

- Find their favorite reading material and read aloud to them—the newspaper; *Reader's Digest,* etc.; the Bible or a daily meditation. Bring a selection of coffee table picture books and discuss them.

- Read the lyrics of songs.

- Read or recite familiar poetry, nursery rhymes together.

- Read inspirational material to them.

- Read old recipes and discuss them.

- Do gentle shoulder massage.

- Brush their hair.

- Massage their hands and feet with scented lotion. Manicure their nails.

- Bring a potted plant and discuss gardening.

- Bring colorful pictures of pets, kids, garden, and food.

- Wind wool with them.

- You do crafts while you visit and discuss.

- Take tiny gifts—three chocolates, soap, piece of costume jewelry, handkerchief, and samples of perfume.

- Unravel old knitting—a sweater—and discuss.

- Tear cloth for braided rugs. Show them a finished rug. Discuss.

- Have the person assist you with braiding.

- Promote bonding with another person nearby.

Through words, we actively construct our social world.

FIGURE 9-8

- Pray with them. Sing with them.

- Spend 5 to 10 minutes browsing through and discussing large picture books—barns, horses, gardens, embroidery, the Royal Family.

- Use old memories to help the person regain control—encourage communication using one of these ideas: pictures and photographs; babies and children; antiques to polish; reminiscing and story telling; pets (brought in by family or staff); familiar objects (lace, shells, buttons, beads, and other jewelry); stamps; coins (collections); hats.

- Try to engage them in: WORK + TALK + REMEMBER!—sorting; cutting paper; folding, cutting up cards; putting paper in envelopes.

- Promote movement. Walk and talk.

- Bring a collection of hats to try on and talk about.

- Bring in an old-fashioned dress, a ball gown or wedding gown or kilt and talk about it.

- Bring in old carpentry and kitchen utensils and tools to talk about.

- Arrange for a roving troubadour to play a guitar, harp, mouth organ, or keyboard.

- Sing and hum favorite hymns and songs.

- Bring a Walkman with earphones.

- Talk about Dame Vera Lynn or some other famous singers and hum their hit tunes.

- Bring a tape and play one lovely piece.

- Have a hymn sing after supper, repeating first verses of familiar old hymns.

- Write letters for them to family members, friends, people within the facility including management (and they should answer!), the editor of local newspapers, the Queen, Prime Minister, MLA, Major, Senator, Congressman (they will answer).

- Set up a mail box.

- Deliver mail.

- Send mail to everyone in the care facility (this is an excellent activity for shut-ins, older volunteers to do); do all year round.

- Help them prepare a few Christmas cards for special friends and family.

—Some items adapted from *Aging is a Family Affair* by Wendy Thompson [Family Books, NC Press Ltd., 1990].

(upper arm movement) or fold children's clothing (manual dexterity) for long periods. They will only pull on a pulley a few times, and then only if a staff member is there to encourage them.

As the disease progresses, winding, tearing cloth or paper, bunching up paper, folding, braiding, unwinding knitting, and similar simple activities maintain upper arm strength. However, Gentlecare tries to keep everyone walking or dancing for as long as possible.

Intimacy/Touch

Dementia robs people of spontaneity—of the ability to reach out and connect with another human being socially or physically.

Gentlecare recommends using the power of touch to cut through this disease-induced barrier. We recommend activities such as massage of hands, feet, back, and head, hugs, dancing, hair brushing, manicures, pets, kids, and babies to help elderly people feel loved and included in the human family. Gentlecare encourages intimacy between spouses and arranges private spaces for them.

Often people afflicted with dementia mistake others for their spouse. If people with dementia bond, and no one is hurt or exploited, these relationships are supported. It is very important to discuss such activity with family members. However, regardless of the feelings of others, the person with dementia has the right to pursue relationships. Staff members need to monitor activity of this nature closely without judging or condemning. Gentlecare experience has shown that the more "legitimate intimacy" is introduced into regular programming, the less need there appears to be for sexual activity. It is not surprising that older people, like anyone, want to be loved and accepted.

Meaningful Activities

Work and leisure activities include special undertakings that require cognition, skills, and a great deal of support. On occasion, emphasizing overlearned, familiar areas of competency, Gentlecare finds that elderly people can achieve success at this level of function.

FIGURE 9-9

WHILE WORKING IN A LONG-TERM *care facility, I particularly noticed an elderly man in a geriatric chair because he was very tall and appeared very uncomfortable. When I talked with him it was obvious that dementing illness had robbed him of significant function. However, he told me that he had operated a farm in the countryside of Ontario, Canada, and that he sold wood for a living. He was confined to the "geriatric" chair because he had a tendency to wander outdoors, and the facility on that day was short staffed.*

Since the man was perfectly fit physically, we devised a care plan for him that involved piling wood into a pile. This activity progressed very well with the elderly man piling the wood by day, and staff pulling the wood pile down by night. One day, however, he became very angry, complaining that "vandals" were messing with his wood pile. We had been caught! So we modified the plan, having the maintenance worker "buy" the completed pile of wood on the condition that the man throw it into the back of the truck. The maintenance staff would then drive off and return to dump a "new" load of wood to be piled. One day we looked out and discovered that the old gentleman was sitting on a stump of wood watching as two other men piled the wood!

Good friends are a comfort.

ONE DAY, A VOLUNTEER *brought in a huge basket of fresh blackberries to a special care unit. But staff looked at it in dismay, not knowing what to do with this gift. An elderly lady classified as requiring total care with grooming and eating activities came into the kitchen and asked if she could make a pie since baking is such a complex activity. I considered the mess we might create, but thought to give it a try. So I put the necessary ingredients out in a row on the counter. With lightning speed, she whipped up the most delicious fruit pie any of us had ever tasted!*

These stories illustrate the power of residual brain function, particularly if the person's longstanding areas of competency are stimulated and supported. Overlearned skills often remain functional even if the person cannot learn new skills, e.g., handshakes, opening doors for women, singing hymns, dancing, cleaning, etc. If staff are skilled and families are supportive, if environments feel like a familiar home, if activities mean something to elderly people, then on occasion magic happens. But it is important when working with people experiencing dementia not to hold out unreasonable hope that this level of achievement will occur routinely.

Meaningful activities require coordination of many levels of skills.

10

Rediscovering the Joy

Tell me—I'll forget
Show me—I may remember
But involve me, and I'll understand
        —Ancient Chinese proverb

I gained valuable insights about dementia from watching my father dig holes in his lovely garden. At first, I was aghast as I watched the destruction. I had always regarded my father as a gardener, and I had a preconceived notion about how he should perform this activity. I could not accept my talented father operating at such a primitive level. I had to do something—draw the problem to his attention, show him how to do it, fix it for him, do it differently, make it turn out the way it was supposed to look!

I think I probably would have continued to think about activity for my father this way had I not been lucky enough at one moment to observe his face as he dug holes: he was as happy as he could be! He laughed and smiled occasionally, and focused on the task with such determination and joy that all the helplessness of dementia—the frustration, confusion, blundering, and ugliness—disappeared. This man was back in control, enjoying a feeling of accomplishment, reveling in an activity that made sense to him.

From that moment I abandoned any notions I had had of ever seeing my father perform at his previous level of functioning. I began to regard all activity as a series of tasks that could be simplified, modified, and broken into pieces that he could find achieveable. For instance, tasks could be shared. I could do the difficult parts and he could manage the simpler ones. If I were sufficiently clever and discreet, he'd never even know we weren't contributing to the task on an equal basis. As I learned more about the destruction taking place in his brain, I was able to devise more and more effective ways of engaging him in activities.

But no matter how creative I was, the activities that he thought up himself engaged him most completely and had the most healing effect. I grew skilled at watching him in action, discovering what it was he was attempting to do, and working along with him to achieve his desired goal.

When my father was involved in an activity of his own choosing, he was not angry or frustrated. He did not swear or throw things about; he was his usual pleasant self. As soon as we moved into an activity requiring me, my mother, or a staff member to be in control—giving instructions, rushing him along, expecting him to perform at levels no longer possible—then the fireworks began. After some weeks of experimentation, I learned to prepare for an activity by leaving objects, supplies, and tasks about for my father to discover on his own. Preparing in that way expanded the variety of things we could do, and gave us both great pleasure. My father liked to do sensible things, helpful things, and messy activities. He liked activities that required him to do the same thing over and over again, like stacking wood or raking leaves. He liked to be outdoors with his dogs. He liked to walk more than I did and watch other people talking and singing. And he loved to have people read to him.

And so I am indebted to my father for early and thorough training in dementia programming. Those experiments from long ago form the basis of the Synergic Program principles that we use in Gentlecare today.

Designing Gentlecare Synergic Programs Using the 5+10 Formula

Activities for people with dementia can be viewed as either simple or complex. *Simple* activities have only one step and are repetitive. Those with a physical component that are related to past life experiences and former life roles are recommended for people with dementia. *Complex*

TEN STEPS THAT HELP A PERSON WITH ACTIVITIES

1. Set the stage: remove distractions; be prepared; and choose an activity within the person's ability to perform.
2. Get the person's attention and agreement to participate before you start.
3. Identify the task.
4. Break the task into its simplest components.
5. Communicate clearly and frequently.
6. Help effectively: assist the person to accomplish the work, rather than doing the task yourself while the person watches.
7. Provide for rest breaks, and praise frequently. Give a nutritional boost during the activity.
8. Watch for fatigue and stress. If you notice signs of fatigue, stop immediately and remove the stressor.
9. Help the person have a successful closure of the activity even though a task is not completed.
10. Celebrate the experience, and praise and validate the effort.

FIGURE 10-1

activities, in contrast, consist of several parts that must fit with one another in order for a task to be completed. They require new learning and sequencing and depend on abstract concepts. They frequently involve large groups of people and the use of complex equipment and supplies.

Complex activities usually challenge performance in ways that may not be possible for someone with dementia. Such activities are often noisy and confusing and contain an element of rush. As a rule, people with dementia find complex activities too difficult and stressful.

In Gentlecare we organize activities indicated by the person's care plan by using the Gentlecare Synergic 5+10 formula. The 15 activities included in the formula are programmed for each individual, and form the basis for each person's daily life. Successful activities for people with dementia are:

- Simple: requires no new learning and consists of one step only without sequencing.

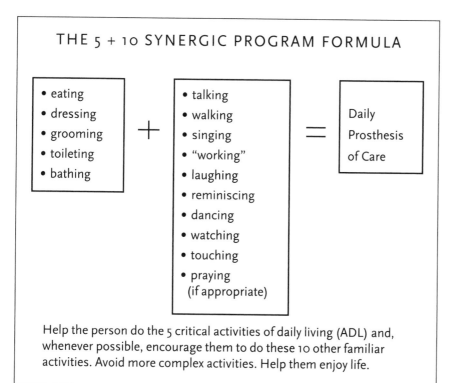

THE 5 + 10 SYNERGIC PROGRAM FORMULA

- eating
- dressing
- grooming
- toileting
- bathing

+

- talking
- walking
- singing
- "working"
- laughing
- reminiscing
- dancing
- watching
- touching
- praying
  (if appropriate)

=

Daily
Prosthesis
of Care

Help the person do the 5 critical activities of daily living (ADL) and, whenever possible, encourage them to do these 10 other familiar activities. Avoid more complex activities. Help them enjoy life.

FIGURE 10-2

- Personal: should provide something that the person with dementia can identify with, that means something to them.
- Realistic: an activity must be a task that "makes sense" to the person engaged in it. It helps if it is a useful activity.
- Stress-free: the activity must be "do-able," and the environment must be supportive.
- Happy and joyful: programs should be fun.
- Successful: the person feels a sense of accomplishment.
- Energizing: not exhausting.
- Brief: lasts no more than 15 minutes, unless the person becomes engrossed in the activity.
- Familiar: based on former life skills, overlearned abilities.
- Functional: related to the person's own needs and life.
- Pertinent and necessary: baskets of peaches or tomatoes that must be used; guests who must be fed or served coffee: a bit of urgency makes the task exciting.

All activities mentioned in this book can be adapted for use at any point in the disease process. In the early stages of the disease, the person can be given greater responsibility, having more functional ability. In the middle stages of the illness, staff and family members need to offer more assistance or simplify the activity. In later stages of dementia, the person may be able only to assist, observe, or make marginal contributions to the activity. The activities indicated are adaptable for use in a person's home, in adult group homes, in assisted living programs, in nursing homes or long-term care facilities, in acute care hospitals, in palliative care situations, and in large psychiatric hospitals.

Dementing illness destroys people's ability to do things—certainly to do things at the level of performance that they formerly achieved. This presents an exceptional challenge for those of us who try to help them normalize their life in spite of dementia: how can we find appropriate, engaging activities that they can successfully carry out, in order to return meaning and satisfaction to their lives?

I have come to believe that the reason it is so difficult to arrange meaningful activities for these people is that we try too hard. We try to engage them in activities that look good, make a big impression, have a recognizable result, and make the person appear normal. We assign responsibility for activity to a few designated people in the organization when we know it takes all of us, families and volunteers included, to compensate for the effects of dementia. We fail to accurately assess and observe the people we work with to see what matters to them and what they are still capable of doing. We create environments devoid of materials or equipment that make normal activity possible. We think people with dementia cannot do anything—and sure enough, given our expectations, they can't!

It's time, long past time, to begin to relax and enjoy these wonderful elderly people. It's time we let them relax and enjoy a normal environment, filled with normal activities. It's time we let them fit in the best way they know how. When we begin to think differently about activity in dementia care, everyone wins.

GENTLECARE ACTIVITIES

These Work	These Don't
Validation: focusing on the person's legacy and accomplishments	Reality orientation
Reminiscing: joining their journey	Current event discussions/quizzes
History maps: large posted maps of local areas with pictures of the person's farm, business, or home. Staff can draw the client's attention to them frequently.	
Role charts: jobs are assigned to each resident with titles attached. For example: Joe—floor cleaner; Molly—juice pourer. Contributions are acknowledged by all.	Bingo
Asset cards: 3 x 5 inch cards, prepared by the family, list interesting bits of information about the person (likes to play the mouth organ, etc.)	Card games/puzzles
Letters and cards	
Hymn sings, war stories, folk songs, lullabies	
Just being in a garden, digging holes, sowing seeds, raking leaves, watering plants, picking flowers, fruit, or vegetables, eating garden produce	Gardening: this is a complex activity, which must be broken down into simple tasks (see list at left). Rules, sequences, specific procedures are too difficult for a person with Alzheimer's disease to accommodate.
Short car drives: in the early stages of the dementia process	Bus excursions: often result in relocation stress, anticipatory anxiety, and exhaustion

FIGURE 10-3

These Work	These Don't
Walking: indoors and outdoors	Aerobic exercises: those that require following directions and mirroring the activities of others
Dancing: with partners, line-dancing, or group dancing	
Marching	Circle groups (see above explanation)
Hugging: shoulder hugs work best	
Touching	Ball toss: or any activity that involves tracking a moving object
Handshakes and greetings	
Laughing: at funny situations, costumes	Sports: or any activity that requires sequencing or good hand/eye coordination
Massage: of hands, feet, back, shoulders	
Rocking chairs, gliders	Fire drills
Story telling	TV
Reading out loud: from Bibles, *Reader's Digest,* weather reports, recipes	Background music (Muzak)
	Stereo as background music or news
Old photo albums, large blow-ups of old photos	Public address systems
Slides: of family outings, animals, children	Large group activities
Small-group sing-songs, hymn sings	Big entertainment groups
Live music with one or two performers (roving troubadours)	
Dogs, cats, ducks, rabbits: all animals must be cared for by staff	Fish, birds: because they can't be touched and require a lot of care
Tasting food: ask a person's opinion; exchange recipes	

These Work	These Don't
Kneading: using pre-mixed dough (good for men)	
Watching cooking: men love to watch cooking, jam making, bread or pie baking	
Baking: prepared mixes, bread mix, making turkey stuffing	Baking: this is a complex task that must be broken down into simpler component parts
Stirring	
Scooping	
Rolling	
Decorating cookies, cake	
Folding, mending: children's clothing rather than towels	
Eating	
Serving	
Braiding, unraveling knitted goods	Crafts, making decorations
Tearing: paper, cloth	Pottery, ceramics
Cutting: paper, cloth	Sensory stimulation activities in kits, boxes, or put away in closets
Polishing: silver, copper, wood objects, jewelry	Aromatherapy in small containers
Moving: boxes, chairs, books	Taking part in organized events that the person must fit into and perform at predetermined levels
Dish washing, car washing: these activities have to be real and dramatic	
Dish drying	
Hand laundry	
Hanging out laundry on a clothesline	
Winding wool or cord	
Scrubbing	
"Helping" someone else	

These Work	These Don't
Rummaging: magazines, purses, old cards, hats, scarves, postcards, jewelry, little boxes; treasure chests filled with pictures, lace, buttons, shells, jewelry, hats, scarves, clothing; chests of drawers filled with treasures	Supplies locked in cupboards
	Activities that must be initiated and controlled by staff
Materials prepared for work activities like tidying, moving, packing in boxes, cleaning, washing	Activities that are abstract (whose end products are not easily understood)
Bookshelves with books and newspapers	Activities that require sequencing, in which one part must be completed before the next part is undertaken
Cupboards with dishes/cutlery, produce	Activities that stress order, cleanliness, tidiness
Hang on racks: rows of purses, aprons, hats, jewelry—as both wall decorations and enticements to activity; fill pockets with little treasures	

Gardening and yard work provide opportunities to do former favorite activities.

This lady was lonely until her "friend" came into her life.

Gardening is very complex so it is good when a friend helps out.

A dog is truly man's best friend.

Polishing a favorite saddle gives hours of pleasure.

Nothing makes people with dementia glow more than children.

A kitchen brings back wonderful memories.

Comfort bags and purses provide safe places for treasures.

Part Four

NUTRITION IN DEMENTIA CARE

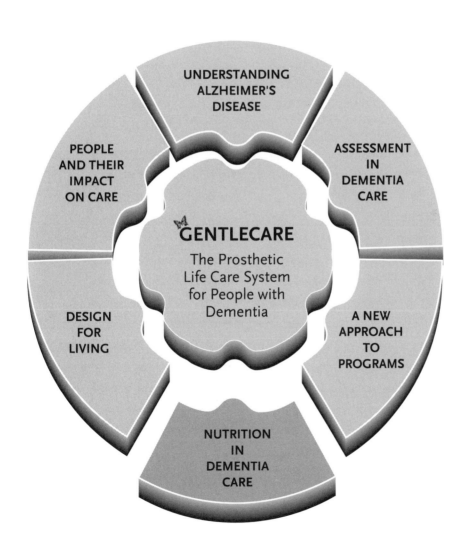

11

The Gentlecare Philosophy of Nutritional Care

(The nutritional material for the Gentlecare paradigm has been developed in collaboration with Lorna Seaman, RD)

*All human history attests
that happiness for man
depends on dinner.*
—Lord Byron

Food is one of life's greatest pleasures, and elderly people are particularly appreciative of mealtime. Throughout history and in all parts of the world, sitting down to a meal has been a time for social interaction, to nourish ourselves and replenish our energy, and an occasion for celebration.

Our work activities are often structured around mealtimes, providing us with a time to satisfy our hunger, rest and visit with friends before resuming our duties. But it's probably the meals associated with special occasions that stay in our memories—the birthdays, anniversaries, and family-friend get-togethers when food has provided the focal point. Many special holidays are linked to certain foods: here in North America the turkey at Christmas, the pumpkin pie at Thanksgiving. Every cultural group the world over has developed its own foods for times of celebration.

Although much of the work with meal preparation and presentation has traditionally been the responsibility of women, men have taken pride in food production and being able to "put food on the table" for their families. Thus when food becomes the focus of therapy, it works equally well for male and female clients.

Across a continuum of planning, production, and celebration, food opens up all sorts of possibilities for involvement and synergic programming. For example:

- discussion of garden designs and choices of produce; meal plans, menus, comparing cookbooks and recipes
- planting, tending, and harvesting the garden; baking and cooking activities such as bread-making, cookie-making; food preparation such as husking corn, peeling potatoes or apples, hulling berries
- activities around meal presentation: setting and/or clearing tables
- planning and decorating for special events such as Christmas; Canadian and American Thanksgiving; Diwali, the Indian Festival of Light; St. Patrick's Day for those of Irish heritage; or Chinese New Year when the greeting is "Kung Hey Fat Choi" (Cantonese for "Wishing You Prosperity")
- planning seasonal socials and harvest fairs such as a strawberry tea, a corn roast, a fall fair

Thus food, in addition to nourishing our clients, becomes a fascinating source of interest and provides opportunities for therapy for older people.

Gentlecare has developed a radical philosophy of nutritional care. The Gentlecare paradigm focuses on using food as a therapeutic tool to help our elderly clients afflicted with aging and dementia issues. Gentlecare considers nutritional care to be a major dementia frontier.

Why are these ideas so radical?

Before we present the Gentlecare view of food, feeding and nutrition I think it helpful to have a quick look at the traditional view of food service personnel and nursing staff regarding the preparation, presentation of meals, and clean up afterwards. A review of the list below indicates that the concerns of the clients are not paramount with either food service or nursing. The problems of food service and nursing include:

- set up time, meal time and clean up time
- clients lined up waiting for meals to be served

- cleaning issues
- clients getting too little or too much food
- noise and crowds
- temperature of food being served
- providing menu choices
- stealing and hoarding of food by clients
- how to get the dishes cleaned in time for the next meal
- management of angry clients

The resolution of problems emerging from food and its consumption always favor the views of management. Little concern is focused on how *food* might help solve client problems. *In Gentlecare the food focus is on the design of a nutritional care plan for each individual that fulfills his or her need for a continuous, even flow of energy and nutrients throughout the day.* Food is seen by the proponents of Gentlecare as a powerful tool to help clients cope with the challenges facing them.

Why is food so important?

The food we eat is essential for life. Millions of cells within our bodies convert food into energy that enables us to manage the myriad and complex activities of daily life. *For the aging person afflicted with dementia, the need for adequate supplies of energy, delivered at regular intervals, is essential to prevent fatigue, enhance performance, avoid nutritional low points, and prevent catastrophic behavior.* Thinking of food as an energy source opens up an entirely new and vital way of helping clients.

How do we use food as a therapeutic tool?

Our goal is to make nutrition as important a therapeutic tool as medication or any other aspect of care.

How often do we talk about the challenge of bathing in health care? We have only to hear the screams of an elder being bathed by strangers, or see a member of the care staff bruised or injured from an altercation with a client upset by the intrusion of a stranger into their personal space.

The Gentlecare theory is that these incidents are often due to exhaustion, metabolic depletion, and unreasonable demands made on clients to perform in ways they are no longer able. Gentlecare practitioners make a direct link between the stress of these performance demands and the client's ability or inability to perform the challenging activity.

We believe that food strategically offered can often change behavior in surprisingly positive ways. Consider the strategic use of a cup of tea or coffee, or a high-energy snack given before a particularly frightening or unpleasant task. Consider the sheer comfort and pleasure of a favorite food or treat that triggers an important memory and attracts the client's attention.

Gentlecare makes a direct connection between the behavior exhibited by the client and the intervention we select to help that client. We suggest a whole new repertoire of food-related interventions that can be substituted for other types of interventions that are not always helpful. Offerings of food and beverages are almost always successful!

Gentlecare proposes a modified menu-planning process.

The total daily nutritional requirement is divided into three small, well-balanced meals and five "nutrition boosts," with approximately the same nutritional value.

These food events have each been given descriptive names to help care staff distinguish the purpose of each one.

The first meal is breakfast, which is served at three separate times (see chapter 12 for all the time suggestions) to three different types of clients, the "Early Birds," "Regular," and the "Sleepyhead."

The second meal, lunch or dinner, is served at midday.

The third meal, dinner or supper, is served between late afternoon and early evening.

The five "nutrition boosts" supplement the three meals and are called:

• Wake-up and orientation boost

- Mid-morning boost
- Mid-afternoon boost
- Bedtime boost
- Night owl boost

The Gentlecare program does not encourage people to eat whatever they want whenever they want and, it should not be confused with "grazing." "Grazing" is the dreadful practice of making buffet food available all the time and permitting clients to eat what they please. The practice of "grazing" is particularly inappropriate for cognitively impaired clients because they lack the judgment needed to make complex choices and are often too physically frail to manage buffet-style eating.

How does Gentlecare suggest making a paradigm shift in the way food is offered?

Try sitting on a low chair at a high table to personally experience how frustrating this can be.

Gentlecare has developed the **Nutritional Care Cycle** which helps care providers organize the nutritional component of the client's care plan.

Step 1: The Personal Profile informs us about each individual's former life patterns:
- wake-up times
- timing of meals and period of time allowed for eating
- favorite foods
- typical amounts of food and drink consumed at each meal
- preferred times for rest and exercise after meals

Step 2: The Clinical Assessment provides information about the client's particular nutritional needs and clinical concerns.

Step 3: reviews external stressors on the client that impede performance.

Step 4: develops the nutritional care component of the client's Prosthetic Care Plan.

The Gentlecare concept of the **24-Hour Nutrition Clock** recommends small, well-balanced meals and nutrition boosts spread evenly throughout the day. See Chapter 12 for a detailed description of this program.

In order to successfully implement the client's nutritional care plan, Dietary Staff must take the lead in changing the way facility staff and clients think about food. As we stated earlier, the primary focus of food preparation and delivery has been from the worker's perspective and not the client's. Clients need help in modifying their eating habits so as to enhance and stabilize their energy levels.

Gentlecare promotes the nutrional needs of the client first. The primary object is the provision of small meals and boosts throughout the day, evening, and night. Meals and boosts that are nutrional, easy to recognize as food, and are served in an appropriate environment. This is the challenge in practicing Nutrional Care the Gentlecare way.

In Chapter 12 the reader will be introduced to the Nutritional Care Cycle and to the concept of the Nutritional Clock and how the use of these structural elements can be exploited for the benefit of the client.

Chapter 13 covers "the magic of Gentlecare meals": how the theory of Gentlecare is applied to the practice of dining.

Before we introduce our 24-hour Nutrition Clock Program, we need to be more knowledgeable about the repercussions of aging, dementia, and mental illness on the nutritional status of the elderly. We also need to review the stages in the physiological act of eating.

Background information on nutrition and aging

Aging and certain diseases that afflict older people can significantly change the experience of eating, affecting both the enjoyment and the nutritional benefits of food. Changes in vision, physical mobility, and the senses of taste and smell affect the older person's ability to enjoy this most basic and life-enhancing activity. Barriers to eating properly—that is, eating the right types of food in the right amounts at appropriate intervals—can dramatically affect both health and quality of life. For example:

- Significant numbers of older people suffer from *dysphagia* (difficulty in swallowing).
- The aging process affects dentition: 50 percent of people have no teeth by age 65, which rises to 67 percent by age 75. Most people

compensate for this problem by using dentures; however, when people are cognitively impaired, management of dentures becomes a challenge.

- As people age, the muscles necessary for chewing lose strength. Eating becomes more difficult and requires more energy. It is harder to control liquids as the tongue, cheeks, and lips become weaker. These difficulties can be made worse by the use of certain drugs.

- The production of saliva (xerostomia) is reduced as people age. This decreases the effectiveness of the digestive process, the transportation of food, and the adhesion of dentures to the gums. Warm environments decrease saliva flows. Some medications decrease saliva flows, but others can have the opposite effect.

- There is a 60-percent reduction in the number of taste buds on the tongue as people age. After age 60, therefore, the sense of taste is less acute, and there is a consequent loss of enjoyment in eating and appetite. In addition to registering taste sensations (sweet, sour, salty, and bitter), the tongue is responsible both for moving food toward the stomach and for cleaning the mouth. The effectiveness of the tongue is diminished with age.

- With aging, there are marked reductions in the senses of smell, taste, and touch, together with a reduction in the cough reflex. These changes lead to increased incidents of aspiration (drawing into the lungs) of food and liquid by elderly people, which can result in pneumonia and even death.

- The sense of taste consists of sensations from the mouth, which are interpreted jointly by the sensory cortex of the brain and the hypothalamus—both of which are damaged by Alzheimer's disease.

- Aging affects vision and perception, making it difficult for older people to distinguish the presence of food on dishes, to differentiate among food types, and to use utensils effectively.

- Finally, it is estimated that the efficiency of metabolic processes is diminished by up to 20 percent as people age. Kidney function can be diminished by half, highlighting the critical issue of dehydration and the importance of hydration programs. The excessive use of medication by elderly people can seriously exacerbate metabolic problems.

The changes due to aging alone are a sufficient challenge to good nutrition. Moreover, the majority of elderly people receiving health care services will also experience dementing illness. Significant numbers of them will also suffer from some form of mental illness, such as depression. The impact on eating of this complex combination of problems requires a fresh look at the role of nutrition in the care of elderly people.

The dysfunction caused by dementia profoundly affects the eating process. As a result, the energy needed for the performance of the complex tasks of daily living is severely compromised. In Gentlecare, we believe this energy drain is a major contributing factor in incidents of catastrophic behavior. People with dementing illnesses live in a world of anxiety, frustration, and fear. Such psychological chaos depletes energy, and if this is not replaced through good nutrition, people become increasingly defenseless in dealing with encroaching stress and turmoil. The factors that cause stress and fear are referred to as iatrogenic factors.

Specific dysfunctions such as *agnosia* (inability to recognize familiar sensory stimuli) and *apraxia* (inability to initiate purposeful movement) make it difficult for people with dementia to access their food.

The syndrome often referred to as "bulimia" is worth a more detailed discussion. The condition "bulimia nervosa" refers to repeated episodes of binge eating followed by purging, whereas a "binge eating disorder" refers to excessive eating that is not followed by purging. The latter is the pattern sometimes observed in persons with dementia. Bulimia is a good example of a complex syndrome which makes assessment and care so challenging.

It is important to note that due to memory loss, the person may forget that he has eaten and give the impression of "bingeing." This is a different issue. If someone forgets having eaten, the Gentlecare practice is to offer a light snack and distraction from food-related activities.

When these problems are combined with loss of memory and degradation of the senses of taste and smell, it is little wonder that malnutrition can occur.

Malnutrition will exacerbate all physical problems and can bring on acute dementia. Acute dementia can be caused by dehydration, malnutrition, a Vitamin B12 deficit, infection, or drug toxicity. Acute dementia differs from chronic dementia in that it will respond to treatment and the effects can be reversed (Review Chapter 4, Figure 4-1). Acute dementia produces symptoms similar to chronic dementia and is often referred to as "pseudo-dementia." If acute dementia is not immediately treated, serious problems, including death, can ensue.

Dehydration directly affects the quality of elderly people's lives. Measuring appropriate water intake is problematic: How often have liquids been given? By whom? How much was actually consumed? Often elderly people cannot indicate that they are thirsty, so caregivers must always assume that they need water or other liquids.

The Act of Eating

Most of us take the act of eating for granted. We eat when we feel hungry. Apart from awareness of the pleasurable feeling provided by our senses, eating is an automatic process. We see food, take what we want, put it in our mouth, swallow it, and feel satisfied. We repeat this process at least three, and often many more, times each day and never stop to consider the complexity of the process. But of the five ADLs, eating is the most demanding in terms of client participation.

A human being swallows about 600 times each day...350 times while awake, 200 times while eating, and 50 times while sleeping.

First Cognitive Stage
- The person who is eating must be aware of the activity taking place. Orienting information must be given frequently.
- The ambiance in the dining area must reflect the purpose of the room.
- The person must be willing to participate in the activity of eating. However, appetite may be reduced, there may be discomfort in eat-

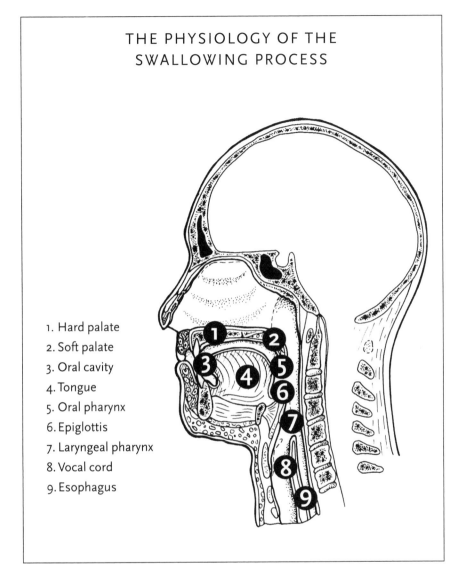

THE PHYSIOLOGY OF THE SWALLOWING PROCESS

1. Hard palate
2. Soft palate
3. Oral cavity
4. Tongue
5. Oral pharynx
6. Epiglottis
7. Laryngeal pharynx
8. Vocal cord
9. Esophagus

FIGURE 11-1

ing with a large crowd; or there may be a perception of being unable to afford to go into such a big "restaurant."

• The person must agree to accept assistance. A bond or relationship needs to exist between the person eating and the person helping.

• The person who is eating must feel comfortable and secure, and must be allowed sufficient time to participate in and enjoy the activity.

Swallowing

The act of swallowing requires coordination of several nerves, 26 muscles of the mouth, the pharynx and esophagus, and the ability of the mind to focus on the activity.

Preparatory Stage

- The person's mouth and teeth should be clean, and dentures (if used) should be in place. Dentures are only effective when they are in the person's mouth!
- Check to ensure that the person has no mouth pain or discomfort.

Ensure that the person is in a comfortable, functional position, with his head in a neutral position or tilted forward and slightly downward: eating occurs in a flexion position.

Chairs that are too low or tables that are too high cause the person to stretch into an extension position, or to strain to raise the arms high enough to reach items on the table. Over time, this will cause exhaustion, which is a significant contributor to giving up on independent eating and requiring assistance at meals.

Ensure that each individual has utensils appropriate to his specific level of function. Where appropriate, try the following:

- Use plates with lips.
- Use sectioned plates.
- Try using deep bowls instead of plates.
- Build up the handles of cutlery to permit a better grip.
- Experiment with specially designed cups and glasses with wide openings and covers.
- Serve liquids in cups or mugs with large protruding handles.
- Use rubber-coated cutlery for people who bite down on utensils.
- Use plain, solid dishes with curved edges.
- Ensure a good color contrast between object and background.

Oral Stage

- The food is chewed and mixed with saliva.
- The tongue gathers food from around the mouth, teeth, and gums.
- The food is formed into a bolus at the tip of the tongue.

- The lips close and the cheeks tighten.
- The tongue squeezes the bolus against the hard palate.
- The food bolus is propelled toward the pharynx.
- The swallowing reflex is triggered.

Pharyngeal Stage

As this stage of eating:
- Respiration is temporarily halted.
- The epiglottis (the cartilage that covers the opening of the larynx) closes.
- The food bolus moves from the mouth into the esophagus by the process of *peristalsis* (contractions and relaxations of the muscular walls of the digestive tract).

GENTLECARE   Best Practice

> Before you assist your next client with eating, take a mouthful of your favorite food and work it through the seven stages of eating. This exercise will help you understand how difficult mealtime is for those elderly people experiencing dementia, and how much time it takes to eat a meal.

Esophageal Stage

- The food bolus is propelled toward the stomach.

Preparation for Digestion

Gentlecare recommends the following strategies to assist in effective digestion:
- The person maintains a comfortable upright position for at least half an hour; or
- The person is involved in a gentle walking program.
  This activity is referred to in Gentlecare as "Rest—to digest."

Cognitive Aspects of Digestion

- Avoid rush, noise, or confusion. There is often a great hurry to clean up dining rooms after meals and return dishes and utensils to the kitchen. Residents may be rushed through meals to accommodate the work schedules of food service and housekeeping staff. It is essential that all personnel understand how important and difficult mealtimes are for elderly people with dementia. Sufficient time must be allocated for staff to carry out the necessary cleaning tasks without cutting into or rushing residents' mealtime.

- Do not immediately involve the person who has just eaten in any complex activity.
- Reduce stress of any kind.

Tips for Safe Swallowing

Assessment

Each person should have had an appropriate disease assessment and an assessment of functional abilities.

Positioning

The person eating should be seated upright, with his head flexed slightly forward. If the person is eating while in bed, ensure that the head and shoulders are supported at an angle of no less than 60 degrees.

In some facilities, housekeeping staff are encouraged to work around people as they would in their own home.

Presentation of Food

- Use a metal spoon, not plastic, or syringes or straws.
- Offer only one teaspoonful at a time.
- Allow sufficient time to chew and swallow.
- Watch for difficulty with swallowing, food drooling out of mouth, coughing, or choking.

- Any client who has been assessed as having difficulties with swallowing should be offered assistance on a one-to-one basis. Do not offer additional food unless food has been swallowed successfully—i.e. the bolus of food has been moved from the mouth to the stomach. This can only be accurately assessed by observation of the client by staff on a one-to-one basis.

Coughing/Choking

When a coughing episode begins, the individual should bend forward at the waist and lower his chin to his chest. Do not cover the mouth with a cloth or napkin as this causes the person to draw back into a position of extension, thus causing a choke.

> **GENTLECARE Practice Tip**
>
> Check each chair and table for an effective functional relationship. Assess each individual to ensure that arms and shoulders clear the tabletop easily, and that all items are within easy reach. Place foam boosters under small or short people, and stools under their feet.

The force of the cough should clear the airway, and the position of the larynx will protect the airway from being reinvaded. Do not interfere unless the food becomes lodged in the larynx and the person cannot breathe. In such a case, the Heimlich maneuver should be performed.

Heimlich Manoeuver

To carry out the Heimlich manoeuver, approach the choking person from behind; reach around the person's body and lock your hands just below the rib cage. Give quick upward and backward jerks to the diaphragm. This provides a blast of air through the vocal cords (airway) which may blow out the obstruction. Refer to policy and procedures of individual institutions for specific strategies.

12

GENTLECARE Nutritional Care Planning

It's good food and not fine words
that keep me alive.
Molière

Gentlecare has developed a process called the Nutritional Care Cycle to help care providers organize the various data and strategies concerning client food intake. This practical plan enables staff to provide elderly clients with dementing illnesses the nutrients necessary for healthy living. Emphasis is placed on both the benefits of sound nutritional choices and the pleasures of the eating experience.

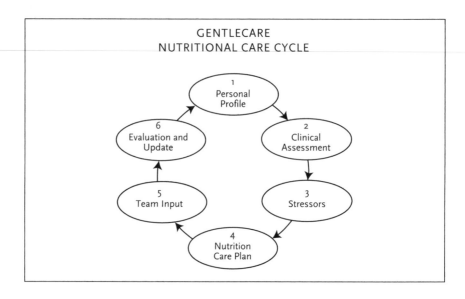

GENTLECARE
NUTRITIONAL CARE CYCLE

1 Personal Profile
2 Clinical Assessment
3 Stressors
4 Nutrition Care Plan
5 Team Input
6 Evaluation and Update

FIGURE 12-1

Step 1: Personal Profile

Family members can contribute essential information regarding food preferences and idiosyncrasies. Their knowledge of the person, advice, and experience provide invaluable information. Posing critical questions helps the staff develop a care plan that truly meets each individual's needs:

- **Who is this person?**
  - What is the extent of family involvement in caregiving?
  - What is the cultural and social background?
  - What are his/her eating habits?
  - Which foods are familiar favorites?
  - Are there any food allergies?
  - Is dementing illness affecting the person's nutritional status as determined by the assessment process?
  - Does the person have difficulty communicating?
  - Which sensory deficits are affecting the quality of life? (e.g., vision, hearing, taste, smell, touch)

Tell me what you eat and I'll tell you what you are.

—ANSELME BRILLAT-SAVARIN

Step 2: Clinical Assessment

*"We do not stop playing because we grow old;
we grow old because we stop playing."*
    —Peter C. Newman

The next step in the cycle is the clinical assessment: a process that reviews the diagnoses, medical history, clinical data, and any physiological issues affecting nutritional status.

Gentlecare practice places emphasis on assessing three different processes which may be occurring in the person at the same time: aging, dementia, and mental illness.

The aging process affects all body systems and each system needs to be taken into account in the assessment.

Three quarters of elderly persons will also experience dementing illness.

*All sorrows are less
with bread.*

—MIGUEL CERVANTES

Researchers suggest that alarming numbers of elders who access health services are experiencing depression. The condition often goes undetected and unmanaged even though effective medications and treatments are available.

When seniors are assessed and asked about what is important to them, they will respond consistently that what they want most is to be needed, loved, and respected. When these needs are not being met, depression may result.

Assessment is a very complex and challenging exercise. If done thoroughly and thoughtfully, this process can result in optimum care for elderly people experiencing dementia. Many issues must be examined:

- **Diagnoses.** It is important to have a clear picture of the person's medical condition and the cause and degree of dysfunction (e.g., cognitive impairment, loss of communication skills) when building the Nutrition Care Plan.
- **Effects of Dementing Illness.** Dementing illness results in deficits that affect a person's ability to manage meals, such as
  – altered consciousness (inability to process information)
  – distractibility
  – poor judgment
  – decreased awareness of and orientation to people, place, and time
  – decreased control of body function (apraxia)
  – lack of ability to distinguish between food and other substances
  – altered vision/perception
  – changes in personality
- **Laboratory data** provide information that can be very helpful in assessing the level of nutritional risk (e.g., albumin, hemoglobin, red blood cells, potassium levels)
- **Medications review.** Medications can affect appetite, ability to eat, bowel function, and absorption of nutrients.
- **Alterations in sensory function**—i.e., deficits in vision, hearing, perception, taste, or smell
- **Musculo-skeletal dysfunction** makes it difficult for the person to get

to the dining room or to position themselves comfortably. Persons afflicted with arthritis, osteoporosis, Parkinson's disease, and Huntington's chorea are particularly compromised.

- A **weight review** will provide important information. Weight loss may be due to a number of factors including:
  - the distress of relocating away from the family home
  - unfamiliar foods
  - confusing or frightening eating situations
  - the expenditure of large amounts of energy in walking due to anxiety, agitation, and night waking
- **Food intake/appetite.** People may binge on food and gain weight. This is not because they have become greedy, but rather is a side effect of the illness. Equally, they may experience an acceleration in metabolism or undertake increased activity and lose weight.
- A **therapeutic diet** is a specific meal plan prescribed by the physician and/or dietitian which regulates the quantities and types of foods and nutrients allowed. These diets form the nutritional component of the treatment of the person's medical condition (e.g., restriction of carbohydrates in the treatment of diabetes or the provision of extra quantities of protein and total calories in the treatment of poor nutritional status). Such diets are sometimes required by people with dementia.

  However, many people with dementia are relatively healthy. "Special" diets can actually *create* eating problems (e.g., when favorite foods are withheld because of a diabetic diet order, resulting in inadequate food intake, lowered energy and strength, and increased levels of stress). Gentlecare recommends that therapeutic diet orders be reviewed very carefully on a quarterly basis by the physician and the interdisciplinary team. Many such orders are carry-overs from another period in a person's life, and the conditions that prompted the diet may have changed in the interim. There is a current trend toward easing the restrictions wherever possible.
- **Swallowing function.** Does this person require modification of food

textures because of poor teeth or condition of the mouth, or has there been a diagnosis of dysphagia? This is a particularly contentious issue: all too often, because of staff or family concerns about choking, all of a person's meals may be pureed.

This precaution can deprive people of much of the enjoyment of eating. It is important to note that one swallowing or choking incident, no matter how frightening, does not represent dysphagia (defined as a swallowing impairment that occurs as a result of an anatomical or physiological abnormality). Assessment by a speech/language pathologist will determine whether the choking was due to a physiological or cognitive dysfunction, or caused by poor feeding techniques, poor positioning, or stress. A recommendation for modification in texture of food and specific feeding techniques will be prescribed on the basis of this assessment.

I ONCE WORKED *in a hospital where every meal was scraped into a bowl, mixed with cold milk, and served as a lukewarm porridge regardless of the people's ability to chew or swallow.*

- **Eating function.** The team needs to determine what, if any, level of assistance the person needs to be able to eat adequately. The following questions must be answered:
  - If food is presented appropriately, can the person manage eating independently?
  - Does the person respond better if food is presented one item at a time? Or is a regular meal presentation more helpful?
  - Does the person only need help initially? Can he then follow through on his own?
  - Does the person need periodic "kick-starts" to combat apraxia (defined as the inability to carry out skilled and purposeful movement)? If so, what type of prompt works best—verbal, physical, or mimed?
  - Does the prompting need to be sporadic only, or given fairly regularly throughout the meal?

THIRST

- Thirst is a signal designed to prevent serious dehydration.
- The part of the brain that controls thirst is the limbic system.
- As the disease progresses and affects the hypothalmus, the person may suffer from a sensation of excessive thirst.
- Other deficits in the brain's function may result in the inability to articulate the need for fluids.
- Thus, it is possible that part of wandering, lethargic, irritable, and confused behaviors can be attributed to unsatisfied sensations of thirst and/or actual dehydration.
- Therefore, provision of adequate fluids when desired and in response to behavioral signals is a high priority.
- An effort to reduce incontinence with the restriction of fluids may result in dehydration, and in fact achieve the opposite of what was intended.

FIGURE 12-2

    – Does the person need total assistance with eating?

    – Does the person need a liquid meal in a cup?

    – Can the person feed himself if bowls, spoons, wet cloths under the plate, or other adaptive equipment is used?

    – Can the person eat independently if offered finger foods rather than foods requiring the use of utensils?

- **Nausea/vomiting.** If nausea and vomiting occurs nutritional status can be seriously compromised. The cause may be a side effect of a medication, or due to stressors or an intolerance of a type of food, such as fatty foods. A persistent problem should be investigated by the physician and the care team to determine its cause.

- **Fluid intake/hydration status.** Dehydration can result in acute dementia. Lack of water can cause symptoms similar to those seen in Alzheimer's disease. People with dementia can't always recognize thirst or ask for a drink if they feel thirsty (see Figures Fig.12-2 and 12-3), so it is important to monitor their liquid intake.

- **Constipation.** Physiological changes that often accompany aging such as a decrease in mobility, activity, and the urge to defecate contribute to the prevalence of constipation in older adults. Other

SIGNS OF DEHYDRATION

- fatigue
- confusion
- IRRITABILITY
- dizziness
- headaches
- low energy
- dry mouth
- dry skin
- loose, wrinkled skin
- sunken eyes
- low urine output (less than two cups)
- weakened muscles leading to falls

FIGURE 12-3

associated factors are decreased fluid and fibre intake, a history of poor bowel habits, laxative abuse, the effects of certain medications, or a combination of several of these factors. In the nutrition assessment the causes of constipation should be identified.

- **Incontinence.** It is a myth that incontinence is a normal consequence of aging. Age-related changes in the lower urinary tract may make older people more likely to experience incontinence, but for most older people, even the very old and frail, incontinence can be treated.

    There are a number of excellent protective undergarments available which can help to keep residents mobile, enhance incontinence management, and protect against the risk of skin breakdown.

    A variety of problems can cause persistent incontinence—for example, weakness of the bladder, the sphincter, or the muscles that support the bladder, or neurological disorders and immobility.

    There are several types of incontinence. Those most commonly found in the elderly suffering with dementia are:

- **Urge incontinence,** defined as the involuntary loss of urine because the person can't control urination long enough to locate the toilet and remove clothing in time. Clients with dementia are helped when doors to bathrooms are clearly marked with pictures, not words or pictograms.

- **Unconscious or reflex incontinence**, defined as the loss of urine without warning or sensory awareness—usually the result of neurological disease.
- **Functional incontinence**, defined as the loss of urine which occurs when people who would have normal urinary control can't get to the toilet in time because their movements are slowed by arthritis or other physical or mental disorders.
- **Skin breakdown with resulting decubitus ulcers or pressure sores** is a major concern in caring for the frail elderly. The nutritional status of a resident is a key factor in assessing the level of risk of skin breakdown.

   Pressure sores are categorized according to their severity by stages as in burn wounds (i.e. from Stage 1 through 4). Identification of the level of risk and/or the presence of a pressure sore and the level of severity should be included in the nutritional assessment.
- **The Braden Scale for Predicting Pressure Sore Risk** developed by Barbara Braden and Nancy Bergstrom is an excellent tool used in many long-term care facilities as a component of the quarterly assessment process (see Figure 12-4).
- There is **loss of body mass** in the late stages of dementia. It is important to note that no amount of supplementary feeding can reverse this deterioration.

Collection of this data will help care providers assess the person's level of nutritional risk. In Gentlecare practice, the person's level of risk is measured not only by physical status, but also by cognitive abilities, leading to a much more effective Nutritional Care Plan. See Classification of Nutritional Risk (Figure 12-5) to determine the level of risk for each individual.

BRADEN SCALE FOR PREDICTING PRESSURE SORE RISK

Mild Risk: Total Score = 15–18   High Risk: Total Score = 10–12
Moderate Risk: Total Score =13–14   Severe Risk: Total score = or <9

Patient's Name_____   Evaluator's Name_____ Date__/__/__ Score_____

SENSORY PERCEPTION Ability to respond meaningfully to pressure-related discomfort	**1. Completely limited** Unresponsive (does not moan, flinch, or gasp) to painful stimuli due to diminished level of consciousness or sedation *or* limited ability to feel pain over most of body	**2. Very limited** Responds only to painful stimuli. Cannot communicate discomfort except by moaning or restlessness *or* has a sensory impairment which limits the ability to feel pain or discomfort over half of body	**3. Slightly limited** Responds to verbal commands, but cannot always communicate discomfort or the need to be turned *or* has some sensory impairment which limits ability to feel pain or discomfort in one or two extremities	**4. No impairment** Responds to verbal commands. Has no sensory deficit which would limit ability to feel or voice pain or discomfort	
MOISTURE Degree to which skin is exposed to moisture	**1. Constantly moist** Skin is kept moist almost constantly by perspiration, urine, etc. Dampness is detected every time patient is moved or turned	**2. Very moist** Skin is often, but not always, moist. Linens must be changed at least once a shift	**3. Occasionally moist** Skin is occasionally moist, requiring an extra linen change approximately once a day	**4. Rarely moist** Skin is usually dry, linen only requires changing at routine intervals	
ACTIVITY Degree of physical activity	**1. Bedfast** Confined to bed	**2. Chairfast** Ability to walk severely limited or non-existent, cannot bear own weight and/or must be assisted into chair or wheelchair	**3. Walks occasionally** Walks occasionally during day, but for very short distances, with or without assistance. Spends majority of each shift in bed or chair	**4. Walks frequently** Walks outside room at least twice a day and inside room at least once every two hours during waking hours	
MOBILITY Ability to change and control body position	**1. Completely immobile** Does not make even slight changes in body or extremity position without assistance	**2. Very limited** Makes occasional slight changes in body or extremity position but unable to make frequent or significant changes independently	**3. Slightly limited** Makes frequent though slight changes in body or extremity position independently	**4. No limitation** Makes major and frequent changes in position without assistance	
NUTRITION Usual food intake pattern	**1. Very poor** Never eats a complete meal. Rarely eats more than half of any food portion offered. Eats two servings or less of protein (meat or dairy products) per day. Takes fluids poorly. Does not take a liquid dietary supplement *or* is NPO (receiving no foods by mouth) and/or maintained on clear liquids or IV for more than five days	**2. Probably inadequate** Rarely eats a complete meal and generally eats about half of any food offered. Protein intake includes only three servings of meat or dairy per day. Occasionally will take a dietary supplement *or* receives less than optimum amount of liquid diet or tube feeding	**3. Adequate** Eats over half of most meals. Eats a total of four servings of protein (meat, dairy products) per day. Occasionally will refuse a meal but will usually take a supplement when offered, *or* is on a tube feeding or TPN (total parenteral nutrition or intravenous feeding) regimen which probably meets most of nutritional needs	**4. Excellent** Eats most of every meal. Never refuses a meal. Usually eats a total of four or more servings of meat and dairy products. Occasionally eats between meals. Does not require supplements	
FRICTION AND SHEAR Abrasions caused by contact with clothing, bedding or other surfaces	**1. Problem** Requires moderate to maximum assistance with moving. Complete lifting without sliding against sheets is impossible. Frequently slides down in bed or chair, requiring frequent repositioning with maximum assistance. Spasticity, contractures or agitation leads to almost constant friction	**2. Potential problem** Moves feebly or requires maximum assistance. During a move skin probably slides to some extent against sheets, chair, or other devices. Maintains relatively good position in chair or bed most of the time but occasionally slides down	**3. No apparent problem** Moves in bed and in chair independently and has sufficient muscle strength to lift up completely during move. Maintains good position in bed or chair		
TOTAL SCORE					

Source: Barbara Braden and Nancy Bergstrom. Copyright 1988. Reprinted with permission.

FIGURE 12-4

CLASSIFICATION OF NUTRITIONAL RISK

COGNITIVE RISK FACTORS	PHYSIOLOGICAL RISK FACTORS
LOW RISK	
Early evidence of: • memory loss • confusion • disorientation regarding time and place • distractability • hyperactivity • alteration in appetite, thirst control mechanism • alterations in perception of sensory stimulation • heightened sensitivity to stimulation	• no recent significant weight change • moderately underweight and stable • overweight, not on redusing diet and no other concerns • eats independently, able to walk, sit at table • consumes > ¾ of food and fluid at each meal • fair appetite and intake, no other concerns • uses regular utensils and dishes • consumes a variety of food types and textures from all food groups • no food allergies
MEDIUM RISK	
• increased memory loss • no sense of time • increased confusion • loss of orientation to place • visual field neglect • inability to read • minimal to moderate evidence of agnosia, abulia, aphasia, anomia, and apraxia	• chewing/swallowing difficulties • needs prosthetic aids and/or assistance for eating • chronic constipation/diarrhea • persistent nausea and/or vomiting • moderately underweight and stable • poor or erratic appetite/food intake • poor fluid intake/mild dehydration • multiple food allergies/intolerances • decubitus ulcers (Stage I, II) • diagnoses that impact on nutritional status: recent cardio vascular accident (CVA), chronic heart and lung disease, chronic renal failure, edema, stable diabetes mellitus, chronic infections (e.g., urinary tract infections [UTIs], pneumonia), osteoporosis, recent surgery, fractures, progressive neurological disease • tube feeding – stable, no complications • significant food/drug interaction • poor compliance with therapeutic diet
HIGH RISK	
• severe depression • advanced stage of Alzheimer's Disease or other dementia • severe agnosia, abulia, aphasia, anomia, apraxia • inability to initiate movement • increased difficulty swallowing • total inability to move voluntarily • inability to communicate and/or respond to verbal cueing • dehydration • all systems closing down	• significant unplanned weight change: .5% in 1 month; >7.5% in 3 months; 10% in 6 months • severely underweight (BMI < 18.5) with ongoing weight loss of >20% over last year • inadequate food/fluid intake to meet nutritional needs, or consuming < 50% of food for >72 hours • frequent nausea/vomiting lasting >72 hours • dysphagia; chewing, swallowing, or choking problems which require assessment • anorexia, failure to thrive • complications r/t morbid obesity • abnormal laboratory values • diagnoses which impact on nutritional status: advanced cancer, acute heart disease, advanced liver failure, renal failure, renal dialysis, unconktrolled diabetes, gastrointestinal bleeding, blood in the stool, bowel obstruction • severe skin breakdown, pressure sores, decubitus ulcers (Stage III, IV) • tube feeding, new route with complications

FIGURE 12-5

Step 3: Stressors

In this step, the impact of stress in the life of the client is assessed. These stressors are described as "iatrogenic" issues (defined as "the consequence of medical care") and also refer to stressors caused by other human interventions and by the environment.

A careful consideration of these iatrogenic issues is very important because the degree to which the client is stressed is controlled not by the disease process, but by staff, families, and the environment.

One of these issues is so critical that it has been given a name:

- **Sundown Syndrome.** For people with dementia there appears to be a nexus between times of performance expectation, accumulated stress, and catastrophic behaviors. A common instance is late after-noon/early evening "sundowning," which occurs when people with cognitive impairment seem to hit a low point and cannot summon the energy to manage daily life challenges appropriately. At that point, performance expectations placed on them can cause them to go out of control. Often this phenomenon is misinterpreted as aggression and blamed on the client, rather than being correctly identified as the consequence of making demands on the person which he or she is no longer capable of meeting. Sundown syndrome can be attributed to the following:
  - fatigue
  - lack of staff support during shift change and preparation for the evening meal
  - lack of light in the environment
  - drop in metabolism
  - pain
  - other factors
- **Pain.** Studies show a distressing lack of pain identification and management where elders are concerned. There is evidence that elderly persons and cognitively impaired people in particular are undertreated for pain.

  Cognitively impaired older patients with less effective communication skills are in need of strong advocates who assess skilfully and then intervene with appropriate medication for pain control.

Pain affects every aspect of living including appetite and food intake and should be carefully monitored.

- **Medications** are a major stressor which affect appetite, ability to eat, and nutritional status:

  – Neuroleptic or psychotropic medications can be the cause of swallowing problems in significant numbers of elderly people, so their effects must be thoroughly assessed by the pharmacist or physician.

  – Antidepressants, anti-psychotics, sedatives, and other similar drugs can cause dry mouth, reduced motor coordination, extrapyramidal side effects, sedation, inattention, and drooling, all of which can affect the swallowing function.

  – Anticholinergic medication can have side effects, including decreased appetite, nausea, and vomiting, which can seriously compromise food intake.

  – Many drugs, when taken over a long period of time, can produce vitamin and mineral deficiencies in the elderly that may severely compromise nutritional status and result in decreased general health and resistance to disease.

  It is important to encourage a regular review of medications if a client's deteriorating health is suspected to be a result of an iatrogenic (medically-related) condition.

- **Environmental Stressors** that affect eating: these are the stress factors present in the macro-environment such as the size of the room in which meals are served, the number of people dining together at one sitting, the level of noise, the appropriateness of the furniture, lighting quality, the amount of glare from the lights, the temperature of the room, and the air quality.

  Unsuitable seating arrangements can affect residents' stress levels, so careful attention is recommended in placing compatible eating companions together. Menus posted on white boards in pastel colors using small print and no pictures are worse than useless! Residents cannot read or understand them.

- **Family and staff attitudes.** Being fed by someone else is a most unpleasant experience for most adults. Thus assisting a person with dementia to eat is a most challenging task requiring knowledge, skill, and patience on the part of family and staff.

Some excellent courses in low-risk feeding techniques developed and sponsored by clinical facilities are being offered in Canada and the United States. Information is available on the Internet or from the dietitian or speech therapist in your facility.

Training is an ongoing process that requires supervision. The pace at which the food is offered, the positioning, and the communication and interaction between residents and those assisting with feeding are key factors that need to be monitored on a regular basis.

GENTLECARE Best Practice

Gentlecare recommends that anyone who will be assisting others to eat would benefit from the experience of having a meal fed to them. Further basic training in the art of assisting with eating is highly recommended. One of the reasons that elderly people with dementia lose eating ability is that inappropriate feeding techniques are used.

Staff have traditionally seen "feeding" as a job that has to be completed three times a day and rushed through as quickly as possible in order to get back to "real" clinical duties. They may feel pressure to complete tasks to meet a deadline, which may be either self-imposed or somehow perceived as a requirement of the job. For example, clients must finish meals and be out of the dining area as quickly as possible to make way for housekeeping staff to clean, for dietary staff to do the dishes, for nursing staff to complete their routine ADLs, and for activities staff to run their programs.

This may appear to be in conflict with Gentlecare which asks staff to make dining a memorable experience! Staff may not see the provision of meals as an important therapeutic tool, and mealtimes as the most important events of the resident's day. Staff may justifiably claim that they've been hired for one job and then asked to do another. This is an area where the need for interdisciplinary teamwork and Gentlecare training is of great importance.

Gentlecare believes strongly in involving family at mealtimes to normalize the experience of eating and enhance social interaction. However, family members may need help in learning how to assist appropriately. They may have had lifelong experience feeding children or recent experience with their afflicted family member, but this will not necessarily have given them the skills to cope with the complexity of that person's illness. It is important that family members not demand a level of performance that the person has lost his capacity to achieve (for example, eating with utensils). In addition, visitors may over-help or over-feed; they may provide too much distraction or direction. Sometimes coming into the facility or taking the family member out to a mall or a busy restaurant for a meal may cause anxiety and actually raise stress levels instead of being the wonderful visit that helps so much.

After a good dinner, one can forgive anybody, even one's own relations.

—OSCAR WILDE

Families are often asked to come in and "feed" their family members. Gentlecare recommends that the emphasis should be on normalizing the eating experience (i.e., a wife having lunch with the husband, rather than "feeding" him). To create this atmosphere, Gentlecare recommends that the visiting family member arranges to have a meal or part of a meal or a beverage available to consume, thus making the experience as normal as possible. Staff are encouraged to arrange private seating for the family group, rather than asking the spouse or visitor to stand and assist with eating at a table occupied by other clients.

Families are under stress when they are caring for their loved ones; and almost without exception they feel guilty about having their loved ones in an institution. No matter how often they are reassured that there is little basis for this feeling, guilt occurs. One of the ways we may relieve guilt is by offering food. Sometimes, a favorite food brought from home can really brighten a person's day. On the other hand, food may be offered at inappropriate times or in inappropriate ways, so staff and families need to strike a balance that works for the afflicted person.

One of the most troubling dilemmas is when a client asks to go home, whether for a meal or a family visit.

Every time this occurs, the person experiences separation anxiety that causes them to relive the devastating experience of leaving home. Gentlecare recommends that the family bring the event to the person rather than the person to the event, whether it be a wedding or a picnic.

This is one of the times when carers are put in real conflict. It seems so cruel to deny anyone the pleasure of a visit to their home, but the anxiety and stress caused by visits can interfere with the person's adjustment to the facility. They simply won't know which place is their home.

Step 4: Nutritional Care Plan

Once we have gathered all the relevant information and considered the stressors on the individual, we can develop a nutritional care plan. This is a plan of action that not only provides energy and good nutrition, but will delight the individual with a meal that looks, tastes, and smells like one eaten at home.

The following factors need to be considered:

- **Personal meal planning**
  - Is this person someone who habitually eats a big morning meal, and then lighter meals during the rest of the day? Or is this someone who has never eaten breakfast, but habitually eats around lunchtime with a big dinner later in the day?
  - Does this person prefer several small meals offered throughout the waking period?
  - Are there favorite and least favorite foods?
  - Are there other food preferences to be considered and worked into the meal plan?
- **The therapeutic diet order** is based on a quarterly review of the client's current medical condition by the dietitian, physician, and care team.
- **Modification of Textures**
  Food must look like food if a person is expected to eat it! Texturing food removes the context, eliminating the visual cues that guide a client and help them enjoy the meal. If a person has problems

A man seldom thinks with more earnestness of anything than he does of his dinner.

—SAMUEL JOHNSON

eating certain foods, Gentlecare recommends trying another food from the same food group.

For example, if a person has choked on toast, soft pancakes or muffins can be safely substituted while still giving the pleasure of different food textures. If a person has choked on an apple (or had difficulty eating one), other, softer fruit such as pears, berries, and melon or cooked fruit such as applesauce can be substituted.

Experiment with a variety of food textures, from soft to chopped, minced, pureed, or liquid. Remember that a person may be able to manage several different levels of food texture, depending on the food itself, the assistance available, the temperature, etc. For example, a person may require assistance with porridge, but be able to eat finger foods (like pancakes or muffins) independently.

Remember: texture, color, and presentation can often make up for the loss of taste and smell.

It is very important to remember that a diet adapted to the client's condition is of no value unless it is eaten.

—DARLENE WEGER,
CAREWEST, CALGARY,
ALBERTA, CANADA

GENTLECARE Best Practice

The language we use around mealtimes for elders is very important. When we refer to them as "feeders" or "total feeds" we dehumanize older people. We feed animals — not our grandparents!

When we refer to help as "assisting with meals" we open up an avenue of help to elders without making them feel helpless or useless. Best Practice staff help each other monitor the language we use around our clients.

• **Need for Assistance with Eating**

The majority of people with dementing illness need some help with eating, thus a wide range of assistance should be available as determined by the nutritional care plan. Wherever possible the client should be encouraged to eat independently if possible, in order to improve nutritional status and delay deterioration in function. Better nutritional status will prevent weight loss, help resist infections and skin breakdown, and provide dietary fiber to combat chronic constipation problems.

Prosthetic dishes and utensils

To compensate for physical or cognitive deficits, offer appropriate utensils:

– utensils with non-slip, built-up grips
– metal spoons—never plastic
– plates with lips
– non-slip mats or wet cloths under plates
– colored glasses to provide visual contrast
– a variety of designs for drinking glasses and mugs

A number of rehabilitative services offer prosthetic dishes and utensils that can help people maintain independence while eating. Your facility will probably have catalogues available. However, much of this specialized equipment is very expensive, and often does not survive its first tour through the institutional dishwasher. Gentlecare recommends that staff and families search through stores specializing in equipment for kitchens, children, and sports, to find creative solutions for the necessary adaptive equipment. Searching for and finding such items can also be made into a special assignment for volunteers/families.

GENTLECARE Best Practice

Remember: Half the world eats exquisite foods with their fingers! Finger foods are a lovely way to eliminate the need for utensils. See Figure 12-6 for menu suggestions.

Physical positioning

Physical positioning of both the person eating and the person assisting are critical for successful nutritional intake.

– The person who is eating should be positioned to be able to both see and reach food. If the person is eating in bed, raise the bed to an

GENTLECARE FINGER FOODS

PROTEIN SOURCES
Cubes/slices of cheese

Cheese balls

Chicken nuggets

Strips of cooked meat or chicken

Fish sticks/sausage rolls/meat tarts

Hard-cooked eggs (halved)

Small meat balls

Crisp bacon

Sandwiches (egg, meat, chicken,
    peanut butter, tuna, etc.)

Grilled cheese sandwiches

Crackers with cheese, peanut butter

SWEETS
Doughnuts, doughnut holes

Cookies

Squares, brownies

Cupcakes, muffins

Biscuits with jam or jelly

Granola bars, yogurt bars

Ice cream, frozen yogurt cones

Popsicles, fruit juice bars

BREADS, ETC.
Toast fingers/cinnamon toast

Melba toast

Bread sticks

Pretzels/potato chips

Toasted English muffins

Lemon/banana/fruit bread

Cinnamon buns/rolls

Digestive biscuits

Pancakes

Arrowroots/social tea biscuits

VEGETABLES & FRUITS
Florets of broccoli, cauliflower

Mushrooms

Zucchini

Cucumber

Dill pickles

Cherry tomatoes

Home fries (warm)

French fries

Green or yellow beans

Carrot/celery sticks

Cubes of cooked turnip, potato

Apple or pear sections

Orange sections (no seeds)

Banana sections

Melon balls/wedges (no rind)

Strawberries/peaches

Seedless grapes

ETHNIC TREATS
Egg/spring rolls

Samosas/chapatis

Crepes/waffles

Almond/fortune cookies

Cornbread/polenta

Hors d'oeuvres

Scones

Cornish pasties

Fish and chips

Note: Some of these foods are not appropriate if the person has restrictions on diet due to medical problems. Most people with dementia can eat these items to improve nutritional status, prevent weight loss, resist infections, and provide dietary fiber.

FIGURE 12.6

angle of at least 60 degrees and place firm pillows behind shoulders and neck. The person should be positioned in a slightly flexed position with chin down to close the airway.

– If the person is seated in a normal chair and their food is on a table in front of them, it is critical that both their shoulders and their arms are well above the table top. Chairs that are too low for the table in use or tables are too high for the chairs are a significant cause of decreased eating function. Over time an uncorrected seating/table relationship will cause the person to lose upper arm strength, will be unable to reach for food, and eventually will give up trying to feed himself.

– The person who is assisting should be positioned so as to enhance the skills of the person who is eating.

– If total assistance is required, the suggested position is on the dominant side of the person being helped; seated on a moveable stool on wheels that locks at the height of the person being assisted; and slightly ahead of, facing, and at approximately a 45-degree angle to the person being assisted. This position allows the person assisting to check swallowing and chewing activity, which can't be done if the helper is directly opposite the person being helped, or if the helper is working at a feeding table.

– If only partial assistance is required, the suggested position is on the dominant side of the person being assisted, seated on a moveable stool on wheels that lock, and positioned at the side of the person being helped, with both people facing in the same direction. This position allows the person who is assisting to move utensils toward the mouth by guiding the hand of the person being helped. It also permits the person being assisted to mimic appropriate actions. The assisting person may only need to repeat or kick-start activity from time to time, and independent eating can be encouraged.

– Before eating begins, remove all restraints that might impede breathing. Keep the throat and chest area free of towels or cloths used to clean the person's mouth.

– Be sure the person's head is supported and controlled. Eating is a flexion-patterned activity; avoid hyper-extension, as it opens the air-way and may lead to aspiration of food.

Techniques for assisting with eating

If a person has trouble controlling liquids in the mouth, try using the following:

– liquids in slush form

– foods with a high water content

– gelatinized liquids

– pudding, sherbets, ice creams

– popsicles

– frozen fruit juice bars

– commercial frozen snack products

Other ideas:

– Give only small amounts of food with each swallow.

– Ensure that the food is cleared from the mouth before introducing more.

– Use small spoons to introduce foods.

– Do not use the edge of the spoon to clear food from the lips and chin, as the skin in this area is likely to be very fragile, easily damaged, and almost impossible to heal.

– Encourage the person assisting to identify the food being presented after every two or three bites.

– Give clear, simple, concrete instructions: "Open your mouth," rather than "Open up."

– Make use of *hyperorality* (the oral sense providing information) to assist with eating: place a small sample of the food near the mouth to help the person identify the food.

– Check for visual field neglect (defined as inability to visually perceive objects on one side, usually the left) and place items of food within the person's visual range.

– Offer ongoing encouragement.

– Avoid feeding tables. They infantalize older people and lead to staff being placed so that they are not in a position to assist correctly and cannot monitor swallowing. People with dementia often need to mimic the action of staff.

GENTLECARE **Best Practice**

Do not use syringes to assist with eating.

Triggering strategies

When total assistance with eating is required, the following triggering strategies can be very helpful.

a. To trigger mouth-opening:

– Touch both lips with a weighted spoon.

– Give a sip of water.

– Ask the person to open her mouth.

– Place your fingers on the sides of the lips, or apply light pressure on the chin.

– Do not try to force the jaws open.

– Mime the mouth opening.

These techniques will often help to open a person's mouth if teeth are clenched on a utensil.

b. To trigger lips closing:

– Stroke the lips with a finger, spoon, or ice popsicle.

– Apply manual pressure, holding your forefinger just above the upper lip and your thumb under the bottom lip to purse the lips together gently.

c. To trigger tongue movement:

– Try icing the tongue.

– Place a cold spoon lightly on the tongue.

– With a tongue depressor, touch the tissue just behind the lower teeth; the tongue will "follow" the touch. DO NOT USE YOUR FINGERS!

d. To trigger saliva production:

– Try icing the tongue with a favorite popsicle.

– Try plain ice.

– Give sips of water.

– Offer a salty or savory bit of food.

e. To trigger the swallowing reflex:

– Touch the person's chin or throat gently to stimulate the digrastic muscle.

– Give a sip of water. This will often help a person with Alzheimer's disease to understand that food is present in the mouth and that a swallow is necessary.

– If food remains in the mouth, offer an empty spoon to trigger swallowing.

– Try icing the sternal notch and rubbing the back of the neck with a washcloth.

– Lightly pinch the pharynx.

– Bring food into the person's visual range. Identify the food.

– Offer the person the food to see and smell (for example, a piece of fruit or bread).

– Use hot or cold liquids rather than tepid ones.

– Remember that textured foods stimulate swallowing more than liquid or pureed foods do.

– Use discretion if there is a history of choking.

GENTLECARE Best Practice

Remember that many choking incidents are more likely to have resulted from poor assisting techniques and/or poor positioning than from an actual inability to swallow.

• **The Need for Water**

Hydration is a vital part of the total nutrition program.

Remember that handing someone a glass of water only counts if the person actually drinks the water! Many facilities have bottled water available in a central location; everyone who provides care should make it a practice to offer people water at every opportunity: As often as possible, stop to talk to elders. Offer water to begin or end an intervention, at the beginning and ending of programs, during meals, and during social events.

GENTLECARE **Best Practice**

The best way to get a client to drink water is to drink with them. Remember that staff and families need hydration too! People with dementia may not be able to see water, so try coloring water with several spoonfuls of juice or use colored drinking glasses. Remind ladies that water prevents wrinkles. Be creative!

A few clients diagnosed with dysphagia will not be able to drink regular fluids. These clients can be helped to achieve an adequate intake by offering thickened fluids of the consistency that has been prescribed.

Some elderly people simply don't enjoy drinking water, especially cold water. Gentlecare suggests the following substitutes:

– fruit juice, pudding or Jell-O popsicles

– fruit (watermelon, pears, apple slices)

– soup

– Canterbury tea (hot water with milk and sugar in a china cup)

– lemonade

– sherbet

Liquids can be presented in a sports bottle—this often works for men.

During recreational events, do not substitute the regular china and glassware with Styrofoam cups.

Water (fluid) intake should be charted for all clients.

The offer of water and the monitoring of actual water intake provides a perfect opportunity for conversation, a handshake between staff and client or family and the elder, for a touch, a hug, or a walk.

• **Constipation**

Increased fluid intake and increased physical activity are key components of a bowel management program. (See the Gentlecare Hydration program.) Evaluation of the use of narcotic medications, laxatives, and stool softeners should be part of the assessment process.

> Offer a regular-sized glass of water with medications and
> encourage the client to drink it all in order to prevent
> irritation of the throat. Position the person with head and
> shoulders raised and neck in flexion to facilitate
> swallowing.

Increase the fibre content in the menu:
- add wheat bran to hot cereals and sprinkle on cold cereals
- include fresh fruit for snacks and dessert
- encourage consumption of vegetables
- include lentils and beans in soups, casseroles, and main dishes
- include higher-fibre breads

• **High-Fibre Recipes – Select A or B**

These mixtures are prescribed as needed for clients and dispensed
daily at breakfast in 1 oz (30 ml) or 2 oz (60 ml) portions, but may be
used as a spread for toast, mixed with hot cereal, or eaten on their
own as a side dish:

A. 1 cup All-Bran or similar   1 cup prune juice
   1 cup stewed prunes   1 cup applesauce
   Nutrient content: 1 oz (30 ml) = 21 kcal
   0.5 gm protein, 7 gm carbohydrate, trace fat, 1.5 gm dietary fibre

B. 1 cup wheat bran   1 cup applesauce
   1/2 cup prune juice
   Nutrient content: 1 oz (30 ml) = 16 kcal,
   0.5 gm protein, 5.9 gm carbohydrate, trace fat, 1.6 gm dietary fibre

• **Urinary Incontinence**

Restriction of fluid intake is *not* the answer to incontinence and can
often aggravate it. A low volume of fluid intake can:
- lead to dehydration and acute dementia
- decrease bladder capacity
- produce concentrated urine that may irritate the bladder
- make urinary tract infections worse

• **Skin Breakdown**

Nutrition plays a very important role in maintaining the health of the skin. One of the causes of skin breakdown may be malnutrition. A detailed record of food intake and blood tests for albumin and zinc should be undertaken. If food intake is poor and blood-albumin levels are low, a high-protein high-energy regime is recommended (e.g., extra milk products, meat, fish, eggs and poultry, extra starchy foods like potatoes, breads and rice, and high-calorie desserts and beverages, as tolerated).

In cases of serious skin breakdown (for instance, severe decubitus ulcers) the use of protein powder in drinks, cereals, soups, and desserts is recommended to provide an extra boost.

The Gentlecare 24-Hour Nutrition Clock

Introduction

Now we come to the most exciting and challenging part!

In Gentlecare, all the information collected in Step 4 for the client's care plan is reviewed to design a custom-made "Nutrition Clock" to suit the individual. It spreads that person's daily nutritional requirement equally between three mini-meals and five nutrition boosts throughout a period of 24 hours. It is planned to provide strategically timed metabolic boosts that enhance performance, avoid nutritional low points, and prevent catastrophic behavior.

There are three basic Gentlecare 24-Hour Nutrition Clocks: the "Early Bird, "Regular," and "Sleepyhead"; the "Night Owl" feature can be incorporated into each of these. Most clients will conform to one of these versions, with a small percentage being Early Birds or Sleepyheads and a larger percentage being regulars.

• **The Early Bird** is frequently a female client: the archetypal busy housewife with a life-long practice of rising early and dressing, preparing breakfast for the family, packing lunches, doing farm chores, cleaning the house. The urge is to be working; the response of staff are often to tell her to sit down, and be quiet, and not make a mess.

The day gets off on the wrong foot when the client's natural inclina-

GENTLECARE 24-HOUR NUTRITION CLOCK
FOR "EARLY BIRDS"

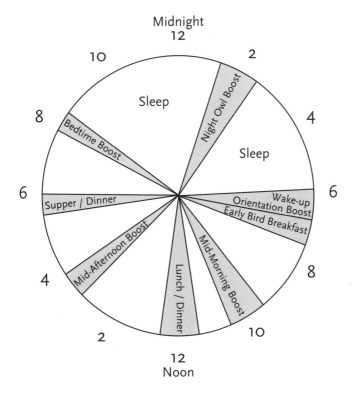

FIGURE 12-7

tion to activity is discouraged. If the morning starts well, the whole day tends to flow smoothly.

The Early Bird begins her day with "wake-up and orientation": a light nutritional boost and hydration when she wakes up—for example, a juice or a hot beverage with a mini-muffin—accompanied by orientation to time and place.

This client often enjoys a breakfast-related activity.

A number of facilities have gardens or atriums: what a great way to start the day with a cup of tea and a muffin, sitting in this area chatting about the day and puttering around in the garden!

After completion of her "work," a continental breakfast of cereal with milk and fruit or toast/roll/croissant or muffin, yogurt, or cheese and a hot beverage is provided. In the mid-morning, we provide a beverage and a biscuit or small muffin and a slice of cheese or a serving of yogurt. At 12 noon serve a small meal. In the mid-afternoon, another

CHAPTER
TWELVE

GENTLECARE 24-HOUR NUTRITION CLOCK FOR "REGULARS"

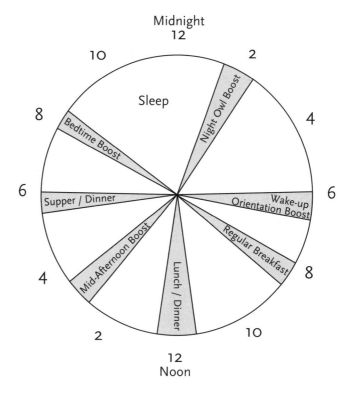

FIGURE 12-8

nutrition boost is offered consisting of a hot or cold beverage with cookies/fruit loaf and fruit or ice cream. At 6 in the evening serve a small meal. In the mid-evening, a bedtime boost is provided. Here we introduce the concept of "comfort foods"—the old familiar foods enjoyed from childhood such as a hot non-caffeinated beverage like Ovaltine, cereal with milk, a pudding, a peanut butter and jam sandwich, or cookies with hot milk. If possible, these boosts should be served "family-style" from the kitchenette on the floor rather than in pre-packaged form.

• **The Regulars** are the people who always eat the same menu at the same time, in the same place. They always come to breakfast dressed and groomed for the day. Nothing unusual or irregular should happen. Our job is to maintain the stability in their program.

A special note: This group should never be troubled by being told that the facility is "short-staffed." When you say that to elderly people who have a strong work ethic, it scares the daylights out of them if they think that something is going to disturb the routine or the safety of the way they've always done things.

They need routine and consistency.

I REMEMBER WORKING in a facility where an old gentleman had been accustomed at home to having one and a half pieces of toast at breakfast. When his wife tried to get this for him, the staff said, "Oh, just let him eat as much as he wants."

But you see, somebody who is a "regular" would not ordinarily leave behind half a slice of toast on the plate. That would not be right. He would either be forced to be "wasteful" or to eat more than he wanted.

We recommended to the staff that they should cut the second slice in half and not put the second half on his plate.

At "wake-up," the Regulars are provided with orientation and a juice or hot beverage and mini-muffin.

Then at the same time every day, they go to the dining room for a small balanced breakfast. The rest of their day is structured to include mid-morning and mid-afternoon boosts between breakfast, lunch and dinner, and a nourishing bedtime boost.

If possible, these clients should be involved in the meal planning and preparation process. For instance, if the food service department receives produce like corn on the cob or fresh berries in bulk, staff should bring it to the unit where they can show it to the residents and talk about how it will be prepared and when it will be on the menu.

• **The Sleepyheads**

CECIL WANTS TO WATCH the hockey game and then the late news. The staff person assigned to his evening ADLs has eight residents to care for and wants to check him off her list. A conflict erupts between them at the end of the day which drains his energy. She "wins" the battle of wills: he is taken to his room and arbitrarily assisted with evening ADLs, including being changed into his pajamas.

GENTLECARE 24-HOUR NUTRITION CLOCK FOR "SLEEPY HEADS"

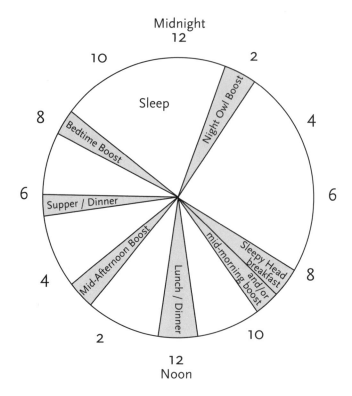

FIGURE 12-9

He is angry and upset. He stays wide awake late into the night. The later it is the hungrier he gets. He needs a snack but he won't ask and no one offers him one.

Finally out of sheer exhaustion he drifts into a deep sleep. Remember that the latest sleep research indicates that older adults have their best sleep between 5 and 8 a.m.

Then, early in the morning, a new care provider comes in to wake him up.

Awakened abruptly out of a sound sleep, he is angry and disoriented: he strikes out at the care aide with his fist. She calls in another staff member for assistance in restraining him.

It's a very dangerous time. His anger is at red alert.

And he's hungry!

Throughout this incident of catastrophic behaviour, the staff are so involved in crisis intervention that neither one thinks to offer him a nutritional boost. By the time they get him settled down and assist him with morning ADLs, it's lunch time and he still hasn't anything to eat.

This sets the scene for "Sundown syndrome."

The Sleepyheads present staff with puzzles to be solved.

These are residents who like to stay up late to watch the news, sports, etc.: they like go to bed later than the other residents. Many Sleepyheads will miss the Early Bird and Regular breakfast times. But it has been observed that when left to their own devices, they will adjust their nutritional and sleep requirements naturally.

When they awaken, they are offered a wake-up and orientation boost.

Their Sleepyhead breakfast is served later and is usually light but nourishing: it could include juice, a protein source like milk or yogurt, cereal and/or bread or toast, with a hot beverage. The energy that had in the past been expended by both staff and resident in conflict can be redirected to ADLs and to fostering the client's independence and emotional control. These clients often become more independent and easier to look after because they are rested, calm, and open to encouragement and support in trying to help themselves. When we provide kitchenettes in their units, we make it possible for them to prepare food independently. The clients who were most prone to catastrophic behaviors are now choosing for themselves to supplement the light Sleepyhead breakfast with a Mid-morning Boost.

During the rest of the day, they are provided with boosts between lunch and dinner and at bedtime. See Figure 12-9 for the Sleepyhead Nutritional Clock Sleepyheads are usually candidates for the "Night Owl" program.

• **The Night Owl Program**

An additional feature of the Nutritional Clock program is to provide nutritional boosts during the night if a resident is wakeful and hungry. Residents are encouraged to feel comfortable asking for "mini-meals" or nutrition boosts during the night. Gentlecare calls this care strategy the "Night Owl" program.

GENTLECARE **Best Practice**

In selecting foods for elderly people, be aware that caffeine is not well tolerated. It is a stimulant and may cause adverse symptoms such as wakefulness, irritability, an irregular heart rate, gastric upsets, and diarrhea. It is found in beverages such as coffee, tea, cocoa, soft drinks, candies with milk chocolate or dark chocolate, prescription drugs like Soma Compound or Darvon Compound, non-prescription drugs such as weight-control aids, alertness tablets, analgesics/painkillers, diuretics, and cold/allergy remedies. All of these contain sufficient caffeine to warrant their avoidance.

It is fitted into the Early Bird, Regular or Sleepyhead Nutritional Clock as needed – see figures 12-7, 12-8 and 12-9.

This feature includes reassurance, quiet conversation and/or a suitable Gentlecare activity, a warm blanket, and nourishing comfort food like a bowl of instant hot cereal with milk and sugar, a dish of pudding, a glass of milk, or a cup of Ovaltine or hot chocolate with a cookie or a slice of toast. See Figure 12-10 for sample Boosts and Mini-meals.

Once settled back in bed, the residents are allowed to sleep until they wake up naturally. At that point they are offered wake-up and orientation.

Gentlecare Meal Additions and Alternatives

Gentlecare offers these suggestions to carers throughout the whole spectrum of care: to the person caring for a family member in the home; to staff in a group home, nursing home, or hospital setting.

• Appetizers

Use special treats to trigger the eating response. Serve them with water before meals.

- small pancakes with jam
- crisp bacon strips
- curly, seasoned potato fries
- potato chips
- cheese cubes
- fruit juice popsicles
- salty crackers

CONVERSATION BETWEEN *an old gentleman and his wife in the lounge just before lunch:*

    Her: "I'd love just an egg sandwich for my lunch."

    Him: "Oh! No! Give me roast beef, mashed potatoes, and gravy any time!"

• Small tasty meals that encourage appetite

If a person is disinterested in traditional main-course foods (meat, potatoes, and vegetables) or simply finds eating a full-course meal too complex or exhausting, try the following:

- buttered zucchini and date loaf with cheese, hard or cream variety
- plain yogurt garnished with cut-up fruit and oatmeal/peanut butter/chocolate chip cookies or digestive biscuits, or bread with peanut butter
- milkshakes made with whole milk, skim milk powder, and fruit (banana, etc.)
- applesauce with warm gingerbread and a glass of milk or a scoop of ice cream
- banana bread with peanut butter and a glass of milk
- puddings: milk, tapioca, rice, or bread, fortified with eggs, milk powder, and/or a nutritional supplement and garnished with jelly, jam, or syrup
- a dish of fruit with raisin or cinnamon bread and butter and a chunk of cheese
- banana split with ice cream or frozen yogurt, custard sauce, and canned or fresh fruit

Gentlecare seeks to make mealtimes as pleasant, relaxing, and complete a social experience as possible for each individual— regardless of his degree of dysfunction.

- hot cereal (oatmeal, cornmeal, cream of wheat) fortified with wheat germ and/or bran and a nutritional supplement, with whole milk and brown sugar
- baked custard with caramel sauce, maple syrup, or jam
- mini quiches filled with vegetables and/or meat or fish
- chicken or fish strips, nuggets, or sticks, with bread and butter and pickles
- thick cream soups with meat, fish, and vegetables
- "chunky" soups (split pea soup with ham, fish chowder, corn chowder) with crackers
- baked beans with a hamburger or wieners, cut up, with chili sauce added
- assorted sandwich plates (egg salad, minced ham, chicken salad, peanut butter and jam, etc.)
- poached or scrambled eggs on toast
- creamed peas on toast, or creamed salmon on toast, with pickle or chili sauce

*Some of these suggestions are obviously not applicable if there are strict diet restrictions in fat, sodium, potassium, protein, or total calorie intake.

Health care budgets and staffing schedules certainly don't encourage staff to take time to offer these helpful, creative mini-meals. However, these ideas should be viewed as possible therapeutic interventions that will break through poor eating patterns and achieve marked improvement in nutritional status. Most of the alternative meal suggestions contain a combination of protein, fat, and carbohydrates that is approximately equivalent to a moderate serving of the traditional first course of a meal.

Families are often willing to help with provision of special foods if they understand the meal plan that the staff are attempting to implement.

• The Eating Environment

We have already considered the profound affect of stressors in the environment on the well-being of the resident. It follows that the eating

GENTLECARE Best Practice

These ideas are not just "frills"! Rather, they are creative therapeutic strategies that will enhance a person's nutritional intake.

environment is a critical component of the nutritional care plan. Elements that affect the experience of eating are:

- room size
- number of people in the dining room
- seating arrangements
- noise levels including audio stimuli such as TV, PA systems, background music
- appropriateness of furniture
- lighting quality, glare
- heating
- contrasts in table settings

Effective nutritional care begins with changing the way we *think about* and implement meals for people experiencing dementia. Significant system and environmental changes will be needed if we are to enhance nutritional opportunities and decrease progressive dysfunction, excessive disability, and escalating costs. These changes include the following:

- designation of a specific dining area for people with dementia
- use of warm mid-range colors to promote appetite and enjoyment
- separation of people in the dining area according to their levels of dysfunction and cognition
- relaxation of rigid mealtime schedules to allow sufficient time for the person with dementia to function or to be properly assisted. This is especially critical during the breakfast period. People may be confused or disoriented on waking and need extra time to adjust.
- ensuring that all assisting personnel are trained and skilled in evaluating aging and dementia dysfunction, offering assistance, and reducing stress.

GENTLECARE Best Practice

A good breakfast often makes the difference between a pleasant day and a catastrophic one.

- **Environmental Strategies**
  - Information may need to be repeated and reinforced in several ways to ensure that the client understands that at mealtime, the appropriate activity is eating. For example, dining areas should look, smell, and feel like places where one would want to eat.
  - Avoid presentation of food on trays. Loss of smell, taste, the ability to visually identify objects, and problems with motor coordination may make it impossible for a person with dementia to understand that the tray contains a meal.
  - Dining areas should be small, quiet, comfortable, and stress-free. Large dining areas should be subdivided to reduce confusion; planters and strategically placed furniture (e.g., hutches or a piano) are useful in this regard. Half-walls (pony walls) can be confusing because clients can see only the upper half of people walking by.
  - Lighting should allow clients to see food items and the people who are assisting them; light levels should be three times normal amounts. Lighting materials and floor finish should be chosen to avoid glare.
  - Ventilation and heat control should provide a comfortable ambiance.
  - Since eating is a complex task requiring great concentration, eliminate distractions such as noise, TV, loud music, loud conversations between staff members, special entertainment during the actual meal hour (use music before or after meals but not during), medical rounds in the dining room during mealtime, and the distribution of medications at mealtime. Gentlecare recommends gathering clients in a social area before or after the meal to distribute medications.

---

10 GENTLECARE SUGGESTIONS FOR GOOD NUTRITIONAL CARE

1. Educate your staff to see eating as a principal therapy, and train them to assist with eating skillfully and gently.

2. Make food and meal-related activities part of the program for each day.

3. Find creative solutions to difficulties with handling food. Provide appropriate seating, utensils, and dishes to make independent eating easier. Try finger foods.

4. Provide appropriate, attractive eating areas.

5. Be flexible and creative about mealtimes, menus, and food textures.

6. Provide frequent, high-energy nutritional boosts.

7. Reduce noise levels/stress.

8. Watch for possible dehydration problems.

9. Keep nutritional assessments and care plans up-to-date for each individual in your care.

10. Set up ongoing communication between departments to promote Gentlecare strategies and problem-solve quickly.

FIGURE 12-10

Step 5: Team Input

Once the nutritional care plan has been developed it must be reviewed by caregivers and family members who know the person well. Before the plan is finalized, everyone must agree that it is a good one, especially if they are to take part in carrying out the recommendations.

Once the plan is agreed upon, everyone is expected to comply with it. It is the treatment plan.

• **Documentation of the Plan**

The vital information in the plan should be easily communicated to anyone who works with the resident.

In a long-term care facility, the responsibility for documentation usually rests with the dietitian and/or the food service manager, following consultation with the team and the physician.

But depending on where the person lives, and who the carer is, the care plan may contain all or some of the components of the nutritional care cycle.

Gentlecare solicits the assistance of all staff, family members, and volunteers to help elderly people with dementia whenever food is offered.

Nutrition is a serious business!

Food should be viewed as a powerful tool to help elderly people with dementia to manage their lives.

Step 6: Evaluation and Update

The final step in the nutritional care cycle is the evaluation and update of the nutritional care plan. Dementing illnesses and problems associated with aging are transitional diseases: the nutritional care plan must change as often as is necessary to address alterations in a person's needs, clinical/nutritional status, and level of nutritional risk.

Any concerns or proposals for change must be reviewed by the team, agreed upon, and documented so that everyone involved is aware that a change has been made.

A general rule of thumb is to complete a monthly review if the person is assessed to be at high risk, quarterly if assessed to be at moderate risk, and semi-annually if at low risk. The nutritional care plans for all residents in a facility are usually reviewed on a routine basis by the team as part of the process of quarterly reviews and annual multi-disciplinary family conferences.

The continuous repetition of the nutritional care cycle helps ensure quality in the overall management of nutritional care.

Gentlecare tries to bring back the joy people associate with eating.

13

The Magic of Gentlecare Meals

"It's the loveliest time of my day."

In Gentlecare, we regard meals as providing more than just sustenance; they are special events in the day and can be powerful therapeutic intervals. The enjoyment derived from eating and drinking can be used to smooth over the difficulties caused by ever-present clinical problems. The energy boost gained from these pleasurable interludes helps residents cope more effectively with the challenges of aging. For those residents who have mental illness and/or dementia in addition to their aging challenge, eating is often the only calm spot in an otherwise confusing and complicated day.

The stomach supports the heart, not the heart the stomach.

—OLD ENGLISH PROVERB

Chapter 9 introduced the four main groups of daily activities: core, necessary, essential, and meaningful activities. There are five core activities—eating, toileting, bathing, dressing, and grooming—which are referred to throughout this book and in most health care facilities as the Activities of Daily Living or ADLs. (The terms "core activities" and "ADLs" are used interchangeably.)

This chapter focuses on the important relationship of eating with the other ADLs, or core activities, and how eating can support the other three main activity groups. Gentlecare believes that eating is an incredibly powerful tool that can be used to increase the effectiveness of all other activities. How is this possible? Let's have a look.

FIGURE 13-1

Eating as a Core Activity

The goal of Gentlecare programming is to use eating and the other ADLs as the basis for therapy instead of viewing therapy as something that comes in from the outside or is administered by some other external group. Food therapy idea #1: Food should be provided not three times a day, but as many times as necessary to accommodate the appetites of the hungry and minimize the impact of dips in energy. Meals and boosts should support main meal periods and should be available upon awakening, in the morning, in the afternoon, at bedtime, and/or during the night. Where possible, these meals should be offered in quiet locations and in conjunction with relaxed family visits.

Eating's support of Necessary Activities.

Natural sleep, rest, relaxation, and privacy are all necessary for health.

In order to maximize the beneficial contribution of eating to these activities, rest periods should be scheduled before and after mealtimes. Rest locations should be away from dining areas, and should incorporate music, fresh air, reading aloud, playing of family tapes, and/or wrapping in blankets. All of these rest supplements will help to reduce stress. Privacy and intimacy have proven to enhance both the enjoyment and the function of eating, so mealtimes should be held in small, intimate dining spaces. Nutrition boosts before and after normal meal periods enhance rest and sleep.

Eating's support of Essential Activities.

The activities of communication, movement, social interaction, and intimacy make a significant contribution to a person's health.

Food therapy idea #2: Social interaction should be encouraged. Buddy relationships (bonding with another person) should be fostered. Often residents can be introduced to a buddy and prompted to look for each other and remind one another of mealtimes, to walk to the dining room together, and to sit together at the same table.

Take care with your language at mealtimes and avoid such terms as "feeders," "feeds," and "bibs," which tend to infantilize the client. Use words like "clothing protector" or "apron" and continue to promote the use of refreshing hot towels before and after meals.

EXTENDING MEALTIME
ACTIVITY THE GENTLECARE WAY

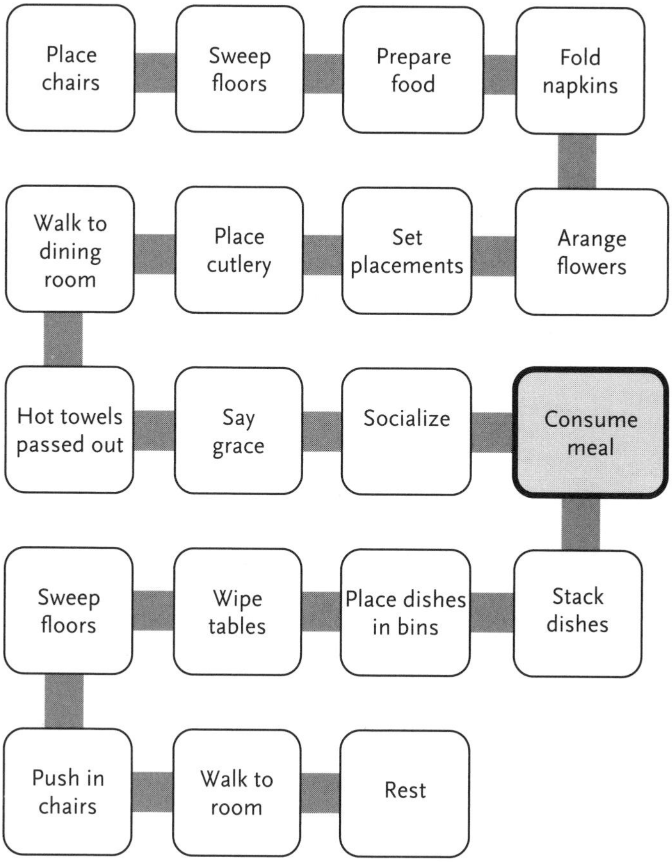

Place chairs	Sweep floors	Prepare food	Fold napkins
Walk to dining room	Place cutlery	Set placements	Arange flowers
Hot towels passed out	Say grace	Socialize	Consume meal
Sweep floors	Wipe tables	Place dishes in bins	Stack dishes
Push in chairs	Walk to room	Rest	

Any of these activities will make
mealtimes more meaningful and pleasant.

FIGURE 13-2

People should be walked to and from meals—preferably in the open air. Sometimes people can be danced to their meals. Marching also works well, especially if led by a piper. Regular chairs should be used, and seating arrangements should encourage social interaction. Avoid feeding people while in their wheelchair, and don't use feeding tables. Gentlecare recommends the use of stools for persons who are assisting residents with their meal. Do not hover over residents with dementia. Involve the family in meals whenever possible—not to "feed" their loved ones, but simply to share in the meal period. Use family events, such as birthdays and anniversaries, as reasons for special meals. Talk to the resident about family, meal preparations, favorite foods, food costs, food products, and recipes from the past.

Maximize opportunities for intimacy whenever possible. Encourage family and staff to touch client's shoulders, arms, or hands while setting up for a meal. Such gestures promote a feeling of comfort and inclusion.

The use of touch can be a controversial issue. Information derived from a detailed assessment will guide staff as to the degree of intimacy that would be welcomed by the client.

Eating's support of Meaningful Activities.

All special events should include food discussion, food preparation, table setting, and flower arrangements in addition to the eating of the food. Meaningful activities can be tied into mealtimes by providing opportunities for residents to help with serving and clearing up after the meals. Recipes can be discussed to sharpen interest in food. Filling the dining area with familiar food aromas has a positive effect.

Meals should follow old rituals and customs, and be made special. Here is a true story told by Sandy Telford of the Deltaview Habilitation Centre:

I phoned a special care unit to ask if I might visit. The charge nurse said, "Sure, come and visit us. We're making pancakes and peaches!"

IT WAS CORN SEASON *in B.C., so we decided to serve corn on the cob in our Gentlecare unit. It was a great hit! Over 50 percent of our people just loved it. Even people who usually have to be fed, or who had not held food in their hands for a long time, eagerly ate the ear of corn. Some sucked on the end of the cob, others had corn and butter all over their faces, and one gentleman ate four cobs. Everyone had a glorious time.*

The staff of Deltaview expanded the simple act of eating into a social and therapeutic event. They achieved dramatically different results than if they had simply served corn niblets as a vegetable. Using corn on the cob in this way took people with dementing illness back to a time in their lives when corn season was a joy for them. People were encouraged to recount their memories of corn. This "remembering" of good times past was empowering. The feelings of comfort, happiness, and competency in former life-roles directly translated into improvements in people's level of functioning.

Here is another illuminating example of how the presentation of food can enhance people's level of functioning.

I visited a huge total care treatment ward several years ago and watched as staff brought more than 100 people into a large dining room. Every person was in a wheelchair or geriatric chair. Every person in the room was served a tray of food, and without exception every person was either assisted to eat, or totally fed by staff. At the end of the meal, staff members returned everyone to their rooms.

The next morning I arrived before the breakfast hour, and was surprised to see people making their way independently to the dining room. Some were walking with the aid of canes or walkers; others were pushing wheelchairs in front of them as support, while still others pedaled their wheelchairs along with their feet. Long before serving time, many people were seated in their places.

Then I noticed that staff members were cooking pancakes and bacon at the side of the dining room. Wednesday morning was pancake morning! The buzz of conversation in the room was louder and more joyful than it had been the previous night at dinner. Many, many people were feeding themselves independently, using spoons and fingers, admittedly, but eating without assistance. People were talking one to another, passing food around the table, asking for syrup, and most significantly, asking for seconds! Very few staff members were involved in feeding activity. As I passed one old gentleman who had been morose the evening before, he looked up at me and grinned. "Good grits!" he said.

Armies march on their stomachs.

—NAPOLEON
BONAPARTE

Health care staff have long been aware that there can be a great deal of synergy between eating and most other activities. Eating can enhance the enjoyment of another activity, and a well-planned activity can enhance the enjoyment of the eating experience.

When food looks like food, tastes like food, smells like food, and reminds people of former pleasurable mealtimes, eating is no longer a chore. Residents' level of competence increases and less staff intervention at mealtimes is required. However, when food is served on trays, in odd-shaped containers with lids that are difficult to open, and is managed by staff members, cognitively impaired people will not recognize the activity as eating. Consequently, if they are to eat, they will have to be fed. Eating then becomes an onerous task to be completed by staff as quickly as possible.

Use color to influence eating patterns. Warm, mid range colors like red, peach, yellow make food look better and people hungrier. Cool colors like blue and gray have the opposite effect.

If we recognize the value of a good eating experience, why do we persist in following systems of food preparation and presentation that result in accelerated dysfunction of the resident, increased need for staff intervention, massive waste, and higher costs? We do this because we are locked into the wrong paradigm of care. We are using the biomedical model of care in an environment that calls for a good prosthetic paradigm. Fortunately, more and more facilities are moving to a flexible, normalized system of meal preparation and presentation to meet the challenge of dealing with aging and dementia issues. Many facilities are changing to buffet-style service, which allows residents to make food choices, and maybe help their buddy to do some choosing. Other units are successfully using salad, dessert, or beverage carts, often supported by residents acting as servers.

Several years ago I visited a unit in the Penticton Retirement Centre in Penticton, B.C. The dinner was being served from a mobile cart by the cook and his assistants, dressed in full whites. The cook went from table to table serving food, discussing choices, and presenting various dishes for inspection. The level of participation, enjoyment, and discussion was just amazing. It is hard not to compare this Penticton example with the typical mealtime involving long, noisy line-ups with staff serving and residents waiting. Over and over again experience has shown that it is no more expensive or time-consuming to offer meals in creative ways. The more normalized the activity the greater the payoff in terms of interaction, increased client functioning, and improved nutrition. There is plenty of evidence to support the notion that when cognitively impaired people are comfortable, in control of their situation to the degree possible, satisfied, and provided with a home-like dining situation, they derive more benefit from their food. Indeed, this is true for any person! A therapeutic nutritional experience can be created every time if staff members are empowered to work in interdisciplinary teams, when effective diagnostic and behavioral analyses are routinely assessed, and when family members are included in problem-solving.

Creative innovations to care plans can be successfully introduced when staff are informed and supported, and when they are encouraged to work in partnership with families.

The best-laid plans for mealtimes are only effective if:

a. The client understands which activity is taking place, looks forward to participating, and is NOT rushed!

b. The plans result in delicious, nutritious, comforting food being offered to each client.

c. The mealtime includes interaction with others similar to the atmosphere around our own dinner tables.

d. The clients are encouraged to feel they are in their own dining rooms, managing their meal to the best of their ability, and encouraged to feel in control—i.e., to manage "seconds," to have another cup of coffee, to assist with clean-up.

The big questions are:

• How do we achieve these objectives?

• How do we feed large numbers of clients?

• How do we feed small groups of clients who have special needs?

• How do we offer choices?

• How do we make people feel it's "their" dining room?

• How do we offer food that looks and tastes homemade?

• How do we make our diners feel special, delighted, comforted?

Many of us approach mealtimes as a job—so many meals to be served, so much food to be kept hot, so many clients who need assistance with eating, dining rooms to be cleaned, and tables to be set up for the next meal. An endless round of thankless, uninteresting tasks.

Some of us try to prepare and serve meals that look and taste like they might have been prepared in our own kitchen. But it is no longer enough simply to present attractive, delicious foods. The combined problems of aging, mental illness, and dementia present staff with a new kind of challenge. We have to acquire a new set of skills. We need to practice in different ways.

The Gentlecare system helps us to make the necessary changes.

The Gentlecare meal aims at providing an attractive, delicious meal that is well served and meets all of the complex clinical needs of the client.

GENTLECARE Dining

In Gentlecare we have come to believe that the organization of the meal is a very important factor in determining the success of the eating experience. It may in fact shape the person's whole day.

If you eat in your own home the gathering is usually small, the environment contains cherished objects, and the practices and rituals are familiar. Residents in facilities should have all of these familiar attributes continued in their new location. How did the resident's meals look and taste before he/she became ill? Family members will tell you all you need to know. To the extent possible meals should look and taste like they always have, and the addition of a "helper/hostess" should be as unobtrusive as possible. The helper should avoid the "waitress model" and should not hover over the food or the table. We suggest the helper sit with the person during the meal, share a beverage perhaps, and use any spare time to converse with the afflicted person rather than bringing an unrelated task to the table. Avoid hanging bibs around the resident's necks (a prime example of infantilization); instead, Gentlecare recommends aprons or vests to protect clothing from spills. Before you start, turn off the TV or other source of noise. Remember that eating is a complex and exhausting activity for the client and requires his/her full concentration. Throughout the meal, try to establish and maintain a situation in which the person feels in control. Encourage the person to help set the table and clean up after they have finished eating. This activity is considered part of the client's therapy program (their "work") and may have to be redone later by the carer.

If the person eats at an adult day care center or an assisted living location they will find themselves dining with a group of other people, many of whom will be strangers. The environment is usually very different from eating at home. Meals are often served at long tables that have been pre-set. There are frequently a lot of competing stimuli in the form of talk, music, TV, etc. Again, staff should focus on minimizing the noise and trying to make the environment and eating experience just like home. The eating area should be distinguished as a special place for dining rather than a "gym with tables." Setting small tables and providing place mats, tablecloths, and centerpieces will help to create the a pleasant ambiance. Such elements of the meal should not be considered "special touches" introduced only for special occasions, but rather should be regarded as providing essential cueing that supports every meal.

If the person lives in a facility, their meals will be taken with everyone else in the facility. This approach is referred to as *one seating*. All residents, regardless of diagnosis, are served at the same time. Those clients who are cognitively impaired or needing individual supervision may be seated in specially designated areas or be mixed with other clients. Although most meals will arrive at the same time, assistance with eating may not be available when needed. If the resident must wait his food will get cold. In such cases the resident may wander away from his table, eat other residents' food, be noisy, cough, choke, spit, or practice other unacceptable social behaviors which will have a negative impact on those around him. These dining areas are often noisy, high-stimulus areas characterized by lots of rush. Staff has little time or inclination to personalize the meal. It is difficult to estimate how much food or drink the resident has actually consumed. This environment is not conducive to assisting and supporting the individual client.

An alternate approach to the *one-seating* meal is the *two-seatings* meal, whereby residents are divided into two groups. One group is made up of cognitively alert residents who are fed together in one seat-

GENTLECARE Best Practice

The use of a tray changes the context of a meal. Residents with dementia may not recognize a tray of food as their dinner! Encourage staff to support the eating activity with information about the meal and cueing as needed. The need for a tray may be a sign that the client is having some new problem—a troublesome buddy, a bad seating arrangement, or perhaps the flu or a cold. Check it out.

ing. The second group consists of cognitively impaired or physically dysfunctional residents who are fed together in the other seating. *All staff should assist with both seatings.* Family members and volunteers may be trained to assist. (Gentlecare recommends that staff volunteers and family members who assist with eating be given a course of instruction in low-risk feeding techniques—many facilities offer such a course.) Gentlecare also recommends that cognitively alert clients be served at the first seating because they are often impatient, require little to no assistance, and appreciate a quiet, clean, and orderly dining room. They usually eat quickly and leave. At the George Derby Centre in Burnaby, B.C., these folks are known as "the come-and-goes"! Once they have finished eating they are assisted to use the bathroom, if necessary, and to rest and then to take part in one of the activities being offered.

Clients for the second seating should wait in their rooms or in the living room or lounge area until first-seating clients have vacated the dining room. This arrangement provides staff with more time to help cognitively impaired clients and reduces noise and confusion. Once their meal is concluded, this group is assisted to use the bathroom, if necessary, and then rest in their rooms until they are ready to participate in one of the day's activities.

The two-seating meal is Moyra's favorite arrangement!

Tray service may be used if the client is too ill or too frail to come to the dining room. Tray meals must be supervised to monitor for chok-

GENTLECARE Best Practice

GENTLECARE recommends a 30-minute rest period following meals.

ing episodes and to provide assistance with eating, and are thus labor intensive. Tray service may not be required for all meals. However, clients should never be forced to travel to a dining room if they feel un-well. Meals should be simple, and comfort foods should be provided. Due to the challenges of their illness, some clients may find eating in a health care facility dining room just too difficult. Despite efforts to re-duce noise, rush, crowds, etc., the client is over-stimulated,and staff must then find creative ways to adapt. Sometimes the easiest solution is simply to adjust the timing of the meal for that individual, to better suit his or her functional ability. Appliances such as microwaves and fridges on the units enable staff to serve meals at times that meet clients' special needs.

As decision-makers recognize the importance of the meal as a prin-cipal therapy, the use of the "two-seating model" is becoming more widespread. Those responsible for renovations or new construction are encouraged to review this model before designing dining space. The dining space should be built to accommodate a maximum of 30 people at each of two seatings. Facility managers with more than 50 to 60 beds are encouraged to renovate space for dining on each unit/floor/wing in order to take advantage of the benefits of the two-seating model. Social spaces such as pre-dining and post-dining areas need to be developed so that there are alternatives to remaining in the dining room after the meal is finished.

We cannot overstate the importance of preparing and serving food as a therapeutic activity. Eating is classified as one of the core activities, but it affects the success of all the activities in each of the four groups. It is also essential to make mealtimes look and taste like they did years ago...as the resident remembers them. By triggering his memory in this way you have given him a strong therapeutic boost that will pave the way to a helpful rest break. When a resident's meals—big or small, early or late, served in their room or the dining room—are properly managed, the day assumes a natural rhythm and residents are more likely to be in top form for each new activity.

PART FIVE

DESIGN FOR LIVING

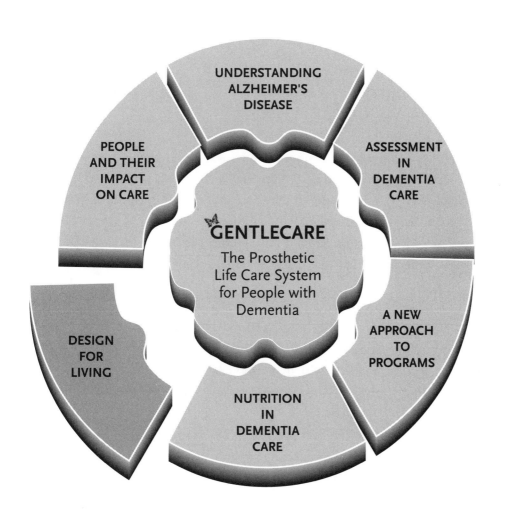

UNDERSTANDING ALZHEIMER'S DISEASE

PEOPLE AND THEIR IMPACT ON CARE

ASSESSMENT IN DEMENTIA CARE

GENTLECARE
The Prosthetic Life Care System for People with Dementia

A NEW APPROACH TO PROGRAMS

DESIGN FOR LIVING

NUTRITION IN DEMENTIA CARE

14

Homematch

We shape our buildings,
and then they shape us.
—Winston Churchill

Home is where the heart is. Home is a magic word. In each of our memories there is a special place that we regard as home. It may be the place where we grew up. It may be the first home we lived in when we were married, or the place where we raised our children. It may even be a new location at the end of a busy lifetime. Home, in fact, may not be a building at all, but rather a place, treasured possessions, or a feeling of comfort and ownership.

I have been thinking a great deal about the notion of home and what it means to me. For me, home is the beautiful old stone house I lived in for the first 20 years of my life. I recently visited it for the first time in many years, and felt the rush of memories: my parents, my friends, my wedding. Each stone and tree held a story that I felt impelled to relate to my traveling companion!

Home is also the first home that my husband and I lived in. How could I forget the wallpapering experience? Developing our first garden? Or the place where we raised our son? For the last 20 years, though, I have lived in a big old house on Canada's west coast. Surely, this is home! This is where my family lives, where my dogs are, my plants, my books, all the significant memories of my adult life.

And yet, due to the nature of my work, I live much of my life in hotels. Are they my homes too? I can only say that the way I organize the hotel room is very important to me. Before I even think about working or answering telephone messages, I must unpack my bags, place my pictures and books just so, arrange my tea-making utensils and all my safety equipment, place some flowers in view, and organize my pillows. Then and only then, with this illusion of home around me, am I ready to take on the world.

If this is my experience, could the importance of home affect others in a similar way? Could the place they live in be an important factor in the way they view life?

Hospitals used to be the places one visited in a medical emergency, to recover from disease, or to have some dysfunction repaired. Despite feeling unwell or frightened, there was always a mystique about hospitals—the stuff of life-and-death TV dramas. There is always a sort of magic or fascination attached to a brief visit to hospital. And we always knew we would be going home again soon.

However, hospitals have now assumed functions other than the treatment of acute illness. Together with a variety of care facilities, hospitals have become places where some people stay for a very long time. In fact, many people—elders especially—live out their lives in these essentially institutional buildings, which have become their home. Within the complex organization known as a health care facility, elderly people now must attempt to find their room, their bed, their bathroom, their bouquet of flowers. For people experiencing dementing illness, this is a virtually impossible undertaking.

Hospitals are essentially designed as places where health care personnel work. The complex medical, institutional, and technological nature of that work inevitably results in settings that are counter-therapeutic for residents who must, instead, use the facility for daily living.

Recognizing the need to modify this workplace setting so that residents can feel at home, long-term care facilities have for some time now attempted to create a residential character by using home-like furniture and decorating styles. Unfortunately, many such efforts do not

You are a King by your own fireside, as much as any monarch in his throne.

—CERVANTES,
   DON QUIXOTE

INSTITUTIONAL AMBIANCE

Typical views from the living space of older people who reside in health care facilities.

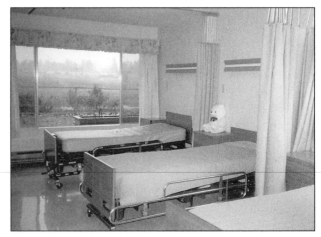

Ask yourself this question: "If I stepped out of my room into these corridors would I know where I was, or where to go to spend the rest of my day?"

RESIDENTIAL AMBIANCE

Example of attempts to develop a residential ambiance in the living space of older people within institutions.

A typical living room and bedroom in the home of an older person.

extend beyond front lobbies. They are often only window dressings—a marketing strategy rather than a sustained effort to create a domestic setting that people can control. For the most part, health care facilities for elderly people are places where residents know they should stay out of the way and be as inconspicuous as possible.

I have worked in a facility where a huge chain is placed across the dining room whenever meals are not being served so the room can be cleaned and remain tidy for the next meal. Such practices raise the question: When was the last time you were prevented by a chain from entering the dining room and food preparation area in your home? How would it make you feel to be excluded from an important part of your home? Would you feel in control of your life? Or would you feel like an intruder in someone else's space?

This is the dilemma facing elderly people when they live in health care facilities: how much like home is home? Only recently have there been serious efforts to assess the damage inflicted on people, especially elderly, cognitively impaired people, by the typical health care environment.

An example of removal of a door to a bathroom and replacement by a curtain.

The negative effects of noise, glare, confusion, and rush are becoming matters of great concern to health care planners— and at the same time, the notion of the positive potential of the environment as a therapeutic force has everyone excited. What if, by changing the places where demented people live, we can change their behavior? For example, what if we move the television out of the main dining room (as a large psychiatric hospital did recently) and as a result, people stop yelling? What if we change the current practice of bathing people by undressing them, draping them in a sheet, and wheeling them on a chair lift through crowded corridors to a room that looks like a car wash, and instead help them undress in a room that looks and feels like a bathroom? What if we find that they then actually enjoy their bath time?

What if we design bedrooms for elderly people that feel like regular bedrooms instead of hospital rooms? Might they then be more comfortable, content, compliant?

The possibilities of supportive environments are endless; they are limited only by our imaginations and creativity. For the most part, they are feasible and affordable. Putting a picture of a toilet on a bathroom door, taking off the bathroom door and replacing it with a curtain, improving the lighting between bedroom and bathroom—these approaches certainly cost less than using drugs or restraints to control an old gentleman who is searching for a bathroom, or worse still, devising his own toilet alternative.

Environmental adaptation does not cure dementing illnesses, but until a medical cure is available, developing people-friendly facilities goes a long way toward empowering cognitively impaired people. If we begin shaping buildings that people can enjoy living in, perhaps we can truly help people live through the devastation of dementia with some degree of comfort and dignity.

Let's examine the design principles that inform current building practices in health care. Space is typically allocated in descending order of priority:

- reception/administration
- nursing station/medication/records
- kitchen/food services
- dining room
- activity/dayroom areas
- rehabilitation/treatment areas
- patient rooms/bathrooms
- bathing areas
- cleaning/storage/utilities
- indoor/outdoor movement areas

Typical large surveillance station.

This environment is designed with a view to providing health services as quickly and effectively as possible. Safety, cleanliness, infection control, and surveillance are the operative words. The large, centrally located nursing station is perhaps the best example of inappropriate and archaic design, one that informs the culture of a facility. None of us has any area in our homes that remotely resembles this design feature. Such an arrangement of space and equipment speaks loudly of hospital, not home. Nursing stations are focal points in a hospital because staff are located behind them. Staff are people's major support system: most people depend on staff members to monitor their health, give them instructions, and liaise with their physicians. Staff control discharges, money, meals, bath times, cigarettes, and contact with families.

When people suffer from cognitive impairment, this kind of control becomes a life issue. If a person has no area of independence, he must keep his support system in view at all times; without these key individuals to feed, dress, toilet, and communicate, only the black pit of dementia exists. How better to keep one's support system within reach than to sit in a convenient row of chairs placed in front of the nursing station? Across the barrier, one can keep help in sight at all times—even speak to someone once in a while, or be spoken to as staff members move back and forth behind the counter.

Meanwhile, behind the barriers, staff members are absorbed in the tasks of charting, telephoning, and discussing health status. The exhausting effort of talking to cognitively impaired people, trying to get them involved, dealing with the needs of families, or working on relationships with fellow employees—those challenges can be put aside in favor of the comforting routine of paperwork.

And so the architectural barrier, the nursing station, begins to shape the way we work and the way residents live. Professional caregivers become abstract managers of paper and things, and cognitively impaired people become voyeurs and supplicants, waiting patiently for that one magic moment of contact when someone happens to emerge from behind the counter.

When I ask architects why they build these "air traffic control centers," as I call them, they cite the need to meet numerous technical requirements: a need for staff to have an unlimited view, for surveillance of large numbers of people; a need to protect confidentiality; security; and prevention of unacceptable resident access to computers, telephones, etc. However, everyone agrees that quality dementia care happens when staff mingle with residents. And we are all aware that sitting in a glass control center is an outdated practice. What facility has staff members available to sit and do surveillance anymore?

Most people would agree that security and confidentiality can best be achieved by the provision of an enclosed, out-of-sight room. Small, well-designed communication rooms where staff members can carry out essential phoning or charting activity, in relative calm, are beginning to replace traditional nursing stations. Not surprisingly, when staff can work in privacy, residents begin to use more appropriate living spaces, indoors and outdoors, abandoning the line of chairs in the corridor.

A new order of priority in long-term care facility design is beginning to emerge:

- resident room/bathroom
- activity areas
- social/dining areas
- bathrooms
- indoor/outdoor movement areas
- communication room for use by multi-disciplinary team
- kitchen/food services
- rehabilitation services
- cleaning/storage
- administration/reception

An example of a well-designed communications room.

This new emphasis views design from the perspective of the person who lives in the space rather than as a work space for staff. It attempts to address the reality that many older people no longer simply pass through health care facilities, but rather live out their lives within them. There is an effort underway to capture the spirit and comfort of "home" as a means of combating the destructive interaction of dementia and institutionalization.

As we begin to assess the potential for harm or for help that exists within environments, some basic principles emerge:

- Design should be sensitive to the needs of the users. Elderly people appear to be best served when they are in a home-like environment.
- Design should reflect the type of building being planned, as well as who will occupy the building. What will this building be used for?

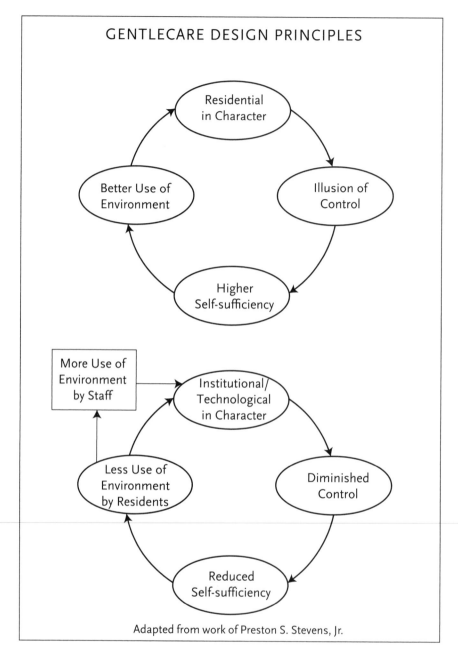

GENTLECARE DESIGN PRINCIPLES

Residential in Character

Better Use of Environment

Illusion of Control

Higher Self-sufficiency

More Use of Environment by Staff

Institutional/ Technological in Character

Less Use of Environment by Residents

Diminished Control

Reduced Self-sufficiency

Adapted from work of Preston S. Stevens, Jr.

FIGURE 14-1

- Design for social organization. Does this building permit or discourage social interaction?
- Design should respect the individuality of people, especially older people. No one design fits all.
- Design should take into account the effects of the disease process on the people who will use the building.

- Aging is a multi-dimensional process. Design should take into account the functional ability of each individual resident in terms of biology, psychology, and social reactions.
- Design for aging people must reflect sensory changes, especially auditory and visual changes.
- Design features should stress wellness, not illness.
- The scale of the building should not be overwhelming, but rather should be designed as manageable space for older people.

In the Gentlecare system, the physical environment is one of three critical elements (People, Programs, and Physical Space) that together make up the prosthetic program for people with dementia. Often, the physical space of Gentlecare is one element that people attempt to implement—because it seems easier, more concrete, quicker, and cheaper. But design of a prosthetic physical environment goes far beyond the installation of colored toilet seats or the use of non-glare wax.

The following design criteria (adapted from the work of Preston S. Stevens, Jr.) are fundamental to building the Gentlecare environmental prosthesis:

- The more residential the character of a building, and the more it resembles home, the more comfortable the person living there will be.
- The higher the comfort level within the building, the more people will feel in control of the spatial situations in which they find themselves.
- The greater the illusion of control people have, the more functional they will be. One's level of self-sufficiency increases proportionately to the sense one has of control over one's destiny.
- The more intact a person's level of functioning, the better the chances of them making use of the environment.
- Finally, the more we live in and use an environment, the more we will shape it into our personal version of home or residence.

Unfortunately, in the design of most health care facilities, the exact reverse of this process is the norm. As Figure 14.1 indicates, typical health care facilities are institutional in nature, highly technological, and designed for work efficiency and staff use. Residents who live in such facilities feel uncomfortable and experience no sense of control. Residents are heard to say: "Is this my bed?"; "Can I sit here?"; and "Is it okay if I go out?"

As a result of their perception that they are interlopers in an institutional setting, they are reluctant to assert their abilities. They are afraid to look after themselves, explore their environment, or make unilateral decisions. As they become more helpless, they make less and less use of the facility's space; typically, they sit for long periods in corridors, in dayrooms, or in their bedrooms. The phenomenon of alienation from the environment holds true for family members, as well.

Since people make little use of living space within the facility, staff members begin to use it as work space. Corridors become filled with laundry, housekeeping materials, medication carts, and storage boxes. Areas are blocked off for dining only, or cleaning, or charting. Residents are moved to the periphery of the space. The physical environment becomes more and more institutional in nature: more and more technology is put in place such as public address systems, alarmed doors, wander-guards, even special sensors attached to people to alert staff when they move about. As time schedules, routines, and staffing patterns lock into place, they create a circle of influence that tightens and tightens, choking off any home-like ambiance of the structure and defining its use.

The feeling of place is a power within us.

—JAMES REANEY

A TOUCHING THING HAPPENED *in a facility recently. I was working with a very imposing-looking gentleman who was a stranger to the facility, as I was. We were approached by an elderly lady who said, "Are you the government man?" My associate acknowledged this by saying, "Yes, I do work for the government." "Do you have a ticket, then?" she asked. "A ticket?" "Yes, I want to go out to that concert in the park," she said.*

Tragically, residents often refuse to eat because they are afraid that they cannot pay the bills in the fancy restaurant. Or they are afraid they are in the way. Or they think the chair, the room, or the garden belongs to someone else. All these perceptions, engendered by the environment, contribute to iatrogenic illness. By focusing on changing the physical environment, the Gentlecare system attempts to engage the remnants of personal power behind the disease in an effort to make cognitively impaired elders feel more comfortable and in control of their lives.

A DIRECTOR OF NURSING SERVICES *called me to say they had recently moved their cognitively impaired residents to a quiet area of the facility where they could move about indoors and in the garden if they wished. The staff had no budget to decorate or remodel the area in any special way, but they thought they would take this first step. She said, "Moyra, we simply couldn't believe it! Overnight we noticed changes in people's ability to eat, and groom, toilet, and dress themselves. They seemed so much happier and content. We can hardly wait to begin to make some real changes."*

15

Designed to Heal

In the fifth century B.C., Hippocrates, the father of medicine, was said to have taught his students outdoors, under a tree. The aesculapiums (the ancient temples of healing) were places to treat both body and soul. Greek patients were soothed by massage, mud baths, and herbal teas. Their minds were stimulated and healed with poetry, music, and drama.

Just as surely as architecture can dehumanize an environment, it can also help to humanize it. Since the major group in most health care facilities consists of elderly people, it is important to reflect on the human needs of these users of the system, and to design facilities accordingly.

Design Implications Due to Changes in Health Status

Research has shown that as people age, five specific spheres of function are affected: vision, perception, sensory integration, motor ability, and cognition. Gentlecare addresses the design implications of each of these functional changes.

Vision

The richest of the human senses, vision provides us with a wealth of information that has a decisive influence on our reactions, our ability to concentrate, our efficiency, and our general sense of well-being or fatigue. For many people, the first overt sign of aging is *presbyopia* (difficulty with near vision resulting from a loss of elasticity in the lens of the eye). People experience an extreme sensitivity to glare. Changes, or perceived changes, in levels of flooring due to colors or patterns can result in falls. Reduced visual acuity means lighting levels must be augmented and colors chosen carefully.

When poor lighting combines with colors, patterns, and texture—especially in crowded areas—the stage is set for elderly people to have problems. As a person's ability to distinguish varying levels of light intensity (as given off by color in patterned flooring, for example) decreases, the pattern gives the illusion of a step. As the elderly person responds to this perception, they lose their balance and fall. At the same time a lack of color or more significantly, a lack of a figure/ground contrast, can give older people the impression of being in a "whiteout." They have an unpleasant feel-

Floor patterns appear as holes or steps to cognitively impaired people.

ing of uncertain footing or an absence of solid footing which is very uncomfortable. Often they stop walking and remain in bed or in a chair in order to compensate.

GENTLECARE Best Practice

Gentlecare suggests staff members work for a few hours wearing very dark sunglasses, while at the same time assessing the effect this has on their functioning levels.

This quickly leads to loss of function. Many new buildings are decorated in popular colors of pink, peach, or beige with no contrast or grounding features to assist older people to move about comfortably.

It is generally agreed that elderly people (especially those with changes to brain tissue) require at least three times as much light as younger people in the same environment. Gentlecare recommends the use of natural light or incandescent light. Floor and table lamps can be bolted in place like those in motels, and track lighting can be used to provide illumination for specific tasks. Strong contrasts in light should be avoided: for instance, a dark bedroom should not connect to a brightly lit bathroom, nor should a bright corridor lead into a darkened room. Do not follow the common practice of dimming lights to reduce anxiety and agitation. Such a practice has the effect of putting elderly people into a blackout, and of course, then they do not move around. All these changes make it difficult to read and interpret the environment correctly.

Perception

As people age, and particularly if they suffer from cognitive impairment, the parietal lobe of the brain is affected. The ability to manage one's body in space and to perceive and understand environmental stimulation is impaired. Environmental design can either support failing spatial perception or further undermine it. Avoid at all costs the use of wall sconces which produce a dangerous pattern of light and dark that disorients older people, causing falls and fractures.

Pattern, juxtaposition of colors, and differences in light/ dark contrast all affect the elderly person's ability to move safely and use space effectively. Every effort should be made to choose flooring without any pattern, and in warm mid-range colors. Carpeting should be constructed with a tight weave and a short strand length; smooth floor coverings should be slightly cushioned and have a non-glare matte finish. Glare is every bit as toxic for a perceptually impaired person as are rush, noise, and confusion. Avoid the currently popular use of dark borders in corridors. Such borders force older people to leap over perceived gaps in the carpeting, causing falls.

Parietal lobe damage also impairs a person's ability to correctly identify objects and locations. Identical corridors, bedrooms, or doors make it difficult for elderly people to distinguish their own room from those of others. Gentlecare recommends the use of good wayfinding cues, in both picture and word form. Familiar objects that break up the length of corridors give important sensory clues to cognitively im-

Glare, color, texture, and confusion all affect a person's ability to move comfortably.

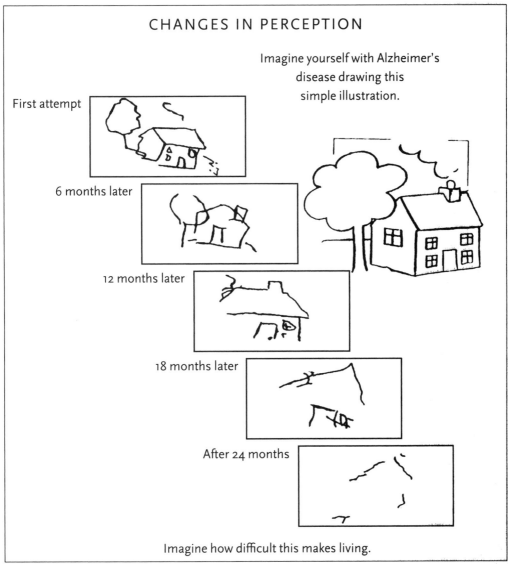

CHANGES IN PERCEPTION

Imagine yourself with Alzheimer's disease drawing this simple illustration.

First attempt

6 months later

12 months later

18 months later

After 24 months

Imagine how difficult this makes living.

FIGURE 15·1

paired elderly people. As the brain ages (and all of our brains are aging!) our ability to perceive, identify, and integrate sensory stimulation (shapes, colors, textures, figure/ground definition, depth perception, and sounds) is impaired. A dark color may be perceived as a hole or drop-off; shiny floors may become lakes or skating rinks; and ordinary sounds can become oppressive and frightening. Most importantly, sensory integration is slowed down. Thus, elderly people who are rushed or in crowds cannot decipher stimulation quickly enough to be able to re-act appropriately, and are thus at risk for falls. They may also be frightened and anxious, due to misinterpretation.

Motor Function

As people age, muscular/skeletal difficulties occur. As a result, balance is impaired and reaction time is slowed. The ability to lift one's feet and manoeuver is compromised. Patterns, textures, colors, glare, rush, noise, crowds—all these combine to cause elderly people difficulties in mobility and functioning.

Elderly people lose muscle strength, and this is exacerbated by the fact that they often just sit for long hours. It becomes harder for them to move through large spaces, down long corridors, and around huge outdoor spaces. Muscle contractures, joint fusion, pain, and edema combine to prevent the older person from moving freely and making full use of the living environment and outdoor spaces. Designers must take this into account, arranging for smaller spaces, easier access, and safer footing.

Cognition

As dementing illness destroys memory and memory-processing ability, the critical life function of learning is lost. A person with Alzheimer's disease cannot process new information. Thus a new location, new people, new procedures, and unfamiliar routines make life terribly challenging and difficult for a person with a dementing illness. People with dementia cannot remember directions; they cannot follow directions, or problem-solve their way out of strange places. They cannot differentiate their room from that of another person, especially if the doors are identical. They cannot find access doors, or even ask for appropriate information. If they do receive useful information, they forget it before they can use it.

People with dementia lose the ability to reason. Thus they cannot understand why they must bathe, or why we use a mechanical lift to assist with bathing. They cannot understand why they must sit in a certain location, or why they cannot lie down on a bed just because it hap-

Alzheimer's disease affects gait patterns and possibly leads to falls.

pens to be assigned to someone else. They do not understand that messages conveyed over public address systems into their "home" do not apply to them, but rather are messages for other people. The ability to use one's mind to problem-solve one's way through a frightening and challenging environment slowly diminishes.

So how can we make a better match between our health care environment and people's special needs? How can we make institutions feel like home? How can we achieve Homematch to limit the effects of illness and support residual function?

Critical Elements of the Prosthetic Environment

Safety and Security

People with dementia live out their lives in the physical space provided by the health care system. Because of the massive damage these people have suffered to memory, reasoning, and the judgment centers of the brain, the area in which they live must be secure and free from significant risk.

People with dementia do not understand why they are being asked to stay in a strange place, and many desperately try to leave—they want to find their home and family and attend to their responsibilities. In health care we give this behavior all manner of euphemistic titles: exterior wanderers, elopers, exit seeking behavior, etc. The hard fact is that the person doesn't feel at home and tries to leave to find his real home.

Thus perimeters of buildings need to be secured. Once this basic safeguard is in place, staff time is freed up to comfort and support the people with dementia, rather than being devoted to enforcement of building exit rules. The widespread reluctance to provide secure perimeters stems from troubling images of locked areas, ghettos, restraints, and prisons. However, if buildings housing elderly people with dementia are not secured, eventually physical and chemical restraint measures will be used to confine these vulnerable people to specified locations.

It is sometimes helpful to compare our attitudes toward secure perimeters around children's daycare facilities, and our feelings about

GENTLECARE DESIGN PRINCIPLES

The Gentlecare system develops living environments based on the following essential elements:

Safety and Security

People with dementia lack cognition, reason, and judgment. Their environment must have safe perimeters and their accommodations must be reasonably free from risk. Security measures must be as non-invasive as possible. Sound alarms should be avoided.

Access and Mobility

Due to confusion and disorientation, access must be clearly defined and lead the person into the appropriate areas. Good access should exist indoors and outdoors. Freedom of movement is critical to good dementia care. Walkways should be inviting, clear of obstacles, and lead the person to where they want to go, or to interesting objects.

Function and Activity

Prosthetic environments exist to be used by the people who live there. Opportunity for engagement, interaction, and meaningful activities should be non-intrusive and not distract from the home-like atmosphere.

Individual Control Privacy Comfort Sociality

People with dementia should be regarded as guests. The environment exists for their enjoyment and use. The physical space should be designed to invite or direct social contact, give comfort, and respect privacy.

Flexibility Choices Change Participation Decision-making

Dementia is a disease in progress. It involves a widely differing group of people. The environment should be designed to accommodate changing needs. The perception that this is the resident's home governs all activity.

FIGURE 15-2

secure perimeters in long-term care facilities. No one would consider placing a child in a program that allowed unrestricted access to busy streets, yet we do not speak of daycare centers as locked units or prisons. It is expected that organizations caring for children arrange for their safety and security. In fact, so ingrained is the practice of securing buildings that house children that we scarcely ever discuss the issue.

Yet every day, health care personnel fight and struggle to keep people with dementia from leaving buildings and wandering into dangerous traffic. Staff members spend endless time running after escaping people and attempting to persuade them to come back. They notify family members, often in the middle of the night, that their loved ones have eloped.

New technology is regularly introduced into health care institutions: alarms, buzzers, and sensors are designed to warn staff that a resident is exiting without permission. The pandemonium that results when the alarms go off drives everyone crazy, residents and staff members alike. Alarms are rapidly becoming the new frontier of restraint. There has to be a better way—and there is.

Dutch doors, murals, or distracting objects can often keep people with dementia from exiting doors.

Many health care facilities use silent key-pad operated locks to provide security at exit doors. The code for the lock is posted, so staff, visitors, and cognitively alert residents can exit and enter at will. Frequently these doors are camouflaged by painting the door the same color as the adjoining walls, or by placing a distracting or interesting

Contrast the difference between these two gardens. One is inviting, while the other could be perceived as a prison.

object in the corridor several feet before the door to engage the attention of residents.

Fences are the best method of securing the exterior perimeters of a facility. If the fence is attractive, natural, and interesting, it can serve as an effective security measure. If the fence is oppressive, bare, and ugly, it may encourage the idea of escape.

People with dementia face other risks as well. In an effort to promote safety, health care institutions often eliminate every conceivable risk factor. As a result, special care units or dementia areas become unstimulating places where people with Alzheimer's disease wander meaninglessly through empty rooms and up and down bare corridors, or walk back and forth on cement walkways outdoors. Plants are forbidden because they might be poisonous. Pictures and curtains are eliminated because people might tear them down. Personal possessions are ruled out because someone might steal them. All small objects are eliminated, because someone might swallow them. Such attitudes subject elderly people to safe but empty, meaningless lives. We would never dream of raising children in such a bleak atmosphere, even though they are certainly capable of all the risk behaviors just mentioned.

Of course it is very important to ensure that elderly people with dementia do not come to any harm. However, experience has shown that the more residential the environment, the more appropriate the behavior of the person with dementia will be. Units that abound with beautiful, interesting, meaningful objects that offer support and comfort to people with dementia bring out the best of their remaining function. Natural plants create a familiar atmosphere that evokes a former life, and provide hours of meaningful work. (See Figures 15-3 and 15-4 for a list of toxic and non-toxic plants to be included in indoor and garden design.) Gentlecare avoids artificial plants, which confuse people with dementia and do not give the same joy as natural ones.

Collections of interesting objects in baskets, trunks, dressers, desks, or hutches provide points of interest and endless hours of rummaging opportunities. Families are urged to supply generic objects or replicas of their loved ones' treasured possessions; thus, if another person becomes attracted to a particular object, it can be replaced without problems or recriminations.

The world begins to exist when the individual discovers it.

—CARL JUNG

Safety is important, but it must be kept in perspective and not be allowed to overshadow the opportunity for a meaningful life experience.

Access, Mobility, and Wayfinding

Freedom of movement is critical to quality dementia care. Walkways should provide appropriate orientation and support to help people navigate their living space successfully. Both indoor and outdoor walking spaces should be provided.

It is preferable that pathways lead people to interesting locations or objects. Seating areas where people can rest are desirable along walking routes.

People experiencing dementia suffer from disorientation. Written signs have limited usefulness for them, so Gentlecare recommends using comforting objects to identify significant spaces or personal rooms: for example, artwork, quilts, grandfather clocks, desks, bookshelves, or large plants.

Life panels, often designed by family members, help people find their rooms, and give them reassurance, ownership, and a sense of being someone special.

Furniture arrangements and interesting objects draw people with dementia into an area without the need for staff intervention. Gentle-

This doesn't look like any typewriter I've ever used!

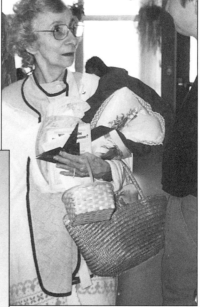

Sometimes small treasures can be found.

Rummaging is a great way to pass the time.

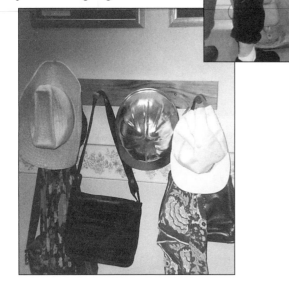

Hat collections are fun and intriguing.

Moving furniture about is a wonderful means of exercise.

care refers to such environmental arrangements as *non-human caregivers,* because of the pleasure and comfort they give and the fact that caregivers do not need to be involved.

WALK THROUGH AREAS *in a facility or home as if you were contemplating living in the space. Check out the rooms for their livability. Are areas clearly defined? Are interesting objects in view? Is the area comfortable, inviting, personalized?*

Design access to the outdoors. Gentlecare recommends providing interesting objects that lead or entice people to the outdoors. Combinations of grass and asphalt provide safe walking experiences. Wooden decks are useful and comfortable.

Small social areas filled with beautiful objects give pleasure all day.

Function and Activity

Celebrate people's competency and remaining function. Provide environmental opportunities for people with dementia to do normal, everyday activities. Try to achieve activity, interaction, and conversation through environmental design. To compensate for sensory deficits:

- Place interesting, fragrant, textured, visually attractive objects within reach of residents. Objects that are placed out of reach do not exist in the minds of people with dementia, and therefore serve only as token attempts to create interesting environments. Furthermore, if sensory-stimulating materials are locked away in cupboards or placed in a special

A familiar clothesline outside a door invites an elderly person to participate in activity.

These objects cannot be seen or used.

Familiar activities like visiting or reading the newspaper are encouraged.

room, access to stimulating activities becomes dependent on staff involvement.

- Personalize.
- Individualize.
- Normalize.
- Stress continuity with the past and former good times through the use of life panels, powerful 8 × 10 pictures of the person at significant times in life—for instance, at his wedding.
- Leave objects in plain sight.
- Display treasure chests, chests of drawers, baskets full of objects.
- Place antique objects in view.
- Use giant fabric flowers, birds, or animals.
- Enlarge photos, especially old familiar ones.
- Place real plants in the room that can be smelled, picked, and watered.
- Arrange tasks that are in progress to entice people to become involved. Any activity is a good one if the person enjoys it, and no one else is harmed.
- Place tools and work supplies in clear view.
- Provide rummage opportunities.
- Design privacy opportunities—small, quiet hide-outs where elderly people can go for rest, serenity, and time alone.
- Design quiet and active areas.
- Design redundant cueing in the environment. Use any method to make information available (verbal, visual, olfactory, tactile). Use pictures, smells,

Beautiful spaces help alleviate the effects of dementia.

textures. Arrange for whiffs of familiar odors: coffee, toast, bacon, ginger, baking (yeast), lemon, tomato, cedar chips, cut evergreens, lavender, flowers, and perfume.

Arabian tents provide inexpensive and effective shady areas.

- Design shady areas protected from the wind. Include rain shelters. Elderly people do not enjoy direct sunlight or drafts. Use arbors, trellises, umbrellas, canopies, and large open, lighted gazebos. People with dementia will not enter small dark gazebo structures.
- Avoid a design that is park-like, or emulates a large public garden, sports ground, or playground ambiance. People with dementia will be afraid to enter such an area because the scale is overwhelming.
- Use a variety of leading points of interest to entice people into the garden and around the walking areas.
- Design walking pathways with edges flush to the ground. Pathways do not need to go in circles. It does help, however, if the path eventually leads people back to the door of the building.

The joy of one's own backyard.

- Highlight existing trees and plant additional ones for shade.
- Hang bird feeders, bird houses, and hanging plants from tree branches.
- Include piles of wood and places to pile wood as part of the garden.
- Install clotheslines against walls so people will not walk into them, with small tables for a clothes basket. Circular clotheslines work well, too.
- Set aside an area of dirt piles, shovels, wheelbarrows, etc.
- Install a dog house.
- Bird baths are magic! Surround them with seating to create a viewing area.
- Avoid fountains, pools, fish, and lily ponds unless you want to be on

People with dementia have a tendency to direct their gaze downward. Objects above shoulder level are rarely enjoyed by them and are therefore of no therapeutic value.

Contrast the ambiance of the institutional emptiness of the space above with the backyard comfort and relaxation depicted below.

Raised flower beds give extra comfort to elderly people as they are easily accessed.

a toileting routine! People with dementia are both frightened and fascinated by water. They will wade in pools and will need to go to the bathroom if they hear or see water.

• Set up a mailbox.

• Create a back porch effect, with shelter and appropriate furniture.

• Use large flowers like daisies and sunflowers, and fast-growing dramatic vegetables like zucchini and tomatoes.

• Cover fences with flowering vines and grapevines.

•Include some grass in the garden, and provide a push lawn mower.

•Some facilities use old cars, motor bikes, or bicycles for a work activity such as washing, polishing, or tire kicking.

•Set up a habitat for rabbits, ducks, etc.

•Consider placing an old-fashioned pump in the garden.

•Camouflage fences with shrubbery. Gentlecare uses flowering vines like clematis, Virginia creeper, or wisteria, and vegetables like beans, spaghetti squash, or sweet peas. Place clotheslines against fences or woodpiles. These designs distract from the feeling of being walled in.

• Outdoor gardens should resemble and feel like an older person's backyard.

• Balance safety with independence. Keep outdoor areas simple and normal.

• Often families or community organizations will sponsor and help care for a garden area. Make sure they understand the concept of a working garden in dementia care, so they don't create a park or a formal garden.

Individual Control, Privacy, Comfort, and Sociality

Low walls give a feeling of privacy in a busy dining room.

- Focus on wellness.
- Get rid of illness-oriented spaces and other reminders of incapacity in the environment. Place nursing stations, medicine carts, dirty linen, housekeeping supplies, supply cupboards, and items for storage in less prominent areas of the facility. Camouflage the doors leading to such service areas, and make the areas as inconspicuous as possible. Avoid medication carts in dining rooms; distribute medication before or after meals, not during them.
- Avoid large open spaces. Design small interesting environments at the entrance to the yard, the dining room, or any large open space so as to entice people into that space on their own.
- Design to a residential, not institutional, scale that is manageable from the perspective of the person with dementia.
- Arrange the life of the person with dementia around family clusters of four to six people, to minimize overwhelming interactions. In Gentlecare, for instance, meals are offered in small family-sized groups, rather than being presented to large numbers of people in large noisy dining rooms.
- Focus on individuality and personal ownership: each person should have some private space.

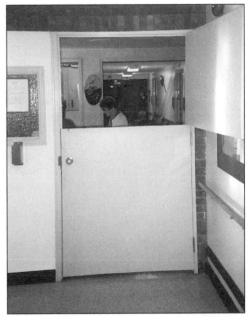

The use of a Dutch door reduces the amount of space and stimuli that a person must cope with, thus reducing anxiety and exhaustion. This is the most benign form of environmental restraint.

Flexibility: Choices and Change

- Use music and TV selectively.
- Place TVs in separate viewing rooms so residents can choose to be in a quiet room if they prefer. Avoid using TV or stereo as background or as a babysitting activity: people with dementia cannot remove themselves, protest, or make adjustments in volume. TVs should not be watched by staff members while they are on duty.
- Design space for family and volunteer use. Make them feel welcome.
- Abandon notions of neatness and order. If they are to achieve activity and interaction, dementia units should have the appearance and ambiance of a well-used home.
- Avoid shiny, polished, patterned surfaces.
- Patterns that have fine details tend to confuse, and should be avoided. Floral patterns that contrast strongly with the background color can increase confusion. Abstract patterns and stripes can appear to move or shimmer. Still-life patterns can be confused with reality, and should be avoided. The same is true of decorative murals or life-size drawings.
- Avoid the use of mirrors and glass blocks.
- Reduce noise pollution, especially in dining rooms. Avoid the use of background music, and turn off public address systems; ask staff to speak softly to one another; reduce the clamor by using rubber-tired equipment; hang acoustical wall hangings; install acoustic ceilings; install wall carpeting to waist height; divide large space with partitions; minimize random noise; and develop a policy of zero tolerance for noise in your facility.
- Color schemes should use warm, mid-range hues; cool colors appear washed out, and sharp color contrasts can be uncomfortable.

Space should be developed for use by volunteers and family members.

- Chairs and sofas should have high seats, sturdy arms, and no support pillars between the front legs. Their functional purpose should be clear. Bean bag chairs are actually a restraint and should not be used, since an older person cannot get out of them easily.
- Furniture should have rounded edges and an uncomplicated design.
- Use tall, sturdy plants for aesthetic interest and to change the atmosphere in a room.
- Boost illumination, especially in the afternoons and evenings. Use portable or standing lights for tasks, and to give a sense of comfort and security. Bolt lamps to tables.
- Illuminate changes in floor surfaces. Avoid sharp color contrasts, confusing patterns, and fine detail in flooring patterns.
- Use indirect and diffused lighting to reduce glare and shadows. Light levels should be consistent across all areas. Use warm white fluorescent light. Use more than one source of light. Illuminate entrances.
- Use cluster furniture arrangements to encourage socialization.
- Develop clear circulation pathways to promote security and competency.
- Use partitions to block the view of larger, potentially frightening spaces.
- Design "bus stops" or rest areas to provide opportunities to stop on the way to and from the dining room. Even a chair to lean on can help.
- Design bathroom facilities in close proximity to dining/activity rooms. Make them easily accessible and have them clearly identified.
- Check the functional relationship between the

Contrast these two living spaces. One looks like a furniture storage area, while the other is filled with interesting things to do.

An example of a non-human caregiver . . . an inviting space.

heights of dining chairs and table height. A person's arm should be able to clear the top of the table easily.

- Arrange hutches and/or sideboards with familiar and interesting objects, pictures, and flowers. Create a mood or theme that reflects the natural lifestyle of elderly people.
- Keep corridors short or break them into sections by placing objects on one side of the corridor only, to facilitate movement.

To assess the perspective of the elderly person, lie on his bed to see what he sees.

- Design to a residential scale, rather than to a hotel or commercial scale.
- Avoid large waiting room spaces in front of the nursing station. Eliminate glass barriers, counters, or enclosures that separate staff from residents. Design to encourage staff/client relationships and interaction.
- Design bedrooms to permit a variety of bed locations.
- Design display panels at the entrance to people's bedrooms to enhance cueing and staff knowledge of residents.
- Focus display boards, picture groups, or furniture at the foot or the side of the bed so that the person in bed can see them. Avoid displays at the head of the bed. Sometimes photos can be more easily seen if they are placed on the ceiling or low down at the side of the bed.

An example of a beautiful dining room.

- Design ledges of windows so that they are wide enough for plants, books, or other objects.
- Use small desks or work tables in rooms to encourage activity.
- Make dining rooms visually appealing and distinctive for older people. This should be a special room; places where people eat should be beautiful, quiet, and relaxing.
- Use square tables for four or round tables for six to encourage socialization and visual contact.

- Place tables at an angle to the wall rather than parallel to it so people can be seated or depart easily.
- Arrange small, intimate dining areas that remind people of home.
- Avoid large institutional spaces designed for dining activity only. They are noisy, crowded, and formidable for people with dementia. Use portable panels or half-walls to break up large dining spaces into quiet, manageable areas. Try using narrow planters mounted on wheels that lock as adjustable partitions. Furniture arrangements can also provide for the partition of space.
- Supervisory personnel should be conveniently stationed but discreet.
- Gentlecare recommends the use of the old-time family kitchen or family room that encourages not only dining activity but socialization and work.
- Use flexible seating arrangements so people have new dining partners at different meal times.
- Avoid the use of feeding tables. Such equipment infantilizes elders, causes difficulties in perception, promotes helplessness, diminishes functional ability, and can cause choking.

Bathrooms

- Bathrooms and bathing areas should be designed to protect privacy, dignity, and safety.
- Fixtures should be color-contrasted with the walls and floor of the bathroom to make them easier to see and recognize.

Contrast the atmosphere of family rooms or kitchens with the ambiance of a feeding table.

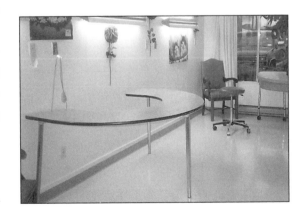

Clearly designate the room's function on the door of the bathroom. Avoid abstract designs.

Fixtures should be contrasted against the wall and floor of the bathroom for easier identification.

• Cupboards for storage purposes should be provided in bathrooms. Rooms should be decorated with hanging plants (we use artificial ones in bathrooms), pictures, and beautiful objects. Include a towel warmer for comfort.

In general, reduce the amount of space and the number of stimuli elderly people must cope with. Anxiety and exhaustion can be significantly reduced if people are protected from over-stimulation. The most benign environmental restraint is the Dutch door; during monitored periods it allows residents to rest, and often to sleep.

Special Care Units have been criticized as serving merely to segregate troublesome dementia victims from other residents, but actually they should be the critical physical space of the prosthesis of care.

Plants: Toxic and Non-toxic

The use of living plants in a facility can make it much more homelike and functional; however, there are concerns about the use of some plants, which can be toxic if eaten. The following lists can be used as guidelines for unsafe and safe plants. Whatever you do, don't deny older people the joy of plants and gardens.

TOXIC PLANTS

The following plants are considered poisonous and possibly dangerous. They contain a wide variety of poisons, and symptoms may vary from a mild stomachache, skin rash, or swelling of the mouth and throat to involvement of the heart, kidneys, or other organs. A poison control center can provide specific information on these plants and others that may not be on this list but can be poisonous. *Many plants do not cause toxicity unless eaten in very large amounts.*

anemone	angel's trumpet (red sage)
apricot kernels	arrowhead
avocado (leaves)	azaleas
betel nut palm	bittersweet
buckeye	buttercups
caladium	calla lily
castor bean	cherries (wild and cultivated)
crocus, autumn	daffodil
daphne	delphinium
dieffenbachia (dumb cane)	devil's ivy
elderberry	elephant's ear
four o'clock	foxglove
holly berries	horse chestnut
horsetail reed	hyacinth
hydrangea	iris
ivy (Boston, English, and others)	jack-in-the-pulpit
jequirtity bean or pea	jerusalem cherry
jessamine (jasmine)	jimsonweed (thorn apple)
jonquil	laburnum
lantana camara	larkspur
laurel	lily-of-the-valley
lobelia	marijuana
mayapple	mistletoe
moonseed	monkshood
morning glory	mother-in-law plant
mushrooms	narcissus
nightshade	oleander
periwinkle	peyote (mescal)
philodendron	poinsettia
poison hemlock	poison ivy
poison oak	poppy
pokeweed	potato sprouts
ranunculus	rhododendron
rhubarb (leaves)	rosary pea
star-of-bethlehem	tobacco
tomato (except fruit)	tulip
wisteria	water hemlock
yew	

Do not further confuse elderly people with dementia by using artificial or silk plants.

FIGURE 15-3

NON-TOXIC PLANTS

The following plants are considered essentially safe and not poisonous. Symptoms from eating or handling these plants are unlikely, but any plant may cause an unexpected reaction in certain individuals.

african daisy	african palm
african violet	airplane plant
aluminum plant	aralia, false
araucaria	asparagus fern
aspidistra (cast iron plant)	aster
baby's tears	bachelor buttons
bamboo	begonia
birds' nest fern	bloodleaf plant
bougainvillea	camellia
Christmas cactus	chrysanthemum
coleus species	corn plant
crab apples	creeping charlie
creeping jenny (moneywort, lysima)	
croton species	croton (house variety)
dahlia	daisies
dandelions	dogwood
donkey tail	Easter lily
echeveria	eucalyptus (caution)
eugenia	fuchsia
gardenia	gloxinia
grape ivy	hibiscus
honeysuckle	hoya
impatiens	jade plant
kalanchoe	lily (day, Easter, or tiger)
lipstick plant	magnolia
marigold	monkey plant
Norfolk island pine	orchid
Oregon grape	pepperornia
petunia	piggy-back plant
prayer plant	purple passion
pyracantha	rose
rubber plant	salal
sansevieria	schefflera
spider plant	Swedish ivy
umbrella tree	violets
wandering Jew	wax plant
weeping fig	zebra plant

Any activity is a good one if the person enjoys it, and no one else is harmed.

FIGURE 15-4

Living space for people with dementia should be:

- normal
- home-like
- therapeutic
- non-technological
- prosthetic
- warm mid-range colors

They should avoid patterns that dominate or move, have comfortable objects and pictures, and be, in short, just like home.

FIGURE 15-5

PART SIX

PEOPLE AND THEIR IMPACT ON CARE

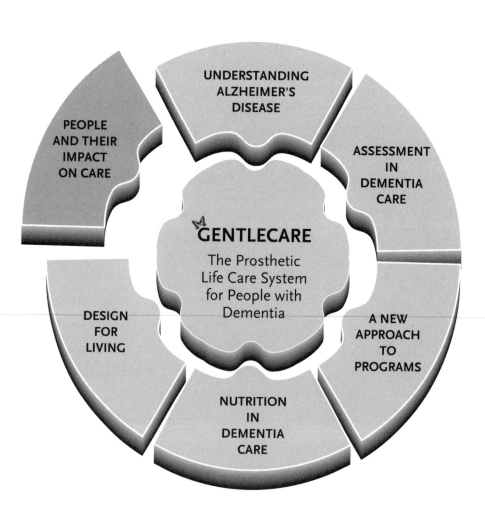

PEOPLE AND THEIR IMPACT ON CARE

UNDERSTANDING ALZHEIMER'S DISEASE

ASSESSMENT IN DEMENTIA CARE

GENTLECARE
The Prosthetic Life Care System for People with Dementia

DESIGN FOR LIVING

A NEW APPROACH TO PROGRAMS

NUTRITION IN DEMENTIA CARE

16

People as Prosthesis

The world breaks everyone, and afterward
many are strong at the broken places....
— Ernest Hemingway, *A Farewell to Arms*

In his lovely book *The Notebook,* Nicholas Sparks writes about Alzheimer's disease:

> *It is a barren disease, as empty and lifeless as a desert. It is a thief of hearts and souls and memories.*

In Gentlecare we have studied dementia in great detail, noting the destruction it creates in its victims. We have shared the horrors of the bleak reality that for many of these diseases there is no known cause, and therefore no cure.

In our search to discover how to help people live through the experience of dementing illness, Gentlecare introduces the paradigm of the prosthesis of care: three critical elements of support that provide families and others who care with a way of helping. These three elements are people, programs, and physical space.

Of the three, the people component is by far the most powerful. People are the therapy.

The world of the person suffering from dementing illness is populated by a variety of people. There are family members; there are many types of professional care providers; there are volunteers and important community service organizations. People in each of these categories have an impact for good or for harm on someone in the throes of dementing illness. People are important in any type of undertaking; but people *are* health care.

Dementia care, wherever it occurs, depends upon quality of service, flexibility, constant problem-solving, and innovation. Quality care is predicated on knowledge, skill acquisition, and ongoing training. It relies on respect, intuition, compassion, and dedication which, in turn, all depend on people.

Good dementia care relies on people working in complex interdependent relationships, giving of themselves, and putting out for other human beings in ways that are quite unheard of in any other relationship or service. Gentlecare believes that the people, lay or professional, who provide health care services to the victims of dementia are more important than the things that are used in the system or than the systems themselves.

Family Members as Carers

From the onset of Alzheimer's disease, the victim's family, and specifically the designated primary caregiver, is intrinsically bound up in the disease process.

Gentlecare regards the family as integral to dementia care, and works to support the family caregiver and sustain family involvement in the care of their relative to the very end of the process. In the course of the illness family members gradually assume responsibility for the person with dementing illness, answering questions, providing information and orientation, speaking on behalf of the person, and managing the person's grief as well as their own. Family life becomes consumed by the disease itself and by the burden of the care that must be taken on. Former roles as wife, mother, daughter, and friend are lost in a new, overwhelming job—caregiver.

This can be disconcerting not only for the family, but also for the person on the receiving end of the care. Without doubt, the sick person needs a caregiver, and yet there is something very sad about the loss of relationship that inevitably occurs when there is such dependency. The phenomenon is often referred to as role reversal, that is, adult children taking responsibility for their parents, or more frequently, a spouse caring for a life partner.

Family members often express their intolerable pain over the loss of interaction and connectedness with their sick family members. They express their grief over the loss of relationship: not having someone there for them, no longer being able to rely on a husband, being unable to confide in a mother. Alzheimer's disease makes these normal activities impossible. The people with dementia, too, often feel acutely the loss of normal roles, which accentuates their anxiety and sense of helplessness. We can hear this in frequently repeated remarks: "I can still do it" and "Don't tell me what to do!" More sadly, we hear it in their despair:

"One of the most difficult things for me is having a body in the house, but no one to talk to, to share news with...."

> "I can't do it. I can't handle it. I'm not asking you or begging you to fix me up so somehow I can but I've got to have some worth. I don't want to lose that too. I'm worth something—something other than this thing. But I don't have the wherewithal to do anything about it. I don't have any way to do it."

Once Alzheimer's disease strikes, the focus shifts from a normal relationship to new roles for both parties: those of "caregiver" and "care receiver." At the same time, family members are expected to assume incredible responsibilities, with little in the way of knowledge or specific skills; in effect, they become pseudo-professional care providers.

The person with Alzheimer's disease, on the other hand, is expected to fit into a new role: that of someone needing and receiving care. Yet we are often surprised when people don't accept that role graciously or willingly! Just at a time when these sick people are terrified and confused, they are asked to abandon former life roles and relationships in favor of a diminished existence controlled by others. As the disease worsens, there is less and less emphasis on normal life activities; the disease eclipses all life roles and functions.

Within the health care system, the family member who has Alzheimer's disease is often thought of in terms of illness, and the family caregiver is frequently assessed in terms of their role in dealing with the illness. In the process, it is sometimes forgotten that these two people have been husband and wife for perhaps 35 years. But when family members of Alzheimer's victims shift out of normal relationships and into new and unnatural roles as caregivers, do we lose a powerful therapeutic force? We all know extraordinary caregivers. Some family members go far beyond what most of us consider humanly possible to support and assist their loved ones. My mother was one of those.

And when I think about such caregivers, I am struck by the observation that their primary overriding focus is on the familial relationship rather than on their role as caregiver.

People are the therapy.

My mother, for example, learned all she could about the disease, and was very innovative in trying different approaches and strategies. But first and foremost, my father was her husband, and she did everything humanly possible to respect him in that capacity to the day of his death. When I listen to other such exceptional caregivers, I hear this repeated over and over:

"Of course, I didn't know Dean while I was growing up, but when she got ill, I wanted to be the daughter she'd never had" (Joyce Wright, of her mother-in-law).

"I plan to keep Wendy with me. She is, after all, my wife" (Tom Pope).

"As long as I am able, I will be here for Andy. That's just my place in life" (Florence Renaud).

"You won't ever leave me, will you?" "No, no . . . I won't ever leave you, George" (Helen Wilson).

Understanding the Dynamics of Family Caregiving

A person experiencing Alzheimer's disease typically lives at home with his family for an average of four years before professional help is sought, but we all know family caregiving can go on for much longer periods. The path of the caregiving experience only too often follows a steady decline into burnout.

At the time the disease is first identified, the family typically is thrown into a state of shock. Often the information is so horrific that there is a tendency to block out the whole issue: denial of the severity of a problem is a human and understandable way of protecting against intolerable pain. However, as the disease unfolds, the family must begin to make important decisions affecting the sick person—at the same time that they must provide increasingly difficult levels of care. They begin to experience anger and frustration over their inability to reverse the diagnosis, find appropriate help, or make the whole disease process simply disappear from their lives. The anger surrounding caregiving is very frightening. It may be displaced in many directions:

I don't like the role of caregiver.

—THE WIFE OF AN ALZHEIMER'S SUFFERER

- toward the medical community, which seems powerless to help;
- toward other family members, who may not be as involved as is deemed necessary;
- toward friends and neighbors, whose lives are untouched by disease; and/or
- toward the person with dementia, who is becoming more needy every day.

It is very important for family carers to understand that anger on the part of caregivers is appropriate! It is how we manage feelings of anger that challenges us.

Such a diffuse and unfocused anger engenders a feeling of being out of control, and that emotional reaction is often misunderstood by the caregivers themselves, family, friends, and professional health care staff. All may consider the reaction to be dysfunctional.

It is very important for family carers to understand that anger on the part of caregivers is appropriate. Dementia is one of the ugliest diseases imaginable, and few of us who have felt its impact on our lives have not felt incredible rage. And rage can occur over and over again; it can lie in wait to sabotage one's emotional life at any point.

TOGETHERNESS

He used to be a part of me:
We shared in all.
He used to tell me what
he thought or wanted,
And I agreed, or argued for my way:

Result: a compromise. It worked!
We walked together and
chose a path we liked.
Then came dementia for him.
He became different —
mostly sad and lost —
And so was I.
We could not freely share;
We could not choose together;
we each were angry and
could not help each other.
Our world turned upside down.
Today it's tragic for us both.
He cannot make connections.
I feel alone;

he resents my helping him.
He cannot see, he cannot hear,
he cannot put his words together
He is adrift in a strange sea
And my little boat holds only me.

If we could only feel together
through this awful sickness,
It would help so much.
If I could only understand him
when he speaks;
If he could only know I want to help;
We'd both feel good again.
But no! Each day seems worse.
We cannot learn to work and
feel together

We fail and struggle hopelessly
in joint dementia.
Only one vague hope remains
Will there be part of me —
A bit of warmth and life and joy —
When he is gone?

— Gil Ludeman

I REMEMBER AN EXPERIENCE of long-delayed anger in my own life. Years after my father died, I was walking along a street and went into an antique shop to browse. I paused to look at an old mirror and was suddenly totally overcome by a rage so overwhelming that I ran out of the store and walked for blocks, trying to get my feelings under control. I remember feeling so angry that Dad was gone, furious that he wasn't here to share our favorite activity of antique hunting. It just wasn't fair. My anger manifested itself physiologically as well as emotionally—and most frightening of all, it was not under my control.

In our culture, anger is not a socially acceptable emotion. From childhood on, all of us, but most especially women, have learned to suppress feelings of anger, to express our rage in alternate ways. But anger not addressed is internalized, causing depression or dysfunctional behavior. Caregivers need to be reassured that anger must be expressed. It must come out. But it is important that we learn to focus our rage in appropriate ways.

People with dementia need families more than ever.

It is not appropriate to direct anger at ourselves. It is equally inappropriate to direct anger at the person with dementia who is totally vulnerable, unable either to understand or to change, and who can suffer terribly in an atmosphere of simmering anger. Sometimes anger can best be expressed through effective advocacy on behalf of our loved ones or for all persons suffering with dementia. Support groups, therapists, grief counselors, and sometimes friends also can help families to understand their anger. Most important of all, the factors causing anger must be changed. The life circumstances that cause us so much distress must be identified and modified. For example:

- if a family member does not seem to be doing an appropriate share of caregiving;
- if a longtime friend never comes by;
- if some part of the disease has not been explained thoroughly;
- if someone who isn't participating in the caring is critical of those who are;

- if the person with dementia does something we don't understand; or
- if the health care system does not seem to be providing appropriate services

then there is a requirement for analysis and resolution of the issue. Otherwise, the anger created will end by undermining your health and performance as a caregiver.

As family members attempt to steer their way through both the maze of dementia and the bureaucratic hurdles of the health care system, they can experience frustration more intense than they have ever felt in their lives. And much of this is due to sheer lack of knowledge. One of the persistent myths of Alzheimer's is that the less people know about the disease progress, the less frightened they will be. Gentlecare opposes this approach, believing that people are never as afraid of what they know as they are of what they do not know. Families need to understand what is to come, or they will never be able to make appropriate care happen.

ONE DAY I WAS CALLED *on the telephone by a very elderly lady who appeared to be in deep distress. She said to me with tears in her voice: "No matter what I do, he gets sicker and sicker every day. I cook his favorite meals. I dress him in his favorite clothes. But every day he gets sicker and sicker."*

I said, "But, my dear, that's the nature of the disease. Alzheimer's is a progressive disease, and you will not be able to alter the fact that your husband is losing abilities day by day."

Her response was, "I didn't know that. No one told me it was going to be like this." Then I said, "It's simply awful. But even though he is going to become less able to do things, there are still all kinds of things you can do that will make your lives more comfortable." And I shared with her some of the strategies we use in Gentlecare. In a much more cheerful and determined voice she said, "I'm going to try some of those things."

A few days later her son phoned me. "I don't know what you said to my mother, but you've saved her life!"

Now, nothing so spectacular had happened; but what I had been able to do was to give her the information and knowledge she needed in order to do the caregiving job more effectively. I was able to empower this already strong, dedicated woman to do her job more effectively.

The anger and frustration of the early stages of the disease give rise to debilitating anxiety and guilt as the family's control over the disease, and consequently over their lives, slowly fades. Not knowing what's happening, not knowing what to do, sensing changes in lifestyle that haven't been planned for or even discussed, watching the sick person slipping away—all these feelings contribute to an emotional paralysis.

Family caregivers feel helpless and disheartened. They question themselves and others, critical of a system they see as contributing to the impotence in which they are trapped. These thoughts lead inevitably to the trademark feeling of the family caregiver: guilt.

Guilt is one of the most malignant of all the kaleidoscope of feelings the family caregiver experiences. It is a heavy, unwarranted burden that saps the caregiver's spirit and steals energy. Arising from unresolved anxiety and helplessness, the expression of guilt appears more socially acceptable than the admission that one's life is being controlled by a relentless disease—and that circumstance makes one very angry.

Family members who may have cared for sick people for hours, days, months, and even years will claim to feel guilty if they take time for a bath; and our social and health care system reinforces this notion of culpability. It's not unusual for people to be urged to keep their sick family member at home rather than seek professional help, even at the expense of their own health. I can vividly recall my mother being counseled by a health professional team: "You've been married all these years. Surely your husband deserves to live at home with you!" Few caregivers can resist pressure of this type. It is often easier to continue an intolerable regime of care than it is to chance public censure.

It is hard to imagine that a family member would feel guilty or would be made to feel guilty if they were seeking medical assistance for a family member's cardiac disorder. However, the stigma of diseases of the mind prevails, and often profoundly informs behavior that affects people's lives. Guilt is a burden family caregivers don't need!

I'm for sure not a sick-a-bed that needs Meals on Wheels! No, come on! I mean, there are other people who need that, and they should get it.

—A PERSON WITH ALZHEIMER'S

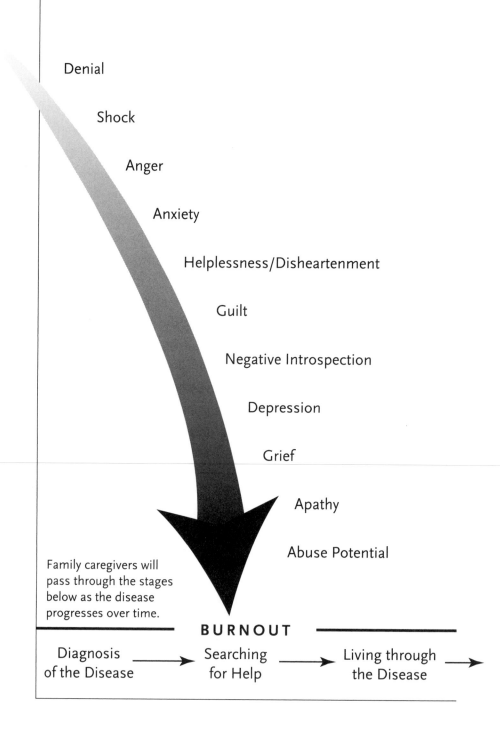

THE DYNAMICS OF
FAMILY CAREGIVING

Denial

Shock

Anger

Anxiety

Helplessness/Disheartenment

Guilt

Negative Introspection

Depression

Grief

Apathy

Abuse Potential

Family caregivers will
pass through the stages
below as the disease
progresses over time.

BURNOUT

Diagnosis ⟶ Searching ⟶ Living through ⟶
of the Disease   for Help   the Disease

THE PATH TO RECOVERY

Review of Life Choices

Stabilization

Healthy Grieving

Constructive Planning

Positive Introspection

Stagnation

Contemplation → Making Life Choices

It is hard to be surrounded by the mini-deaths of progressive dementing illness and not feel oppressed and sad. Without support, caregivers can be overcome by negativity, anger, and helplessness. These negative feelings can lead to profound depression, which can last throughout the course of the disease and beyond.

Family caregivers are greatly at risk for clinical depression and rarely seek or receive treatment for this serious illness. Some research suggests that 40 to 60 percent of caregivers are clinically depressed. Depression not only makes caregiving intolerable for the person offering care, but it dramatically affects the functioning of the person with dementia. People with dementia are acutely aware of the feelings this disease engenders among others in their environment, and are unable to find respite from that oppressive knowledge and burden.

Overriding every other feeling, however, is the smoldering pain of grief. The grief that follows physical death is understood and accepted by our society. But grief associated with chronic illness is frequently ignored or misunderstood. Sometimes family caregivers will say, "I can't understand why I act the way I do; or why do I seem to be crying all the time; or why do I get so mad at him?" Rarely do they identify these emotional outbursts as emanating from prolonged, overwhelming grief.

Mourning someone who has not physically died, and who therefore falls outside the universally recognized rituals of mourning, places caregivers in an odd position: no flowers are sent; no sympathy cards arrive in the mail; no sympathy phone calls are received; and in fact, no one may call at all.

And yet death surrounds the caregiver. With dementia, unlike physical illness, the sick person is physically healthy for much of the duration of the disease process. What is grieved by the family is the death of the personality—the loss of the essential human being.

The grief associated with the small daily deaths or devastating changes (loss of skills, roles, dreams, and hopes) is often submerged in the overwhelming task of just coping with every day. Dementia care leaves little time for introspection. And the opportunity for an open examination and discussion of feelings rarely occurs, because the person with dementia is almost always close by.

So the grief of dementia is clandestine: grief is hidden, repressed, or changed to a more socially acceptable emotion like guilt. If caregivers admit to feeling bereaved, they are often reminded that the person with dementia is still alive. It is easier and more socially acceptable to be guilty than to grieve when you have lost a loved one to Alzheimer's disease.

Caregivers of people suffering from dementia are seldom considered to be bereaved prior to the actual physical death of their family member.

Society provides little opportunity to deal with the acute feelings of loss and grief that families feel throughout much of the process of dementing disease. Caregivers can't mourn decently while the person with dementia is still alive. Even within the family constellation, confusion can exist about mourning: often the spouse, as principal caregiver, is acutely aware of the extent of the disease, while other relatives see the person in social situations where functional deficits are concealed. But it is important to remember that grief neglected, grief ignored, grief scorned, or grief put on hold comes back to haunt us. Any time the pain and sorrow due to loss are not dealt with, the feelings will be manifested somewhere, sometime.

Family members who acknowledge their grief, and receive support and therapy, talk about a weight being lifted from their lives. They speak of renewed energy and a greater understanding of the actions of the sick person.

Help with anticipatory grieving is rarely discussed with families, nor is it readily available. Without such help, families continue down the slippery slope into a state of apathy. This classic feeling of helplessness is the inevitable outcome of chronic fatigue, sorrow, and isolation.

I have come to believe that abuse is a predictable outcome of the experience of caregiving, especially if that caregiving is carried out without appropriate respite, support, and therapy.

Lack of respite is the Achilles' heel of the family caregiver. Abuse occurs, it seems to me, in one of two ways: either the family caregiver sacrifices his or her health in an attempt to meet the needs of the person with dementia; or the caregiver goes beyond the breaking point

You are lucky . . . at least your husband is still alive. Mine died with a heart attack.

—WIDOW, TO AN ALZHEIMER'S CAREGIVER AT A GRIEF SUPPORT MEETING

Guilt is...

- never being able to say no
- never being able to satisfy the expectations of others
- never being able to satisfy yourself
- being angry in a nice way
- not feeling good about your best efforts
- being annoyed by others who expect you to be different, better
- stressful
- putting off making important decisions
- putting off taking action
- grief on hold, not examined, put aside
- expectations out of step with reality
- never being able to enjoy yourself
- feeling a failure
- feeling abused, used, left out
- narcissistic
- lonely
- ugly

Guilt uses all your energy and ruins your life.

FIGURE 16-2

and physically or psychologically abuses the person with dementia. Both types of abuse are systemic and pervasive in dementia care. Frequently the caregiver is not aware of what is happening.

I REMEMBER BEING ASKED *to work with an elderly caregiver who had tied his wife to a tree in the backyard with a rope. When I asked him why he had done this, he said, "Moyra, I just can't keep up with her anymore. I'm too old. She loves being outside, but I can't take her for walks anymore."*

Abuse is an emotion-laden word these days, and most of us are reluctant to admit that caregivers, family or professional, would ever do such a thing. But abuse takes many forms: yelling, criticizing, isolating, restricting movement, leaving people alone, not supplying them with information, forcing them to eat, withholding food or drink, admonishing them, or making them feel responsible for some problem. All of these actions are just as damaging as the more commonly described physical types of abuse such as pushing, hitting, or neglecting.

We all need to become more sensitized to the potential for such action. We need to acknowledge that any one of us could react in a harmful way if we were physically and emotionally exhausted. We need to say to caregivers, family or professional: "Abuse is not OK, but it is understandable; and further, we will help you through this crisis."

Family caregivers who manage alone for years with no respite or support are greatly at risk. Professional caregivers who work with minimal resources are equally vulnerable. The potential for such problems needs to be brought out in the open, anticipated, and planned for, so that the well-being of neither caregivers nor care receivers is compromised.

Regardless of the order or severity of the feelings discussed, the outcome far too frequently is caregiver burnout. Burnout refers to a state of exhaustion, helplessness, and ill health that renders caregivers unable to care for themselves or anyone else. The Caregiver Burden Scale illustrates the typical decline in caregiver health over a five-year period.

The more we know about family caregivers, the more likely we are to be able to support them in their efforts to sustain the person with dementia.

I REMEMBER ONE EVENING, *working for a caregiver support group. As the family caregivers gathered in the room I became aware of a stifling burden of pain and loss pressing down on me. The room was simply filled with sorrow. It seemed to me to be impossible to teach new ideas, or ask these caregivers to talk about their experiences. So I asked my colleague, who just happened to be a pianist, to play some music for us.*

I hope you understand when I say, I wish this would end!

— A CAREGIVER

Let us try to help the family caregiver find their loved one behind the disease.

For several minutes he played "Memory" from Cats for us. As the music filled the room, the caregivers began to cry. I began to cry. And the terrible weight of pain began to lift and recede. Too often, the family caregivers just need permission to be human—to let go of responsibility, if even for a few minutes.

It is significant to note that most of the care for people with dementing illness is provided by elderly women. This fact should shape our efforts to assist caregivers in appropriate ways. For example, when we offer caregivers respite, what type of holiday or rest break do we have in mind? It's important to remember that older single women may not be used to traveling on their own, and may not have the money, clothes, or skills necessary to plan a vacation on their own. And older women are often perceived as half of a couple when they visit relatives or friends.

ONE OF MY CLIENTS, *while visiting relatives, was asked, "Where's Charley?" When she replied that she had left him in a wonderful respite bed in the hospital, they gasped in disbelief. "You left him where?"*

Data from an important study (Isenhart; reported in the *American Journal of Alzheimer Care and Related Disorders and Research,* October 1992) on the differences among family caregivers suggests that men and women offer care differently. In fact, people of different sexes may even offer different types of care. The study further states that mid-life children have different approaches to the task of caregiving. What is significant is the variation in impact of the caregiving experience on personal health of men and women. Women caregivers clearly give more of themselves and become sicker in the process. Men, on the

DIFFERENCES IN KIN CAREGIVERS
OF PERSONS WITH DEMENTIA

Female Spouse Caregivers	Daughters and Daughters-in-law as Caregivers	Male Spouse Caregivers	Sons of Caregivers
Family orientation	Feel moral responsibility	High desire and commitment to relationship	Role confined to decision-making and financial assistance
Nurturing	Use parent-infant model of care	Take charge of care of ill person	Very low stress, depression, and burden
Extension of responsibilities	Keep parents at home for longer periods and at higher level of disability than is wise or appropriate	Motivated by positive forces	Use family and friends to help
May be saddled with care		Few guilt feelings	Use social services more effectively
May feel resentment	Fewer financial and emotional resources	Use assistance from other family members	
More depression	Higher divorce rates	Use social services	
More stress	Tend to refuse outside help	Can afford services	
Accept little or no help	Low rate of use of social services	Can identify problems, assess strengths and limitations	
Do not use social services	Feel guilty and overburdened	Less stress and depression	
Take more responsibility than reasonable	Are stressed and depressed	Action-oriented approach	
Under physical and emotional strain			
May conflict with other family members			
Become isolated			
Most in need of help			
Most difficult to reach		*"She deserves it."*	
		"She cared for me and the family."	
		"It's due her…"	
"No one else could handle him."			—Adapted from the *American Journal of Alzheimer Care and Related Disorders and Research,* October 1992
"I would feel so guilty."			
"This is my whole life…"			

FIGURE 16-3

other hand, view dementia care as a job. They analyze the task, assemble resources effectively, and attack the job with an action-oriented approach. The Isenhart study suggests important insight that family caregivers can acquire to help them offer caregiving more effectively and protect their own health while doing so. Caregiving is clearly a risky business! The following is a summary of some of the factors to take into consideration when undertaking the job of caregiving or assisting someone else in doing so.

I have mentioned the fact that a majority of family caregiving is provided by women, and further, that men and women provide care differently. A significant factor in this difference appears to be the nature of the relationship between the giver and the receiver of care before the person became ill.

Alzheimer's disease affects all members of the family.

If there is no pre-morbid history, as may be the case with in-laws, or if a dysfunctional relationship existed before caregiving began, then the challenging experience of caring for the dementia victim through the disease process will be even more difficult, if not impossible. A great deal depends on the personal health of the caregiver. Caregiving is exhausting, physically strenuous, and psychologically harrowing.

Today she couldn't tie her shoe. Can you imagine? She couldn't tie her shoe! What will be next?

The organization of the living arrangements where care is to be provided is critical. If an aging parent with dementia is to be introduced into the family, consideration must be given to the displacement of other people, a loss of privacy, and the invasive nature of the disease itself, to name only a few factors. Clearly, all members of the family must be willing to participate fully or the arrangement will be unsuccessful.

No matter what the living arrangement, it's important to remember that the person with dementia cannot change behavior, so adaptation must be the responsibility of family members. Not infrequently, several family members are involved in caring for an elderly parent, and this is not easy. If several people are involved, it's very important to decide on the primary caregiver. Then the whole family must support that person's decisions and efforts.

If the person with dementia is to be maintained alone in his own home or in an apartment, arrangements are required for round-the clock support. Often a live-in therapeutic companion can be helpful in this regard. The key to success, however, is stringent screening, thorough training, and supervision of employees.

"Dad looks OK to me! We had a long talk about that fishing trip we took up north."

—A SON

Family Life Stressors Outside of Caregiving

Daily life goes on despite caregiving responsibilities. Interfamily conflict (whether between siblings, spouses, or children) can be devastating.

Caregivers are often faced with the additional task of buffering warring factions, or running interference for the person with dementia. This places an intolerable strain on the principal caregiver and must be resolved at all costs. Sometimes the build-up of losses and stress become too much to bear; often it is the simplest thing that may cause the dam to burst.

Careful scheduling is required if the caregiver must mix care provision with work and family responsibilities. Open communication and effective mobilization of all resources can prevent breakdown. Gentlecare recommends seeking professional assistance with legal and financial aspects of

Nothing replaces the family relationship.

guardianship early in the caregiving process. It is crucially important to remember that no one can provide dementia care alone. Caregivers who learn how to give dementia care and who are supported and loved through the experience remain healthy.

THE UNIQUE GRIEF CYCLE
OF THE CAREGIVER OF PERSONS
WITH DEMENTING ILLNESS

Normal Life

FIGURE 16-4

Throughout life we all experience death in one form or another (loss of friend, a job, a pet, etc.). But after an appropriate time of grieving, our life activities return to balance. We continue to give attention to all of the components in our life (family, friends, work, leisure activities, etc.).

Life While Caregiving for a Person with Dementia

FIGURE 16-5

When caregiving someone with dementia, the caregiver *assumes responsibility* for another person. They are surrounded on a daily basis with the "mini" deaths of dementia, and their grief is overwhelming and largely unacknowledged. Other life activities are obliterated by caregiving responsibilities.

Life After the Death of
Person Under Care

FIGURE 16-6

When physical death finally occurs, the caregiver finds himself alone after years and years of responsibility. They often experience this final death as anticlimactic, or with a sense of relief. Their grief is often muted, since grieving has occurred over many years, and there are few tears left. Society (and other family members), on the other hand, expect overt signs of grief, and many misinterpret the feeling of peace, relief, and freedom that the caregiver may exhibit. The caregiver is now faced with the daunting task of beginning to recreate his or her life after a long period of inactivity.

Caregiver's "New" Life

FIGURE 16-7

Persons who wish to help caregivers after the loss of a family member need to help them reconstruct the balance of life activities, with special attention to health issues, grief therapy, and new relationships.

Caregivers' Perceptions of Giving Care

A great deal depends on how the family caregiver perceives the role undertaken. If the caregiver uses maladaptive coping styles, he or she can seriously stress the person with dementia. Overcaring, for example, can cause the sick person to become excessively helpless or very belligerent. Caregivers need to deal with their own feelings surrounding the illness, and may require professional help to do so. Caregiving can be awful, but much of its unpleasantness and stress can be avoided or prevented. Often it's as simple as making a choice: a choice to ask for help; a choice to rest; a choice to simplify a procedure; and a choice to let go of unreasonable expectations.

Caregiver Knowledge Base and Skills

No element of caregiving is as important as that of information and knowledge. Simply put, caregivers who understand dementia give superior care. And they stay healthier.

There are many skills required of the family caregiver. Sometimes skills developed through former experiences are helpful, but often new skills are required to carry out effective dementia care. For example, caregivers must learn how to communicate effectively with someone with temporal lobe brain damage. They must learn how to decipher a "word salad" conversation or complete a dangling sentence. They must learn how to identify and eliminate stress factors affecting the person they are caring for—whether the factor in question is a too-loud TV or a too-complicated place setting. They must learn how to look at problems from all points of view, and find the positive core of each event. For example, in an effort to help, the person with dementia may make a mess or perform poorly. The caregiver must be able to concentrate on the positive motive or intent, rather than the poorly done task.

Reframing is a neuro-linguistic programming technique adopted for Gentlecare. It helps caregivers transform the meaning of behavior. It is a technique for changing the response to certain behaviors to generate new and more satisfying behaviors to choose from. Reframing creates new alternatives. This story illustrates reframing—looking at a situation and finding a different meaning in it:

FLORENCE AND ANDY *had been great gardeners. When Andy developed Alzheimer's disease, his wife and family helped him to keep on gardening whenever possible. One day Florence decided to cut down a dead tree on the front lawn and enlisted Andy's help.*

Just as they began the task, Florence was called away to the phone. When she finished her call she found Andy sitting watching TV.

"I thought we were going to get rid of that tree," she said.

"It's done," he replied.

So Florence looked out the window, only to see the dead tree standing straight and tall. On closer inspection she found that their favorite tree, a cherry tree, was all cut up and the wood neatly piled.

Later she said, "Moyra, I had a choice. I could either kill him, or laugh about the whole thing. And I decided it simply wasn't worth getting stressed over."

Adult family homes offer a family ambiance to the person with dementia.

One lovely thing that happens when you start telling stories about people with dementia is that it makes you recall all the funny times spent with them. Recalling the story of Andy and Florence and the tree-cutting incident, I'm reminded of another "Andy story."

On awakening, you look inside your mind and see nothing but black.

—A FAMILY CAREGIVER

ONE DAY ANDY AND HIS SON EUGENE *were storing stuff in the loft over the carport. Andy was passing the supplies up to Eugene. Suddenly nothing more came up through the hole, so Eugene stuck his head down to see what the delay was. Not only was his father not in sight, but the ladder was gone! Andy had put the ladder neatly away and was watching TV. It was some time before other family members heard faint calls for help and rescued Eugene!*

Life Factors Outside of the Illness

The normal responsibilities of life are not suspended when a family member has a dementing illness. Caregivers must add their caregiving responsibilities to what may already be demanding lives.

Spouses and grown children may have full-time work responsibilities—and grown children often have children of their own to look after. People have homes that must be kept up, and many have community commitments that mean a great deal to them. The financial expense of care for a family member may be worrisome, and may add to the burden of care. Family caregivers are often called on to advocate on behalf of the sick person, and this takes courage and diplomacy.

But as we have seen, there can be a way out of burnout and despair. *There can be life after dementia!*

No one can provide dementia care alone!

Those who love or admire family caregivers can assist in the rebuilding of life after the death of a spouse from Alzheimer's, and that assistance is needed both before and after the person's death. A caregiver needs to maintain skills, friendships, and community roles throughout the illness of a family member, and moreover, needs to be without feelings of guilt in doing so. Friends and family are potent agents in helping caregivers achieve these goals, but they need to understand that an exhausted caregiver may not be able to reach out for help. Friendship must be offered, sometimes over and over again.

Caregivers need diversion from their caregiving duties. Special activities such as respite opportunities, vacations, overnight visits, and retreats can refresh and energize a caregiver in amazing ways. It is important to remember, however, that caregivers may require assistance to take advantage of such opportunities.

Few illnesses associated with aging are as devastating to the sick person and his family as dementia. Those who wish to help caregivers can contribute significantly by supporting, reinforcing, and respecting their life relationships and the role of the family. They can help caregivers acquire the support, therapy, and knowledge they need to succeed with this incredible responsibility.

And in partnership with them, we can assist the person with

Alzheimer's disease to live as comfortably as possible through the experience.

Professional Care Providers as Therapeutic Agents

In a time of diminishing economic resources for health care services, nothing could be more important than taking a good hard look at the most important resource of all: the people of the health care system. Doing so requires us to think about people in new and different ways, to examine their activities with different goals in mind.

For most leaders and planners in health care, this requires a paradigm shift—a change in the organizing principle that underlies the way we think about workers in health care, as well as the way services are provided.

Management guru Tom Peters, author of *In Search of Excellence*, says, "There are no limits to the ability to contribute on the part of a properly selected, well trained, appropriately supported and above all, committed person." To paraphrase, average health care workers are capable of moving mountains—if only we ask them to do so and construct a supportive environment for them to work in. Current health care practices raise some vital questions:

- What criteria are used to select workers?
- What is the quality of direction and support being given workers?
- What are the resources workers need to get the job done effectively?
- Where is the opportunity for workers to contribute ideas about how to do the job better?

> *It is really amazing what people can do when you let them.*
>
> —GORDON FORWARD, CEO, CHAPPARAL STEEL

The paradigm of hierarchy—the pyramid or classic organizational chart—has up to now informed the way most people think and work throughout the health care system. Within that paradigm, authority (i.e., wisdom) flows from the top down to workers at the bottom, who simply carry out directives received from above. This system works exceedingly well in emergencies, but it no longer serves the complex social circumstances in which health care finds itself today.

No system that limits most people while giving power to a few, fosters competition and territoriality, and limits patterns of action to a formula or set pattern can thrive in a world where everything is subject to change and almost everything seems possible. Some of us even believe we can regenerate the old medical paradigm of health care into a new, more effective model. The most obvious motivating force for a new paradigm in health care is the dramatic change being forced on health care systems by our aging population.

The new model of health care needs to be a cyclical paradigm rather than a hierarchical one. It must embody *interdependence* between the person who is ill and all of us who wish to help, between the afflicted person and his family, and between the care systems and the communities they serve. In her autobiography, *Revolution From Within*, Gloria Steinem speaks of "progress becoming mutual support and connectedness. Progress means interdependence." She proposes an image of an organizational structure that is a circle at rest, and a spiral at work. The cyclical paradigm becomes interdependence.

Finding a professional caregiver who understands is priceless.

Old-fashioned hierarchies, in which a few people at the top wield power, a lot of people in the middle wait for orders, and many more at the bottom feel powerless and resentful, are everywhere being challenged as inappropriate and cumbersome. The shift is toward smaller, more lateral and cooperative work units, often known as self-directed work teams. These units are perceived as a breakthrough system for increasing productivity, sparking innovation, and reducing costs.

The fierce competition for power, money, and status, which has always been a major force in health care, is shifting to the practice of trust, respect, and cooperation. The excitement of learning together, appreciating other people's insights, finding effective solutions together, feeling pleasure in cooperative effort, sensing the joy of truly

The absurd man is he who never changes.

—BARTHÉLEMY

helping people with dementia live more comfortably: the power of these experiences is beginning to chip away at old practices. Each person is beginning to be seen as a unique and capable contributor to effective health care.

AS THE HOUSEKEEPER *for C wing during the first month of Gentlecare, I admit I began a little unsure and apprehensive. In the first two weeks there were a lot of kinks to be improved out, but I must tell you I have come to love it!*

Although it is a busy wing with lots to be done, the new approach has given me a great new sense of fulfillment in my job. I no longer just scrub toilets and mop floors, but have the opportunity to bless the residents such as Sally, simply by letting her help me make the bed or bringing her into the hall to help me dust, when she normally never comes out. To be able to have the opportunity to transform such an anxious person into a happy participating individual, even for a few minutes, is very rewarding for me.

Thank you, Gentlecare, and keep on keeping on.

—Pat Rankin
Housekeeper, 1993

A circle needs no beginning.

—OLD JAPANESE PROVERB

Gerontology, or care of the elderly, has always suffered from an image problem: it is perceived by others and sometimes by gerontological practitioners themselves as acute care medicine's poor step-sister. An element of authenticity, of pride in the work done in support of older people, has always been missing. And gerontological work has always been considered easier than acute care. The qualifications of workers are not assessed as stringently as are those of the workers entrusted with the lives of critical patients. If a person liked old people and had always been kind to grandparents, the person would be considered for employment in gerontology. The practice of gerontology lacked the urgency of more emergency-oriented services. Environment, equipment, and supplies were never truly critical issues, so resources were negotiable. Hanging over all gerontological practice has always been the evil influence of ageism: "Why bother? They are old."

I REMEMBER WORKING ONCE in the long-term care section of an acute care hospital. From time to time, whenever there was a shortage of physiotherapists in the acute care section, I would be asked to send our gerontology physiotherapist to work in acute care. When I protested that we needed his services, I would be told, "But surely it won't matter if old people miss a few treatments."

The new reality of gerontological care flies in the face of such negativism. Anyone who has worked a shift recently in any long-term care facility can attest to the complexity and diversity of the challenges one encounters. With evolving specialization in the management of the diseases of aging has come an awareness that the traditional tools of the medical trade, drugs and surgery, simply do not work in dealing with gerontological problems. The needs of elderly people are changing the practice of medicine. Practitioners are faced with complex social issues that require a body-mind, psycho-social approach to care unlike any previously attempted in Western medical history. There is an urgent need to look beyond symptoms to the context of illness: to considerations of stress, society, family, diet, living arrangements, activity, and emotions.

In that context, the people we choose to work in health care make all the difference. What are their attitudes toward elderly people? What is their level of dedication, their stamina, their professional preparation? Can we give them the knowledge, skills, and resources to do the job required of them? It behooves us to choose excellent people, and then cherish them and LISTEN TO THEM when they tell us about the world in which they work.

What Qualities Should Staff Members Have?

Since staff members who work with people with dementing illness are therapeutic agents, it is vital that they want to work with this type of client. As we have seen, dementia care depends on the ability of staff members to connect with people afflicted with dementia. Consequently, staff who place a higher priority on accomplishing tasks rather than connecting, or who simply don't want to make the effort to meet people's needs over and over again, should not be assigned to dementia care units—irrespective of seniority, shift priorities, family schedules, health issues, etc. If a staff member does not enjoy dementia care, assigning her to a special care unit will be disastrous for the clients and others working with them. I do not know about others, but I would rather work all alone on a dementia unit than work with someone who does not want to be there.

In providing care for elderly people, it is not just a matter of knowing how something should be done, but rather of knowing how something should be done and doing it that way. Staff members assigned to dementia care units should have, as a minimum, current core training in:

- progressive dementing illnesses
- psychiatric diseases
- physical diseases of aging
- communication, verbal and non-verbal
- problem-solving
- task analysis and age-appropriate programming
- family caregiver relations
- strategies for working with volunteers
- how to develop programs and environments as therapy

Choosing Staff

So how do we choose people who have the qualities needed to deliver excellent dementia care?

The Gentlecare system looks for the following characteristics and background in choosing staff members:

Attitude and beliefs

By this we mean the way a staff member regards someone with dementia, and the way they react to them. It refers to the association of ideas the person has developed through life experience with respect to both old age and dementia. Attitude is the outward manifestation of the principles we hold dear, the convictions and sentiments that

There are no obsolete people, just obsolete skills.

—FREDRICK HERTZBERG

inform our actions. As well, people must have enough self-confidence to be effective advocates for those in their care.

Use of language

The way we use language in dementia care is critical, since language shapes the way we act and often the way others act as well. Language must be clear, fair, and objective. It must be used carefully so as not to diminish people. For instance, if someone refers to an old man as violent, that man will be approached in a very different way than if he was said to be upset or frightened.

Preparation

The treatment of progressive dementing illness has only relatively recently become a medical specialty. Staff trained in the biomedical model of care or the psychiatric model of care do not necessarily have the required knowledge base for delivery of good dementia care. In fact, many practitioners speak of the need for such people to unlearn old-style care practices to carry out effective dementia care.

Staff who want to specialize in dementia care require specialized clinical preparation. Since this area of knowledge is still developing, such training must be ongoing. It is important to note that Gentlecare recommends cross-functional training of all staff, volunteers, and family members.

Ongoing training and self-learning are essential to dementia care.

Experience

All of us at one time or another have been children or have helped children develop, so we know what the developmental process is like. Dementia care requires that we learn to understand the reverse of that process and how to support people as they lose skills and functioning. The more positive the life experiences we have had with elders, the more effective we are in supporting them through dementia.

Knowledge

The knowledge base about dementia is changing rapidly. Staff must understand the normal aging processes, the diseases that result in dementia, mental health issues, as well as innovative strategies of care. And learning must be continuous! Gerontological care staff members need to become self-learners.

Skills

Dementia care requires staff members to have skills different from those generally needed in the provision of health care. Strategies or approaches used elsewhere in the health care system are only occasionally appropriate in caring for people experiencing progressive dementia. Specifically, dementia care practitioners require the following skills:

- communication
- problem-solving
- task analysis and presentation
- observation
- stress identification and reduction
- reframing
- distraction
- and more!

Respect

Gentlecare looks for staff members who understand how difficult it is to live with dementia. Respect for brave older people is fundamental to the Gentlecare approach, so staff members must have an intrinsic understanding of the courage and spirit of the people they are helping.

Sense of humor and buoyancy

Despite the huge difficulties it presents, dementia care also offers wonderful opportunities for joy. People with dementia, properly supported, are very funny people who can make you feel very special. It really helps if staff members approach their work with a sense of fun and anticipation rather than a grumpy attitude. Furthermore, a happy demeanor in a staff member changes the way a person with dementia responds.

Knowledge is not power. Applied knowledge is power.

—ERNIE TADLA,
 THE BUSINESS EXAMINER

One should govern people as one would cook fish, poking as little as possible.

—LAO TZU

Designing the Shift

Good dementia care is based on a staff member's ability to enter into therapeutic relationships, to use skills and knowledge to support dysfunctional people, and to develop a prosthetic arrangement of programs and space for each individual in care and the families of those people.

Does this sound like something you can do non-stop for 12 hours? Does this sound like something you can do for a day or two, and then go to a different area in the facility to perform a different job? The job of providing care to persons with dementia is so challenging and complex that the issue of extended shifts and days off must be addressed realistically. It is unrealistic for staff to be able to relate emotionally to a wide variety of people and the public for 12-hour periods. Facilities that schedule staff for this type of shift need to be aware that caregiver burnout is just as prevalent among professional caregivers as it is among family caregivers.

One day with a great teacher is better than a thousand days of study.

—OLD CHINESE SAYING

Furthermore, staff members who work 12-hour shifts have long periods of time when they are not on duty. This means that if these staff members are to know what is happening in the lives of the people in care, then they and everyone they work with must have an enormous commitment to information catch-up. It is far too common for staff not to have necessary information about the people they care for, such as changes in functioning levels, strategies, or activities to avoid, information on family dynamics, etc.

AS A DEMENTIA CARE CONSULTANT, *I often approach a staff member who is dressing someone or assisting a person with eating and ask simple questions: How long has this person been here? Does the family visit? How much dinner can this person eat without help?*

It is not unusual for me to receive the response, "You'll have to check at the desk: I just got assigned here from another ward and I've been off duty for several days."

If people acting as therapeutic agents do not know basic information about people in their care, then they certainly can't deliver individualized prosthetic care.

Staff Assignment

The rotation of professional staff in and out of specially designated dementia care areas is another contentious issue. The problems created by 12-hour shift work are identical to those stemming from staff rotation.

Quality dementia care depends first of all on the relationship between staff members, the person with dementia, and the person's family; secondly, it depends on the knowledge and skill base of staff. Ideally all staff in a long-term care facility would be in a position to deliver prosthetic care, but this is rarely the case. For this reason alone, it is critical to have a stable work group within a dementia care unit.

If someone does something extraordinarily well, videotape them at work, and share it with all staff as a study tool.

Gentlecare advocates that a core group of staff sufficient in number to provide care 24 hours a day for a 7-day week be designated as the dementia care team. This group should be permanently assigned to the dementia unit and given responsibility for developing the prosthetic macro-environment.

Once this core group has been established, it becomes possible to accept new or rotating staff members into the group, with appropriate orientation and training. Such an arrangement also allows dementia care staff to take time off dementia care assignments for periods of time, for career reasons or when personal issues make it difficult for them to interact in such an intense atmosphere.

Training and Development

Knowledge is the key to successful dementia care. The more all staff members know about dementia, the easier and more effective their work becomes. The more family caregivers know, the more willing they are to participate in care, and the more capable they are in supportive roles.

A training program, for example, is used to give staff information about a specific topic, such as how to operate a dishwasher, do a lift, or prepare or serve a meal. Staff development, however, occurs when knowledge is internalized, creating a behavioral change that produces a positive result in both attitude and action. Development is a process, not an event. Development realizes potential; it stimulates growth and change. It releases powers inherent in people so that they strive for effectiveness and excellence.

Training is knowing how to do something. Development is doing it. For example, training is knowing how to put ingredients together into a meal that will meet nutritional needs. Development is presenting that meal to elderly people in a pleasing, serene environment; communicating with them; responding to their concerns; and whenever possible, involving them in food choices and the food preparation process, or in clean-up. Training is knowing how to get eight people up and dressed in time for breakfast, while development is understanding each person's wake-up preferences and performance level; orienting people to time and place; assisting them with their grooming and dressing; and preparing them for and supporting them in the day ahead. These differences in approach are not time related, but rather attitude- and knowledge-based.

Only connect.

—E.M. FORSTER

Inservice must be ongoing and involve everyone.

Involving Everyone

Health care practice often involves confrontation, competition, and exclusion of various groups of people. Often, information is controlled by a small group in order to enhance the power of that group over others. Territories are developed by one category of staff, and others are not welcome in the space defined by the members of that category. Nursing stations are an example of this.

To provide quality dementia care effectively and efficiently, we have to change the way we think and work so that all types of workers, volunteers, and families can contribute. Involvement is the regular, spontaneous taking of initiative. It is the process of looking at work differ-ently—not in terms of "It's not my job," but rather, "Which of us can do this job best?"

In dementia care, an elderly person may reach out to anyone for help, regardless of that person's academic preparation or job descrip-tion. This means that the maintenance staff, the hairdresser, and the food service worker must be as well prepared to respond to a request for help as any other team member. In the eyes of the dysfunctional person, the person who is asked for help is the best one. For instance, if the nearest staff member at dinner is addressed with a remark like:

- "Where am I?"
- "Have the horses been fed?"
- "I've got to get the hay in!"
- "Someone is killing me!"
- "She stole my glasses!"
- "You can't go in there."

it is simply not appropriate, in dementia care, to say, "Ask the nurse."

In Gentlecare units, in all types of staff members who understand dementing illness and have acquired specialized communication skills, we find superb therapeutic agents. Furthermore, support staff people say that they find that such interaction enhances and enriches their daily work.

Involvement means sharing information and skills. Some favorite Gentlecare ways of doing this are:

- holding regular open meetings;
- creating communication books that everyone writes in;
- instituting interdisciplinary rounds run on a democratic model;
- proving cross-training and development workshops for all staff;
- role-modeling dementia strategies and approaches;
- using videos;
- using multi-media materials;
- setting up journal clubs; and
- providing exchange locations for articles, write-ups, texts, and jour-nals in communal rooms such as staff rooms or bathrooms.

When we see how funny we are, we see how dear we are.

—ANNE WILSON
SCHAEFF

That's what learning is. You suddenly un-derstand something you've understood all your life, but in a new way.

—DORIS LESSING

How can you get very far,

If you don't know who you are?

If you don't know what you've got?

And if you don't know which to do,

of all the things in front of you?

Then what you'll have when you get through

Is just a mess without a clue,

Of all the best that can come true

If you know what and which and who.

— A.A. Milne,

Winnie-the-Pooh

Involvement means exchanging stifling bureaucratic structures for an environment in which people feel comfortable taking whatever initiative is required to fix problems and extend first-rate service. This does not mean that everyone does everyone else's job! Rather, it implies a healthy respect for and trust in one's colleagues, and an enhanced awareness of each staff person's unique potential.

Building the Team

Example is leadership.

—ALBERT SCHWEITZER

Health care institutions have traditionally held interdisciplinary rounds in which the members of divergent professions meet to discuss the status and plans for those in their care. Following such meetings, each professional representative then goes to practice in isolation from the other members of the team. This sort of exercise has resulted in a focus on power allocation and territoriality rather than care.

For example, it is not unusual for staff to compete for client time: rehabilitation, recreation, and activities staff schedule their care strategies at times when care staff do not "need" the sick person whether or not those times are appropriate for the person in care. Similarly, food service personnel often decide on the timing of residents' meals, even if the times selected are incompatible with their comfort or with care plans that nurses have developed. Only rarely are support personnel, housekeeping, maintenance, and food service staff included in team rounds, and even then it is usually as observers rather than as full working participants.

Teamwork, on the other hand, involves much more synergy. Teams are democratic, autonomous, highly trained, and have responsibility for problem-solving and for formulating effective care delivery systems. They must work together, not just talk together. The team leader is often the best facilitator, not the most highly trained person.

The Leader's Job

In the new paradigm of care, the role of the team leader (coordinator, unit manager) is completely transformed. It encompasses helping the group articulate a vision and a set of values; group facilitation; people development; quality control; planning; coordination; and creation of a flexible, responsive support system. The leader's focus moves from one of being directive to one of ensuring participation. Tom Peters describes this as a change from "cop to facilitator" or "management by walking around." Of course, such a shift requires that such leaders or coordinators acquire the skills needed to do the job differently.

Good leaders make all the difference.

Changing Organizational Style and Structure

Gentlecare advocates a review of traditional organizational structures that emphasize extreme specialization and

The use of 12-hour shifts, seconded from acute medical practice, does not work in dementia care.

job definition. The power of well-chosen, well-trained, well-supported people working in team-based management is so awesome it is breath-taking. Top-down management style is simply too unresponsive and cumbersome to be practical in gerontological care.

In traditionally structured long-term care facilities, the people who have been entrusted with decision-making are frequently simply not available when action needs to be taken. (This is not true in most acute care treatment situations where the physician as team leader is usually on hand to make critical decisions.) In long-term care, whoever makes the critical contact with the cognitively impaired client or his family must be in a position to respond positively.

THIS REMINDS ME OF A TIME *when an extended care unit reported a problem with swallowing disorders. When I reviewed the unit's feeding procedure, I noticed that staff members used large soup spoons to feed people. I suggested that a small spoon might be less intrusive, and might reduce the possibility of gagging and choking. The staff agreed and said they had asked for small spoons, but the big spoons kept coming up on the trays. I asked whom they had contacted, and they said they had asked their supervisor to check with the dietician, to see if she would ask her supervisor to discuss the matter with the director of care, who presumably could raise the matter with her administrative counterpart. Eight months later, big spoons were still causing swallowing problems.*

It is easy to put people down. It is harder to lift them up.

Gentlecare addresses the challenge of developing quality care by shifting from a hierarchical management style to decentralized, team-based management. The following criteria are built into the management program:
- staff specialization within interdisciplinary, self-managing teams
- adjustments in jurisdictions
- participation by all
- skill enhancement for everyone
- rewarding of initiative
- empowerment of workers, families, and volunteers

Building a Community:
Volunteers as Care Providers

Volunteers are not staff! Volunteers do not do staff work. Volunteers are not replacements for professional staff. Rather, volunteers have a critical and unique role to play in health care delivery that cannot be undertaken by paid workers.

Volunteers are tangible links to the outside, and are not part of the health service community. They are normal, ordinary people, and representative of the dozens of people we all interact with in our daily lives. They evoke memories of times past, good times, and healthy periods in life. They are the bridge between health care institutions and ordinary life. For people suffering from dementia, for whom life in the community has been abruptly truncated, volunteers provide a comforting link to a time that was important, joyful, and under their own control. No matter how diligently staff try, they cannot achieve this sense of naturalness in their relationships with residents, since their work inevitably casts them in a different role, with a different set of functions. Gentlecare regards volunteers as therapeutic partners in creating systems that are comforting and prosthetic for vulnerable elderly people. In such a partnership, there is no limit to what can be achieved. Without volunteers there is no possibility that staff alone can create an environment that meets the needs of dementia sufferers.

It is one of the most beautiful compensations in life that no man can sincerely try to help another without helping himself.

—EMERSON

Throughout the world, volunteers contribute to organizations in myriad ways: fund-raising, direct service, research, transportation, one-on-one visiting, entertainment, education, advocacy, contribution of specialized skills, liaison, emergency assistance, ombudsman service, service to voluntary boards, support groups, activators, organizers, and catalysts ... the list is endless.

One in four Canadians performs volunteer work.

Do these activities sound like tasks that need to be done to support dementia care? Do these activities sound like tasks that professional staff are in a position to undertake? If any one of these activities were undertaken in a dementia care unit, would the workload be eased? Would dysfunctional elderly people be comforted? I think so. I know so. Gentlecare units that work in partnership with volunteers cannot imagine operating without them.

In Canada, 5.3 million people contribute their time in formal organizations, and 13 million people help in informal ways. Volunteers have many redeeming characteristics, but in these days of shrinking economic resources they have one enchanting quality: volunteers are an infinite resource!

Volunteers are available in unlimited numbers. There is no "cap," no predetermined "F.T.E.," no budget restriction, no resource allocation. Organizations can have as many volunteer partners as they can accommodate comfortably and effectively. There is no task that someone, somewhere, somehow in the community cannot accomplish. The secret lies in simply asking.

I do it for myself.

—A VOLUNTEER

I REMEMBER WORKING *with a group of elderly veterans. When any one of these old gentlemen left the hospital, his belongings would be packed either in a garbage bag or a cardboard box. Somehow this just seemed a bit tacky. A phone call to the local Royal Canadian Legion Ladies Auxiliary explaining the problem elicited this response: "Give us a little while." Within hours, a car drove up and discharged a mass of suitcases in different sizes and shapes "for the boys." I can still remember the delight this generous gift brought, and the difference it made at discharge time.*

Volunteers are vital links that keep whole communities together. Volunteers are communities! And they can help us build the vital alternate or surrogate mini-community required to help people with dementing illness live through the disease. Without volunteers:
- Who speaks for your community?
- Who supports families in crisis?
- Who helps create a sense of home and familiarity for our sick elders?
- Who gathers community resources to address urgent needs?
- Who provides the beauty, the music, the spiritual comfort?
- Who goes for walks and takes time to talk?
- Who offers comfort in the dying time?

- Who reads?
- Who has the time?
- Who makes the cups of tea?
- Who knows how things used to be?
- Where are the young with their laughter and their enthusiasm?
- Who do you call when you have a crisis?

In Gentlecare programs, it's volunteers—that's who!

Planning for Volunteering

But good volunteer programs don't just happen. Volunteers do not come out of the walls by osmosis. Volunteer involvement in health care requires careful planning and nourishing. Volunteers are motivated by many factors:

- the wish to learn;
- the hope to do something successfully;
- the new experience;
- the desire to give of oneself;
- the need to exert power and influence;
- the desire to problem-solve;
- the wish to advocate for favorite causes;
- the desire to have fun, to make a difference;
- the urge to meet new people and friends;
- the opportunity to be creative;
- the wish to acquire skills and knowledge; and
- the desire to be useful and competent.

And almost everyone wants to do a good job.

Volunteer systems can be divided into four areas of focus:

Recruitment

The acquisition of volunteers is everyone's business. Although they may be formally welcomed into the organization by a coordinator of volunteers, everyone needs to be on the lookout for suitable candidates. Once volunteers are attracted to the unit, Gentlecare recommends that they be invited to a one-to-one placement interview. During the interview, the volunteer's motivation, skills, and needs can be identified. A volunteer assignment sheet can be completed, and a preliminary placement discussed. Gentlecare advocates an initial trial placement, with an option for either party to renegotiate. The volunteer should leave the interview with a clear understanding of the assignment, the commitment of both parties, and the organizational system within which he will be working.

Would-be volunteers who do not meet organizational criteria should be referred elsewhere. Do not send them to a care unit to see how it works out. This can sabotage the whole volunteer program. If there are any reservations about the suitability of a volunteer, ask the person to work under supportive supervision for a trial period.

Volunteers can be recruited from social or service organizations, seniors centers, universities, colleges, high schools, church groups, special interest groups, talent pools, ethnic groups—anywhere, actually, where people are to be found.

Education
Like any person on staff, volunteers must know what they are doing, and which actions are or are not appropriate. Gentlecare recommends cross-training of volunteers with staff, that is, the inclusion of volunteers in any staff education or development activities. This can be a valuable experience for both groups, and can develop important bonding for work with those in care. In addition to that training, volunteers need to understand how the organization works; who does what; who they can count on for help; confidentiality; and appropriate responses.

They also must learn effective communication skills prior to assignment. Do not send new volunteers to a unit to talk to patients. This is terrifying! The volunteers will disappear and never come back! Instead, suggest they work in partnership with an experienced volunteer until they feel comfortable on their own.

Ongoing education

This is a sure-fire way to engage and retain volunteers. If the process of dementing illness is explained to them, if they understand the behavior it causes, and if they are taught effective strategies and approaches, they will be hooked forever. The strategies used in dementia care make sense to volunteers: they are do-able and they make elderly people who are ill feel wonderful. All these elements make for a successful volunteer experience.

Support

The job of volunteer coordinator is to make sure everyone knows what each volunteer is doing within the organization. *But supporting volunteer efforts is everyone's job.* It is critical that everyone greets volunteers, acknowledges their assignments, helps direct and support them, and thanks them. In order to contribute effectively, volunteers need to feel welcome. It is so very sad, and such a waste, to see volunteers tiptoeing around professional territories, afraid to make a mistake. Would any of us volunteer under such circumstances? Would we feel confident and successful? Support can come in many forms, but as a minimum, each contact person within the organization should say to each volunteer:

If we want to help people change, it's important that we don't push them or pull them— just walk together.

- "It's great to have you here."
- "We notice a difference when you visit."
- "Your help is really appreciated."
- "Thanks for coming."

Regular, honest, helpful feedback is also a source of encouragement to volunteers, as it is to everyone! Don't tell volunteers what not to do; tell them what you need to have them do to help you or the client, and if necessary show them how to do it.

Acknowledgment

Volunteers don't expect to be paid, but like any human being, they appreciate having their contributions acknowledged. I have worked in organizations that have celebrated volunteers with a huge gala dinner or party. These events are costly, take endless hours of staff time to organize, and usually end with everyone wondering if it was worth all the fuss and bother. Gentlecare instead recommends on-going acknowledgement of volunteers in any of the following ways:

- providing an introduction in the organization's newsletter, or posting notices on the bulletin board;
- publicizing the "volunteer idea of the month" or "contribution of the month";
- sending notes of appreciation for special accomplishments;
- making brief presentations to the board of directors or the executive committee reporting on outstanding work; and
- ensuring acceptance of the volunteer as a valuable member of the team.

Gentlecare believes that volunteers are so vital to dementia care that the position of Coordinator of Volunteers should be a full-time respon-sibility, rather than an add-on to some other job.

A Word About Groups of Volunteers

For social and support reasons, volunteers from large service organiza-tions often prefer to visit institutions in groups. This practice is very in-timidating for elderly people, and overwhelming for staff on duty. Often staff attention has to be focused on caring for the volunteers rather than on the people in their care. As well, volunteer groups some-times expect unrealistic levels of participation on the part of residents and staff.

I REMEMBER WORKING *on a dementia unit one evening, and be-coming aware that the ward staff had rounded up some very im-paired elderly people and grouped them around the elevator. When I inquired about what was happening, I was told that it was Rotary bingo night, and that the bingo volunteers always expected a large turnout. Very sick elderly people who couldn't even recognize a bingo card if you paid them were being used to meet perceived expectations.*

This is wrong, but it is also a very common occurrence. Staff are placed in the untenable position of knowing such activity is harmful to their clients, but feeling powerless to object for fear of offending very important volunteers.

It is the care facility's responsibility to clearly outline the needs of its clients, and to specify what help is appropriate. No service organization worth its salt should insist on doing something harmful to people. In most cases, they are only doing what they think is best, or recreating something that they have done for years for another client group (and which no one has talked to them about redefining).

Gentlecare recommends that large service organizations be invited to have their volunteers visit in pairs (two people, that is!), or if they prefer, they may work together as a group *outside the facility* to accomplish a specific task such as letter writing, shawl making, Christmas present wrapping, and fund-raising.

A Further Word about Volunteer Auxiliaries

Over the years, hospital auxiliaries have made magnificent contributions to health care. They are often a source of donations of both money and specific equipment. Traditionally, they have also operated services such as tuck shops, gift shops, and beauty parlors. Auxiliaries are usually associated with acute care hospitals rather than long-term care facilities.

Volunteers are an infinite resource!

With the tremendous increase in the numbers of people with dementia that are appearing in health care institutions, it becomes advisable for the members of auxiliaries to participate in educational programs developed for individual volunteers. For example, auxiliaries frequently get involved in decorating health care facilities; in dementia care units, this work can be greatly enhanced if the importance of environmental adaptation is explained to the participants.

Family Members as Volunteers

Family members often ask to volunteer their services or simply assume volunteer jobs in the course of caring for their family members. Often this is enormously helpful to people with dementia, staff, and the family caregiver. After all, relatives know the problems very well, and have definite ideas about the quality of care that should be offered.

However, it is important to note that in an effort to expiate their guilt and grief, some family members or caregivers nearly live in the facility day and night. These people are already exhausted and in no position to approach people with dementia in a therapeutic way. Staff members need to work with these caregivers to help them focus attention on their own needs and grief.

Family members who volunteer should be registered, trained, and supported just like any other volunteer; being a dementia caregiver doesn't automatically qualify someone for a volunteer assignment. Often their interest can be directed to advocacy or fund-raising, to give them some relief from the grind of personal care. Sometimes it is helpful to match family caregivers with volunteers who have the time and energy to listen and be there for them, and to help them in advocating appropriately for their family member in care. Family volunteers must be assessed carefully on an ongoing basis for exhaustion and burnout.

SOMETIMES VOLUNTEERS HELP OUT *in unexpected ways. In one facility everyone was concerned about the ugly, uncomfortable dining room on the dementia care unit. Staff members were at their wits' end wondering how they could improve the ambiance. They responded to the suggestion to ask the volunteer auxiliary to develop a suitable environment. Working together they created a simply lovely, comfortable room where elderly people felt at home. The last time we spoke, they were beginning to work on the bathrooms.*

Do not send new volunteers to a unit "to talk to patients."

And Others...

Sometimes staff members themselves volunteer in lovely ways. At one facility in Ontario, Larry, one of the housekeeping staff members, brings in his new baby to visit one evening each week. The event is called "Larry's Baby Night," and is a highlight of the activity schedule.

In developing dementia care services, it is critical that we establish a vital link with volunteers and community organizations. We need to look closely at the unique and priceless contribution that only volunteers can bring to health care. We need to recognize the contribution of volunteers as social change agents, as problem solvers, and as prudent managers of resources.

We need to stop regarding volunteers as charming extras, as peripheral assets—nice, but non-essential. Perhaps we need to stop recognizing them one week in every year, and begin to realize that we need them every day of the year if we hope to meet the needs of today's sick people.

17

Working Together in Therapeutic Partnership

She's not my caregiver,
she's my wife!
—a man with Alzheimer's disease

The experience of working with people suffering from Alzheimer's disease or a related dementia is challenging, and often filled with despair. But there are moments of insight and clarity that open new pathways for direction or action. More often than not, this new way of thinking is inspired by the people experiencing the disease, rather than by those who only observe their struggle.

The quote at the head of this chapter—the plaintive cry of a husband: "She's not my caregiver, she's my wife!"—occurred during one of the moments that opened up my thinking. I was listening as a professional staff member explained to the man that his wife had been his caregiver, but now she was tired. Now, they—the facility staff members—would be his new caregivers. His wife was going home to rest. His point, of course, was that this was not a question of merely substituting caregivers, as one might substitute a team player in the middle of a game—but rather that we were separating him from his *wife*. Implicit in his cry was the conviction that no one of us could ever replace her. She was his WIFE!

Family members have always held a place of importance in the health care systems I have designed: they are a source of vital information, they help their loved ones feel good, and they often help out during various programs. But this man was talking about something far more significant. He was saying that in addition to being his caregiver, his wife was his life partner, his soul mate, maybe his best friend, and definitely his major support system. In that moment, it became clear to me that the prescribed role we have developed for the significant family member in health care is not appropriate within dementia care.

The expected role of the spouse or family member is to visit two or three times each week, chat briefly with their loved one, provide some special food treat, and share concerns while we share our observations with her. This places the spouse in the role of "hospital visitor" rather than partner, and diminishes their importance. This ritual, played out day after weary day, does not serve the person with dementia well, nor does it offer support to family members. This approach not only fails to alleviate the guilt and grief of the family, it frequently exacerbates those feelings.

For staff members, family visits simply add one more task to an already busy day. If the family is pleased with the service that is being provided, the visit can be a pleasant interlude. If the family is upset or, perish the thought, in advocacy mode, the burden for staff becomes intolerable.

Certain health care systems simply do not allocate appropriate time for staff to meet with families and develop effective working relationships. Staff members often do not understand issues of caregiving or the grief and pain associated with institutionalizing a family member. Complaints about institutional inadequacies are often taken as personal criticisms. Professional staff sometimes do not acknowledge the legal responsibilities of families nor their role as advocates. Families are often referred to as "the second client," while no provision is made in staff schedules to work with families.

Gentlecare views the significant family member (often the spouse) as the *principal caregiver,* whether the person with dementia lives at home or in a facility. The person who is established in the mind of the person experiencing dementia as the central support person is the principal caregiver. All others who seek to help must do so in secondary

Every day he is slowly dying, and part of me is dying with him.

—A SPOUSE

roles, working always to support and encourage the family member in her arduous role.

If no family member exists, or none is able to assume the role of supporting the sick person, if it is at all possible someone must be found within the staff or volunteer community to serve as a surrogate family member. The person with dementia must feel that there is someone who is there for him, who can be counted on, who will accept him just the way he is, without expectations or judgment.

Professional caregivers often say that their families are absent, exhausted, dysfunctional, or impossible. And this can be true—some families are those things. But by far, the majority of families care deeply about their loved ones. When they fail to express those positive feelings, almost without exception it is because they are experiencing symptoms of caregiver syndrome: extreme fatigue, stress, grief, depression, guilt, poor health, isolation, and burnout. Research has shown that family caregivers reach an emergency state of exhaustion after only two years of caregiving, but most families give care for double or triple that time before seeking help.

It is rare for families to abandon a spouse or parent. With education and support, family members can and do work to achieve a state of comfort and happiness for people experiencing dementia. Because of their history and perspective, they can accomplish things that professional caregivers can never achieve.

Gentlecare seeks to harness this therapeutic potential by developing partnerships with family members both in the home and in facilities. A partnership begins with a written, voluntary contract that clearly outlines the role each party will attempt to play in the life of the person with dementia. It identifies the professional worker who will be the central contact for the person with dementia, and the spokesperson from the family. It outlines concrete ways in which each party will work to support and assist the other to achieve more effective treatment outcomes. In addition to achieving those outcomes, the partnership helps to prevent family caregivers from succumbing to caregiver burnout and illness.

I was out of energy, out of patience, and I was afraid I was out of love, because I was starting to scream at him.

—WIFE-CAREGIVER

The Gentlecare Therapeutic Partnership Contract

Gentlecare designs a contract with families that clearly lays out responsibility.

Family Responsibilities

BE INFORMED

As painful as it may be, family members need information about the disease process their loved one is experiencing. In Gentlecare, families are provided the same educational programs that are delivered to professional staff.

PROVIDE HISTORY

Vital background information about the person with dementia helps staff create the appropriate prosthesis. Such information refers to personality, culture, education, profession, community affiliations, family constellation, habits, skills, interests, idiosyncrasies, spirituality, preferences, and strengths.

IDENTIFY A FAMILY CONTACT PERSON

To ensure effective communication, professional caregivers need to have a family spokesperson identified. As a rule, this person is the spouse or legal guardian.

SPECIFY SERVICES ANTICIPATED

Prior to admission, family caregivers need to discuss their expectations of care with professional staff and physician(s). Issues to be covered in that discussion include at least the following: use of medication, restraints, clothing, nutrition, room partners, activity programs, walking opportunities indoors and outdoors, end of life issues, and so on.

BE HONEST AND OPEN IN COMMUNICATION

Action happens when families talk to the person in the organization who can create change. Complaining to everyone or to no one does not advance the cause of more effective care. Families often feel frightened or impatient when confronted by a faceless organization. They may fear reprisals to their family member if they complain. They are terrified that the person with dementia might be asked to leave the facility

Alzheimer's is a terrible, terrible way to die ... and taking care of people with Alzheimer's is a terrible way to live.

—DR. ALLEN ROSES,
DUKE UNIVERSITY

if the family raises care issues. However unfounded such fears may be, it is a perception that can immobilize family caregivers. On the other hand, family caregivers sometimes complain about every small detail of care as a way of managing their feelings of guilt for having placed their loved one in an institution. Constant complaints often result in no one paying attention when real concerns surface.

Gentlecare encourages families to make detailed notes of their concerns, making sure to include date, time, and a contact person. Often this process alone helps to clarify issues. Once a concern has been validated, it can be taken to the person responsible for that particular aspect of care for resolution.

Every effort should be made to minimize complaints based on hearsay, non-specific complaints, or uncorroborated claims. Techniques such as avoidance of discussion, stonewalling, power trips, manipulation, scapegoating, and buck-passing should also be discouraged.

A good rule of thumb in the management of complaints is to remember always that families and care providers share the same objective: a decent quality of life for the person in care.

NEGOTIATE THE FAMILY ROLE

Family members need to be candid about their relationships with the person with dementia and the scope of their responsibilities. Spouses may take full charge of care or they may share aspects of responsibility with mid-life children or siblings. Long-distance caregivers may be able to provide financial support but may not be able to visit very often. Family disputes or areas of conflict should be identified. Each family is different, and these differences must be respected in planning for care.

MAKE A TENTATIVE SCHEDULE OF FAMILY VISITS

It is very helpful for facility or home support personnel to know when the family caregiver or some other member of the family is going to be visiting the person with dementia. This information is important.

The common view is that this is because staff want to "fix up" the person prior to the visit. Possibly, but this information is important in Gentlecare because staff members create a different prosthesis if family are present than the one they put in place when the person is alone. Schedules allow both parties to maximize resources and build the day around these important contacts.

Families are advised to spend time with the person in care as often as it is comfortable and healthy for them to do so. Visiting schedules vary from every day, three times per week, weekend visits, brief evening visits, to two to three times per year.

It is very hard to visit someone in hospital. Family caregivers need help in determining how often they can tolerate the stress, both physically and psychologically. If families are confident that good care is in place, they feel more comfortable spacing out their visits.

It is important to work with families to determine the best time of day for them to visit; visiting may be best at the time of awakening, or perhaps at bedtime, or again, may best take the form of a shared walk before dinner. It is often helpful to avoid the times when personal care is being offered, since the person with dementia cannot concentrate on several things at once.

Family contact may be the best therapy we can offer. The schedule of family visits should form the basis of any care plan.

ACCEPT CERTAIN DUTIES ON BEHALF OF A FAMILY MEMBER

Caring for someone with dementia is the most exacting task ever undertaken. When we pool efforts and skills, the burden is lightened for everyone, and better care occurs. Family caregivers should be encouraged and allowed to continue to care for their loved one. Care may take the form of regular walks, massage, hair management, nail care, hydration, clothes management, care of personal effects in rooms, assistance with creating a sense of home in the institution, fund-raising, and advocacy. Some families with help find that they can reach out to other sick people who live with their family member.

BE TOLERANT

Caring for large numbers of people with dementia is a daunting task. Most professional caregivers do the very best they can, but health care systems are complex organizations, and problems inevitably occur. Family members who try to understand the issues, and who work with staff to solve problems, will appreciate the much higher quality of care that results.

ASSIST AND FACILITATE IN THE SEARCH FOR RESOLUTIONS

Once families understand their role and are comfortable with it, there is no end to the magic that ensues. In my experience, solutions to most

Come not when I am dead, to drop thy foolish tears upon my grave.

—LORD TENNYSON

serious problematic behaviors have almost always come as a result of family information and collaboration.

Consider this scenario. The spouse of a man whose nutrition is seriously compromised by dementia comments to staff: "My husband always loved raspberries and ice cream." If staff respond, "Wouldn't we all! But this is not a restaurant," the exchange leaves the family member frustrated, angry, and helpless. If only her husband were at home, she could give him all the things he loves, but he can't be at home because he is too ill. The staff member, exasperated by the seemingly extravagant demands of the family, thinks: "Has she any idea what a facility food budget looks like? It's not my fault he is not eating raspberries. I do the best I can for everyone here."

Let's suppose the staff member had responded differently: "Oh! Do you think he might eat that? We don't have ice cream or berries available, but if you bring them in, I'll mix them in a smoothie for your husband, and we will see if he can manage it. Wouldn't it be wonderful if we could get a good protein drink into him?" This response acknowledges the family member's concern; states the fact that the institution doesn't have special foods readily available; gives the family member a critical role; and joins staff and family together in shared responsibility for helping the person with dementia.

Facility Responsibilities

INFORM

Family caregivers need to understand the disease issues fully as much as do general care staff. Gentlecare units include family members in regular staff in-service and educational sessions. It is also useful to create a special education bulletin board for the public, on which current "Info Bites" are posted. Avoid newspaper clippings with the latest and often unfounded miracle cures, and items that are outdated. Regular family information and support meetings are very helpful as well.

RECEIVE INFORMATION

Families are the major source of vital information about individuals with dementia. Efforts to include families as part of the treatment team are rewarded over and over again by help in constructing better prostheses.

COMMUNICATE EFFECTIVELY

Families need information and stories about their family member to assuage their pain and guilt, ease their loneliness, and to survive. They do not need to hear horror stories, complaints, or disasters. After all, if they had been able to manage problematic behaviors, the person with dementia never would have been institutionalized in the first place. Furthermore, in today's climate of economic restraint, stories of cutbacks, staff shortages, reduced services, and closures are terrifying for the family caregiver, who dreads harmful changes for the person in care.

IDENTIFY A CONTACT PERSON IN THE FACILITY

The Gentlecare system suggests that each family needs a facility liaison person who is responsible for keeping family members informed, transferring information and stories, listening to complaints, and referring caregivers to appropriate sources of help. This liaison person is responsible for identifying a substitute contact person for the family when the assigned liaison person is not available.

IDENTIFY ROLES/DUTIES FOR THE FAMILY

Families are often frightened or awed by hospital or health care organizations. To make sure that family members are comfortable working in dementia care areas, it is critical that staff members identify items of work in which the help of families would be appreciated.

I remember a situation where a wife asked me, a visiting consultant, "Is it all right if I give my husband a drink of water?"

One facility I know solves the problem by simply posting signs such as: "We need help with the garden. We need books for the living room. Does anyone know where we can get a turkey?"

Oh Moyra! I wish it would end.

—AN ELDERLY
CAREGIVER

RESPECT FAMILY CONCERNS AND RESPONSIBILITIES

All staff need to be aware of the family's relationship to the person in care. In Gentlecare we find it useful to review this information at team conferences or when major changes in care plans are contemplated.

UNDERSTAND THE FAMILY'S SORROW

Dementia devastates families! The anxiety, pain, and grief caused by the progress of the disease are overwhelming; it is not uncommon for family caregivers to feel rage, frustration, and impotence; and whether the person with dementia is institutionalized or at home, the responsibility of the family remains exhausting.

All these factors have an impact on the family members' relationships and interactions. Compassion and empathy from those of us on the sidelines is very helpful.

CONTRACT FOR SPECIFIC SERVICES

Staff members need to be candid and specific in identifying special requirements such as help with bathing, assistance with walking at specific times, and special nutritional needs.

Unfortunately, specific requests are unusual; it is more common for a family to hear, "We need someone with the person all the time." The usual result of that kind of request for help is that a person untrained in dementia care is hired by the family to watch the person with dementia. This is an expensive, demoralizing, and ineffectual way to provide dementia care.

IDENTIFY THE INSTITUTION'S ROUTINE AND EXPECTATIONS

It is important to sit down with families and explain the routines, policies, and procedures of the institution. In Gentlecare we do this on an individual basis and in writing, although the information may also be provided during support group meetings or on bulletin boards.

Every family caregiver hears information differently!

ACCEPT THE FAMILY'S COMMITMENT TO THE PERSON IN CARE

For the most part, families are deeply committed to organizing the best quality of life possible for their loved one. It behooves staff members to understand this, and work with the family to achieve this mutual goal.

Joint Responsibilities
RESPECT THE PERSON WITH DEMENTIA AS AN ADULT HUMAN BEING WHO IS DYSFUNCTIONAL

Health care organizations that undertake the care of elderly people with dementia should be held accountable for regarding their clients with respect, as they would any other sick individuals.

Unresolved complaints help no one . . . not the person with the disease, not the family member, nor the staff. Resolutions, on the other hand, are a source of joy for everyone.

DISCOVER THE LEVEL OF ABILITY OF EVERY PERSON WITH DEMENTIA

Appropriate assessment procedures should be undertaken to determine each individual's needs and strengths. Only then can an effective prosthesis be designed.

PROVIDE A PROSTHETIC ENVIRONMENT (PHYSICAL/EMOTIONAL/SPIRITUAL)

Health care organizations that offer care to people with dementia have a responsibility to provide an environment that compensates for physical dysfunction and offers emotional and spiritual care. Families have a responsibility to collaborate in this effort.

APPRECIATE EACH OTHER'S RESPONSIBILITIES

Both family caregivers and professional caregivers have responsibility for the person with dementia. Great care happens when everyone respects the contributions of one another.

SUPPORT AND ASSIST EACH OTHER

Staff often argue that there isn't time to look out for families. In my experience, when help has been extended to families everyone's job is made easier; clients function at higher levels; support for dementia care increases; and staff feel excited about going to work on Monday.

ACKNOWLEDGE THE CONTRIBUTION OF EACH

The exciting health care organizations that I visit acknowledge good work—no matter who does it. They do so through employee-of-the-month citations; caregiver-of-the-month privileged parking; idea-of-the-week recognitions; Gentlecare strategy-of-the-week awards; and volunteer-we-can't-manage-without awards.

COMMUNICATE CANDIDLY AND CARINGLY

Honest, sensitive communication encourages people to perform in outstanding ways and risk failures. Staff should feel comfortable asking families, "How do you think we're doing?" And families should not fear to ask, "What could I do to be more supportive of my family member?"

When stars work in your organization, everyone shines!

TIPS FOR DEVELOPING
A RAPPORT WITH FAMILIES

1. Prior to admission, provide families with an understanding of the facility's philosophy, and always remember the grieving that occurs at the time of placement.

2. Keep admission day simple and low-key. Enjoy a cup of tea with the new resident and family members.

3. Always phone the family the morning after admission to tell them how the first night went.

4. Keep them informed! Encourage phone calls. Initiate phone calls to an ailing caregiver.

5. Set up a buddy system with another appropriate family member.

6. Encourage flexible visiting times and help them understand what is too little or too much for their loved one, depending on the adjustment of the resident.

7. Make a point of talking to every family member when they visit.

8. Provide an area for families to visit comfortably.

9. Help families feel comfortable on the unit and help them adapt to the behavior of other residents.

10. Friendly reminders of the atmosphere we wish to create is sometimes necessary if families visit with active toddlers or large numbers of people.

11. Always make time for a family member.

12. Remember that a complaining family is a hurting family.

13. Encourage participation in a family group.

14. Provide freedom of information.

15. Involve family members in care planning.

16. Provide reassurance regarding appropriate clothing to bring, lost articles, etc.

17. Encourage participation in educational sessions.

18. Help family understand that this is their unit, and encourage participation in projects.

19. Share with families your special moments experienced with their loved one.

20. Send photos to out-of-town family members.

21. Encourage family members to stay for a meal or a special occasion.

—SANDY TELFORD, RN, DELTAVIEW HABILITATION CENTRE

FIGURE 17-1

18

Cherishing the Memory, Living the Reality

To live in the hearts we leave behind is not to die.

For family members the final physical devastation of Alzheimer's disease happens at a time when their resources are virtually depleted. It is hard not to get caught up in the last slow, painful chapter of dementia. Families must watch as one body system after another closes down, and death appears imminent with each labored breath. But as all of us who have sat these vigils know, the human spirit clings tenaciously to life. Sometimes it can seem a lifetime between breaths before the last one.

Families struggle, too, with end-of-life issues: medical intervention or no medical intervention; antibiotics; intravenous feeding and hydration; resuscitation; relief from pain. Each family, with the aid of their advisors, must make these difficult decisions.

During the first six stages of Alzheimer's disease, Gentlecare is focused on correctly identifying and maximizing the afflicted person's remaining strengths. However, in the final stage of the disease, when the mind as we know it is lost, Gentlecare strategies are designed to ensure the comfort of the dying person through hydration, nutrition, massage, spiritual care, and respect. The critical efforts of the Gentlecare program shift: the goal now is to assist and support the family in achieving a serene passage from life to death for their beloved family member.

The family is encouraged and supported in the effort to be with the dying person through the final mysterious stage of life. Family members are helped to reach the person on a sensory level through the use of strategies that include massage, holding, wrapping, rocking, and cradling. Strategies to reach the person on a spiritual level include the use of music, prayer, readings, hymns, and words of endearment. Each activity must be chosen carefully to appropriately reflect the culture of the individual.

Often when there is little or no response from the dying person, family members feel discouraged, grief stricken, or even foolish in their efforts. Those of us in roles of support, whether home support personnel, neighbors, hospice workers, facility staff, or family members, need to role model and encourage efforts to reach the sick person: there is evidence that at some level, the person with dementia can be reached and afforded a sense of peace; and without doubt, families who engage in such activity through the dying time of dementia feel comforted and effective.

Today is a good day to die for all the things in my life are here.

—CHIEF CRAZY HORSE

I WAS PRIVILEGED *to be present at the dying time of a man with whom I had worked as he and his family lived through the experience of dementia. He and I had shared a love of dogs, and had spent many lovely times together swapping stories and playing with my dogs. As he lay curled up in the final stages of life, the grief and loss of his family was devastating. They felt unable to reach him in any way. No vestige of the man they loved remained. With the family's consent, I decided to bring my big basset, Michael, to visit. As the man lay curled up on the bed, we placed the dog in his arms beside him. Big Mike of course loves to cuddle, and made the most of this comfortable place. Gradually as the dog's warmth and softness permeated his skin, the man began slowly, ever so slowly, to stroke the dog's fur. How could this be, when no purposeful movement is possible at this stage? And yet, as the family watched the tiny familiar gesture, they were flooded with memories of their loved one—in different times, in better times. Suddenly he was with us again.*

Let me not to the marriage of true minds admit
impediments. Love is not love
which alters when it alteration finds,
Or bends with the remover to remove:
Oh No! it is an ever-fixed mark,
that looks on tempests and is never
shaken.

It is the star to every wandering bark
whose worth's unknown, although his
height be taken.

Love is not Time's fool, though rosy
lips and cheeks within his
bending sickles compass comes;
Love alters not with his brief
hours and weeks
But bears it out even to the edge
of doom.

If this be error, and upon
me proved

I never write, nor no man
ever loved.

—William Shakespeare

By far the greatest effort to be made is celebrating the memory of the person—the person who was, before dementia began its dreadful course. Families need to be helped to remember, through stories and pictures, the deeds of kindness, contributions to community or profession, talents, favorite jokes, oft-recounted experiences. When family caregivers are exhausted, bereft, and possibly even ill, it is hard to re-

CONSENT

I wait for death,
Not mine but Aila's.
How strange to wait for death
of another.
It puts a period on the sentence of life.
The very concept means acceptance,
And yet acceptance means consent.
Have I agreed to let her die?
I wait for death.
By what right have I agreed
to see it come?
Come it will, but must I consent?
Can I not reach out and hold her,
perhaps keep it at a distance,
to disperse its power with my presence.
I am indeed a fool to believe
that I can stay the last
pinpoint of ink upon the page.
An accident of motion could
make the pinpoint drop,
finish without consent the final line.

—Arthur Olson,
The Dying of the Light

member those good times. Friends, relatives, and neighbors can help
to rebuild these precious memories.

I REMEMBER RECEIVING A PARCEL *and a letter from an associate*
of my father's who lived on the other side of Canada. In the parcel was
a gallon can of maple syrup. The note said: "Your father did me a
great favor once. This is a small gift to express the esteem with which

CELEBRATE AND LIVE
Dedicated to Moyra Jones

Celebrate the memories! That was what you, my mentor, said.
I do, I do—celebrating's easy!
I have such lovely thoughts of our togetherness
From before year one of our marriage until now—year fifty-three.
We've enjoyed each other in so many ways:
He taught me how to let go, to laugh, to play, to love
Even to cook, although he couldn't,
and I'd avoided that necessity.
So how can I easily give him up to Alzheimer's?
Memories are always fun to celebrate, but not alone!
Live the realities! That's tough and disciplined and real!
I've always been romantic and a dreamer;
This helps me to escape realities.
I still see my love as a dear and funny guy.
I need him to nourish me—
To help me with the pitfalls I find all too easily.
I need him to brighten up the world and love me.
I do not want to give him up
Although I know he's vanishing—piece by piece—
into Alzheimer's.

—Gil Ludeman,
Journey into a Caring Heart

I remember him." I never did learn more about this story but suddenly my father was there vividly in my mind, and for a while the burden of his loss was lifted.

Staff, too, have wonderful stories to tell. It is not unusual for professional caregivers to be welcomed into family circles; after all, they play an intimate role through all the stages of dementia. Staff members suffer bereavement too, repeatedly losing people they have grown to care for over many years. Sharing stories and memories helps everyone heal.

Once death has occurred, facilities that practice Gentlecare find many creative ways to celebrate the person who has gone. Some conduct memorial services, or wakes during which everyone exchanges stories about the person in order to celebrate his life. Some move the life panel or significant picture from the bedroom into a memorial hallway. Some burn a special lamp for 24 hours. More and more families dedicate living memorials to their loved ones; these may take the form of a therapeutic garden, a resource library, or a fund for dementia education or research. These important bequests enhance the life of a wide circle of people, and are a vital way to remember a loved one lost to Alzheimer's. One of the most effective and courageous memorials is created when family members volunteer their services and advocacy after their loved one has gone.

Of course, the best memorial of all is a healthy caregiver who is left with the strength to build a new life. This would be the wish of every person who has ever died of dementia. But recovery from caregiving is a long and difficult process, and it helps if caregivers don't have to experience it alone.

Do not stand at my grave and weep; I am not there. I do not sleep. I am a thousand winds that blow. I am the diamond glints on snow. I am the sunlight on ripened grain. I am the gentle autumn's rain. When you waken in the morning's hush I am the swift uplifting rush Of quiet birds in circled flight. I am the soft stars that shine at night. Do not stand at my grave and cry: I am not there. I did not die.

—Mary Frye

DON'T LEAVE

Don't leave my love, not yet.
What will I do without you?
Who will share my thoughts?
Who will I laugh with?
Who will hold me and love me on
cold winter evenings when the windows
are iced and the sheets snow?
Who will share my dreams if you go?

Give me your hand.
Don't leave, not yet.
Don't leave.
Please!

　　　—Arthur Olson,
　　　　The Dying of the Light

Time does not heal. It just pushes things into the
back of our consciousness. What heals is what we
do with time. Grieving heals. The way home is joy
through the heart of our pain. We have to grieve
until we come out the other side of it.

　　　—Deborah Duda,
　　　　Coming Home: A Guide to Dying at Home with Dignity

Epilogue

Plus ça change,
plus c'est la même chose.
—Alphonse Karr, 1849

A great deal has changed in the years since dementing illness destroyed the lives of my father and mother. And yet far too much remains the same.

Earlier this year a woman phoned me in what can only be described as utter despair. Her story is all too familiar to those of us who advocate for people experiencing dementing illness, and their families.

Suzanne had been caring for her husband at home. At 61, he was in the throes of Alzheimer's disease. Although functioning well enough to attend a Victorian Order of Nurses day care program, Ted was becoming increasingly anxious and agitated. He was experiencing awful pressure to move around. This anxiety and restlessness resulted in his being unable to remain at rest long enough to eat, sleep, use the bathroom, or relax. This excessive need to walk and walk and walk was having a harmful effect on his health and that of his wife.

Suzanne decided to seek help. With the aid of her family physician she admitted her husband to a specialized, government-sponsored program for dementia assessment and treatment. It was her hope that medical specialists could somehow relieve the pressure that was causing her husband to be so restless and uncomfortable.

The following events are described from *the family's perspective*. Of course, there are always two sides to a story. The family's story is told here because for too long this perspective has been ignored and not heard.

What follows is the way one family felt…was made to feel. This was the agony and uncertainty they experienced. This terror and impotence shaped their "days of hell."

DIRECTLY ON ADMISSION, *Ted was administered medication to reduce his anxiety. This medication was increased, discontinued, and other drugs were substituted. The family did not know which medication was given or in what quantity, since this information was never discussed with them.*

What they can describe are the changes they saw in their husband and father.

Ted quickly became frightened and hostile. He resisted staff's efforts to care for him. Most of the time he was comatose. Within days, despite or because of medication and physical restraint (depending on your perspective), he had become belligerent, pushing and hitting at staff and other patients. He was described to the family by staff as violent and dangerous. Although designated as an institution providing specialized assessment and treatment for dementia, the staff appeared at their wits' end to manage behaviors that Ted was now exhibiting.

Several days later, he was transferred to the psychiatric unit of the acute care hospital. The staff on the psychiatric unit described Ted as too aggressive to manage, and told the family that they "feared for their lives."

I'm not sure that it is possible for anyone who has not experienced it to imagine how devastating it is to hear a beloved member of your family described this way.

In such circumstances, a family caregiver is buffeted by emotions of anger, denial, shame, and guilt: anger that anyone could ever say such things; denial that a family member could behave in such a way;

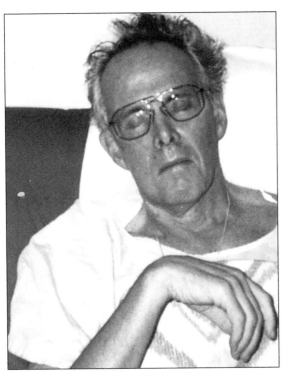
Ted under the effects of medication.

shame that your family is being seen in such compromising public circumstances; and guilt...overwhelming, recriminating, energy sapping guilt, that you ever allowed such an experience to happen in the first place.

Suzanne thought:

- "Why did I ever complain about the behavior that was occurring at home?"
- "How could I have thought it was a problem compared to the mess we are in now?"
- "Are there other, better places I should have taken him?"
- "Are these the best doctors I could have engaged?"
- "Should I speak up more?"
- "Am I failing him?"
- "Are my actions going to result in his suffering and death?"

THESE THOUGHTS SWIRLED *through Suzanne's head as she prepared to attend a case conference to discuss Ted. She found herself alone in the conference with 11 professional staff. Although she had gone to the meeting prepared to present Ted's side of things, and armed with some resource materials she thought might help the staff, she was soon overwhelmed. She describes how even her normal gumption and good sense drained away, leaving her uncertain and vulnerable.*

The psychiatrist who presided at the conference explained that they planned to move Ted to another hospital, since the present location did not have the proper environment. This was very evident to Suzanne, but also puzzling, since the unit he was in was specifically designed as an assessment and treatment resource center.

The psychiatrist informed Suzanne that it had been necessary to invoke the Mental Health Act and have Ted certified as mentally incompetent. This action was not discussed in advance with the family, though at least one member of the family had been with Ted every day; nor were the implications explained.

Suzanne's power of attorney was swept aside with this legal manoeuver. She was to learn later that only a specifically convened review panel could examine an appeal on her part. And this action enabled the staff to apply four-way restraint to Ted and to confine him to a darkened room.

Suzanne now saw her husband in a darkened room, physically restrained hand and foot, nearly comatose with medication, and virtually unable to eat or drink.

What had she done?

How could this be happening?

Where could she turn for help?

At this point, Suzanne was approached by a care attendant who told her about a workshop she had attended where the Gentlecare system of dementia care had been presented as an alternative approach. Suzanne called me. I advised her that, working with her physician, she must quickly find alternate care for Ted. I suggested she visit a privately owned, specialized dementia care facility that had a few government-sponsored beds. Here she would find specially trained staff, a dementia-specific environment, and appropriate care strategies and programs. Because the facility used the Gentlecare model I also knew that no physical or chemical restraints would be used. I further provided her with information regarding a few legal advocates that work on behalf of people's rights within the health care and mental health systems.

Suzanne knew the moment she stepped inside the door of the facility that practiced Gentlecare that this was the place for Ted. Here he could move about freely through spacious indoor rooms and a beautiful outdoor park. Here the staff were not afraid, but interested and supportive. They understood how Ted was feeling; they felt his pain and confusion and appreciated how difficult life was becoming for him.

Most importantly, here they knew how to build a prosthesis to compensate for his dysfunction. Here was a physician who could monitor Ted's care over time in conjunction with family and staff. And signifi-

Ted with staff member: the joy of having someone you can count on.

cantly, here Suzanne had found a haven for her family. This was a place where her feelings were important, her knowledge critical to Ted's care, and her presence vital to his very life. Within a few short miles, she had gone, in her own words, from "hell to heaven."

TED'S PHYSICAL CONDITION CHANGED *quickly and dramatically. And most surprising of all, his cognitive ability began to return. Within a day he was walking with help, and was soon out in the garden with his wife. He began to bond with and trust staff members who were able to assist him with all his activities of daily living. All of us began to enjoy Ted's courtly manner and funny conversations. Slowly his life returned to normal—normal for someone experiencing dementia.*

Ted's family moved from a place of darkness to a place of hope, from impotence to empowerment. They clearly see a possible quality of life for both Ted and themselves as this horrific disease plays out its course. Suzanne's own health has moved away from the brink of illness as the burden of stress is relieved.

Nothing makes Alzheimer's disease OK. But knowing that your afflicted family member is comfortable and supported in his attempts to manage life activities is a help. So does having staff members who respect the family's position and listen to them. Knowing that you can move ahead with your own life without sacrificing your health and happiness helps too. All of these factors make it possible for family caregivers to join with professional staff in a creative partnership of caring to support people living with dementia.

How many Suzannes and Teds must there be before we stop replaying this costly scenario? When will health care planners understand that the biomedical model just doesn't work for people with dementing illnesses? When will our physicians and psychiatrists become aware of alternatives to the biomedical model, which work miracles for people with progressive dementia—over and over and over again?

Is the fact that almost no research into care strategies is being undertaken the reason for lack of support for alternative approaches?

We are not documenting the staggering costs incurred when our health care system turns people like Ted into totally dysfunctional individuals, and turns family caregivers into new consumers of health services because their own health breaks down. Families are simply too weary and frightened to search out different care.

Those of us who advocate for people experiencing Alzheimer's disease or other dementias can only believe that the chaos swirling around dementia care will eventually evolve into humane and effective ways of responding to the needs of these vulnerable people.

Places like the haven that Ted and Suzanne found must replace the highly technological acute care approach that utterly destroys families living with dementia.

They cost less.

They work.

But isn't it time we began to really help victims of dementia? After all, who are these people?

Who am I?

You may wonder.

I am someone you know very well.

For I am every man you meet.

I am every woman.

I am you.

Ted and Suzanne enjoy a daily walk in the garden of the facility where he now lives.

(This is a true and recent story. Only the participants' names have been changed. Ted now lives in a lovely facility in the Lower Mainland of British Columbia, Canada, visited regularly by his wife and family.)

Index

The letter *f* following a page number denotes a figure.